A Thyme to Remember

GENERATIONS OF RECIPES HANDED DOWN FOR TODAY

80th Anniversary Special Edition
by the Dallas County Medical Society Alliance

Copyright © Dallas County Medical Society Alliance
The Aldredge House
5500 Swiss Avenue, Dallas, Texas 75214

The Dallas County Medical Society Alliance is an organization of the physicians' spouses committed to promoting health education through community programming. Its purpose is educational and charitable. The proceeds from the sale of this cookbook will benefit DCMSA philanthropies.

Library of Congress Catalog Number: 98-73313
ISBN: 0-9664895-0-0

Designed, Edited, and Manufactured by
Favorite Recipes® Press
an imprint of

FRP™

P.O. Box 305142
Nashville, TN 37230
1-800-358-0560

Book Design: Starletta Polster
Art Director: Steve Newman

Manufactured in the United States of America
First Printing: 1999 10,000 copies

Healing Hands

The Dallas County Medical Society Alliance is proud to dedicate this 80th anniversary edition cookbook, *A Thyme to Remember*, to the medical profession. As highly trained professionals, physicians are dedicated to their work and dedicated to ensuring the best possible medical treatment for all their patients. The time-trusted physician/patient relationship has been preserved for today and must be preserved for generations in the future. Through projects such as Health Check, Latino Wellness Fair, Live and Then Give, Infant Immunization Programs, Science Place, Science Fair, Nursing and Science Scholarships, and Domestic Violence Programs, the physician spouses (DCMSA) join the doctors' crusade for a healthier, better educated, and safer Dallas. We have a giving, caring heritage. Together, we can build a better tomorrow.

The members of the DCMSA are proud of their physician spouses and the opportunity to work by their sides to promote good health. Thank you to all the volunteers who made this cookbook possible. Thank you to the generations of medical families who have had faith in the medical profession.

Cookbook Committee

Chairmen
Shannon Callewart (Craig)
Sarah Hardin (Mark)

Recipe Testing Chairman
Carol Bywaters (Theodore)

Recipe Testing Section Chairmen
Jean Bremner (Normand)
Wendy Hansen (Phillip)
Barenda Hino (Peter)
Carey King, M.D.
Lucille King (Carey)
Gail Loeb (Peter)
Susan Scott (Troy)
Karen Wang (Stanley)
Tina Westmoreland (Matthew)

Copywriters
Barbara Bradfield (John)
Emily Clark (Peter)
Sarah Hardin (Mark)

Marketing
Elaine Agatston (Stephen)
Melanie Cancemi (Mark)
Tara Chittoor (Sreeni)
Linda Coon (John)
Marty Curtis (R. Stephen)

Mary Geisler (Gerald)
Sonja Goudreau (Jeff)
Barenda Hino (Peter)
Kay Hyland (John)
Nancy Montgomery (James)
Amy Pruitt (Bryan)
Annette Rutherford (Charles)
Nancy Shelton (James)
Kimberly Yamanouchi, M.D.

Advisors
Alicia Cheek (John)
Marty Curtis (R. Stephen)
Lynn Hamilton (J. Kent)
Ann Jones (R. Ellwood)
Patricia Snoots (Wynne)
Karen Burns (Robert)
Sandra Secor (John)
Tina Westmoreland (Matthew)

Treasurers
Susan Bruck (William)
Karen Burns (Robert)

Photographer
Linda Lux (Nicholas)

Stylist
Judy Blackman (Clint)

Recipe Testing Committee

Elaine Agatston (Stephen)
Mary Ann Blome (Bruce)
Barbara Bradfield (John)
Jean Bremner (Normand)
Diane Brooks (John)
Carol Bywaters (Theodore)
Theodore Bywaters, M.D.
Carol Cain (C. Reasor)
Shannon Callewart (Craig)
Craig Callewart, M.D.
Melanie Cancemi (Mark)
Susan Candy (Errol)
Sally Chandler (Mathias)
Linda Coon (John)
Marty Curtis (R. Stephen)
Diane Dopkins (Chris)
Linda Dysert (Peter)
Pam Edman (Clare)
Glenda Folker (Randy)
Mary Geisler (Gerald)
Mildred Geist (Frederick)
Sue Gilbert (John)
Debra Green
Terri Griffeth (Landis)
Lynn Hamilton (J. Kent)

Wendy Hansen (Phillip)
Sarah Hardin (Mark)
Betty Hayes (H. Thomas)
Barenda Hino (Peter)
Felecia Hoeschele (Mark)
Susan Hughes (John)
Kay Hyand (John)
Ann Jones (R. Ellwood)
Lucille King (Carey)
Carey King, M.D.
Ann Kraus (William)
Laurie Latson (Terry)
Nancy Liebes (George)
Gail Loeb (Peter)
Marion Luecke (Percy)
Judy Matson (James)
James Matson, M.D.
Christine McDanald (Conway)
Kate Meler (J. D.)
Silvi Millard (Mark)
Sheryl Miller (Mark)
Donna Monk (Joe)
Barbara Munford (Robert)
Joanna North (Robert)
Janet Nylund (Jack)
Kasi Pollock (Todd)
Todd Pollock, M.D.

Sara Porter (Louis)
Amy Pruitt (Bryan)
Sarah Rathjen (Kurt)
Annette Rutherford (Charles)
Cathy Schultz (Tom)
Geri Schwartz (Michael)
Susan Scott (Troy)
Nancy Shelton (James)
Marcia Simon (Theodore)
Judy Skinner (Walter)
Randi Smerud (Michael)
Virginia Sone (Law)
Carol Stevenson (W. Daniel)
Karen Vandermeer (Robert)
Jane Viere (Robert)
Tammy Vines (Victor)
Jenny Waddell (Gary)
Sally Wagner (K. James)
Karen Wang (Stanley)
Tina Westmoreland (Matthew)
Kimberly Yamanouchi, M.D.
Kristen Zafuta (Michael)

Table of Contents

Helping Hands

The Dallas County Medical Society Alliance, founded in 1917, is one of the oldest medical support organizations in the U.S. From its beginnings, the Alliance had a simple but ambitious mission: to provide a year-round program of service to the medical profession and to the entire community. By its example, our organization has been instrumental in the formation of other local medical alliances, the Texas Medical Association Alliance, and the American Medical Association Alliance.

The DCMSA was born in the living room of a doctor's wife; its headquarters and meeting place today is a stately historic home—Aldredge House—which was completed in the same year the Alliance was born and donated to the group in 1974.

Although the mission of the DCMSA has remained the same throughout its 80-plus-year history, our focus has evolved with the times. During World War I, the Auxiliary (as it was then known) joined forces with the American Red Cross to help soldiers overseas and at home. Our members packed Christmas boxes for soldiers in France, opened their homes to aviators stationed near Dallas, and sewed hundreds of operating gowns and caps at the Red Cross Sewing Room.

Between the wars, the group expanded its mission to include aid to underprivileged children, sewing clothes, providing free milk, and establishing a prenatal clinic at a local hospital. During World War II, the DCMSA devoted countless hours to the USO, bond sales, Red Cross sewing, and the ration board; members volunteered as Grey Ladies and nurses' aides.

As projects changed to meet the changing needs of the ensuing decades, the mission to support, serve, and sustain remained constant. New activities included the establishment of the Edith Cavell Nursing Scholarship Fund, mental health and cancer prevention projects, medical self-help education, and geriatric care support.

From its Swiss Avenue headquarters, the alliance—some 800 members strong—today continues to serve the Dallas community with ongoing projects such as Health Check, the Science Fair, and the fall fashion show, which help raise money for other Alliance philanthropy projects.

Throughout its history, the Alliance has never been a static organization. We have always felt strongly to change is to grow. The Alliance has evolved, along with medicine and the Dallas community, without losing sight of its original mission: to support physicians and their families, to foster strong doctor-patient relationships, and to strengthen the ties between medicine and the community. The DCMSA has grown from a small group of doctors' wives in 1917 into a strong, multi-faceted organization with a solid reputation for reaching out to the community it serves. Dallas has grown from a small, sleepy southwestern city into a diverse, energetic financial and cultural powerhouse. The Alliance has expanded to reflect this diversity and energy, while maintaining its traditions of service and support.

So, while our organization is more than 80 years old, it retains the spirit of its original founders; the energy of the Dallas County Medical Society Alliance today is as fresh as it was in 1917. With the publication of *A Thyme to Remember*, we hope you'll see how much we've changed— and how much we've remained the same.

Handed Down Recipes

Medical practice is an ancient tradition; one physician/teacher passes on the knowledge to a willing apprentice, thereby expanding the art and the science of medicine…And so the practice of cooking is "handed down" from one cook passing on knowledge to a willing apprentice, thereby expanding the art and skill of cooking. To some, the kitchen can be as intimidating as an operating room. To others, the kitchen is a source for tender loving care expressed toward family and friends. As a physician gives care to patients, a cook gives care to loved ones through the preparation of meals.

No cooking school can educate a cook on how to instill nurturing and love into meal preparations. Creativity flows with the anticipation of meal enjoyment. Cooking can be an opportunity to reinforce tradition, a "time to remember" family and past generations. In tribute to the DCMSA's 80th anniversary, our members have collected *handed down* recipes in acknowledgment of the "loving cooks in our pasts." The "loving cooks in our pasts" have enabled us to become the modern cooks we are today. Although our recipes have been updated to fit today's busy lifestyles, we use the learned skills, hints, and homespun attitudes of past generations. It is important to preserve these precious culinary gifts for tomorrow's cooks. Cooking today is a blend of the past, present, and future. *A Thyme to Remember*, a thyme to prepare for tomorrow…hands outreached through time.

The special recipes, which are "handed down" or are completely original recipes developed by members of the DCMSA, are identified by the hand icon.

A Handful of Savors

APPETIZERS AND BEVERAGES

"I enjoy my patients immensely. I love to hear about their families, their past and present experiences, and future plans. Being able to be a participant in a person's life is such a great privilege. Few professions allow one to do that!"
—Melissa M. Carry, M.D., Cardiologist

Asparagus Sandwiches

1 (15-ounce) can cut
    asparagus, drained
6 green onions
1 (5-ounce) can sliced water
    chestnuts
1 tablespoon mayonnaise

8 ounces cream cheese,
    softened
1 teaspoon garlic powder
1 teaspoon Greek seasoning
Salt and pepper to taste
1 loaf light rye bread, toasted

🌿 Mash the asparagus; combine with the onions, water chestnuts, mayonnaise, cream cheese, garlic powder and Greek seasoning in a food processor container; process at medium speed until smooth. Season with salt and pepper. Spread on light rye bread toast. Top the asparagus mixture with additional rye bread toast and cut sandwiches into quarters.

Yield: 48 servings

Antipasto

3/4 cup olive oil
1 1/2 cups vinegar
2 teaspoons mustard
1/3 cup sugar
2 teaspoons salt
1 teaspoon dried oregano
1/2 teaspoon pepper
1 head cauliflower, broken
    into small florets
3 green bell peppers, cut into
    1-inch cubes

3 carrots, sliced
4 ribs celery, sliced
1 jar pickled onions
1 (12-ounce) can water-
    packed tuna, drained,
    flaked
2 cloves of garlic, crushed
8 ounces mushrooms, sliced
1 (8-ounce) jar sliced stuffed
    olives, drained
Lettuce leaves

🌿 Whisk the olive oil, vinegar, mustard, sugar, salt, oregano and pepper in a small bowl until well blended. Combine the cauliflower, bell peppers, carrots, celery, pickled onions, tuna, garlic, mushrooms and olives in a large bowl, tossing lightly. Add the vinaigrette and toss gently. Chill, covered, in the refrigerator for 12 hours; drain. Arrange attractively on a lettuce-lined platter. Serve with crackers.

Yield: 8 servings

These make deliciously

different finger

sandwiches for a party.

May top sandwiches with

crisp-fried bacon slices.

Spinach and Feta Phyllo Triangles

2 tablespoons olive oil
2 shallots, finely chopped
1 pound frozen spinach,
  thawed, drained
4 ounces feta cheese,
  crumbled
1/3 cup walnuts, chopped

1/4 teaspoon grated nutmeg
Salt and pepper
4 large or 8 small sheets
  phyllo
1/2 cup melted butter or
  margarine

❧ Preheat the oven to 400 degrees. Warm the olive oil in a skillet over medium-high heat; add the shallots. Cook for 5 minutes or until softened, stirring. Squeeze the liquid from the spinach, a handful at a time. Add the spinach to the shallots. Increase the heat to high. Cook for 5 minutes or until all excess moisture has evaporated, stirring frequently.

❧ Remove the spinach mixture to a bowl; let cool. Stir in the feta cheese and walnuts. Stir in the nutmeg; season with salt and pepper. Cover the phyllo with plastic wrap and a damp towel to keep it from drying. Lay 1 phyllo sheet on a work surface. Brush on some butter. Lay a second sheet atop the first. Cut lengthwise with scissors into 3-inch wide strips.

❧ Place a tablespoonful of the spinach mixture at the end of 1 strip of phyllo pastry. Fold a corner of the pastry over the filling to form a triangle; continue folding over the pastry strip to the other end. Stack, fill and shape the phyllo sheets until all the ingredients are used. Arrange the triangles on baking sheets and brush with butter. Bake for 10 minutes or until crispy and golden brown. Serve hot.

Yield: 12 servings

I love to cook because it is my chance to be Merlin the Wizard in the kitchen.

Cooking is my creative outlet. I love to experiment. I never cook a recipe the same way twice. Every meal is an adventure to me.

Sarah Hardin

Onion Puffs

2 loaves sliced white bread
1/2 cup butter, softened
16 ounces cream cheese,
  softened
1/4 cup plus 2 tablespoons
  mayonnaise

2 green onions, chopped
Cayenne to taste
Salt and pepper to taste
1 (8-ounce) can grated
  Parmesan cheese

❧ Cut circles from the bread slices. Butter both sides; arrange on baking sheets. Broil until golden brown, turning to brown both sides. Remove to wire racks to cool. Mix the cream cheese, mayonnaise and green onions in a bowl until thoroughly blended. Season with the cayenne, salt and pepper. Spread over each toast circle. Top with the Parmesan cheese. Arrange on baking sheets. Broil until puffed and golden.

Yield: 20 servings

Parmesan Chips

1/2 cup butter, softened
1/2 cup Parmesan cheese
1 cup flour
1/2 teaspoon baking powder

1/2 teaspoon salt
2 tablespoons butter
1/4 cup Parmesan cheese
2 tablespoons whipping cream

❧ Preheat the oven to 350 degrees. Cream the 1/2 cup butter in a medium bowl until fluffy and soft. Mix in the Parmesan cheese until well blended. Sift in the flour, baking powder and salt; mix well. Roll into a circle, 1/8-inch thick. Cut out 1-inch circles and arrange on a baking sheet. Bake for 8 to 10 minutes or until done. Remove to wire racks to cool. Combine 2 tablespoons butter, 1/4 cup Parmesan cheese and cream in a small bowl, stirring until well blended. Spread on half the baked Parmesan cheese circles; top with remaining cheese circles.

Yield: 24 servings

A Thyme to
Remember

May be made ahead

and stored, covered,

in the freezer.

Shrimp Rémoulade

1 bunch parsley
2 ribs celery
2 cloves of garlic
1 tablespoon minced green
    bell pepper
1 cup Creole mustard
2 tablespoons prepared
    horseradish
1 cup red wine vinegar
1 teaspoon Worcestershire
    sauce

4 tablespoons paprika
1 teaspoon Tabasco sauce
Salt to taste
1/4 teaspoon black pepper
Cayenne to taste
2 cups vegetable oil
4 cups shredded lettuce
2 pounds shrimp, cooked,
    peeled, deveined
2 lemons, quartered

Combine the parsley, celery, garlic and bell pepper in a food processor container; process until partially puréed. Remove to a large bowl. Stir in the mustard, horseradish, vinegar, Worcestershire sauce, paprika, Tabasco sauce, salt, black pepper and cayenne. Add the oil in a fine stream, whisking constantly until smooth. Chill, covered, in the refrigerator for 24 hours. Arrange the lettuce on 8 chilled salad plates. Place shrimp on individual plates. Spoon the mustard sauce over the shrimp. Serve with the lemon wedges.

Yield: 8 servings

This is a classic

of Creole cuisine.

Often New Orleans

residents will judge a

restaurant by the way

it prepares this dish.

Mexican Swirls

1 cup sour cream
4 ounces green chiles, chopped
1/2 cup chopped green onions
1/2 teaspoon garlic powder
8 ounces cream cheese, softened

4 ounces chopped black olives
1 cup shredded Cheddar cheese
Salt to taste
6 flour tortillas
Picante sauce

❧ Combine the sour cream, green chiles, green onions, garlic powder, cream cheese, black olives and Cheddar cheese in a bowl until well mixed. Season with salt. Spread on the tortillas. Roll up and cut into 1-inch slices. Serve with picante sauce.

Yield: 16 servings

Mexican Egg Rolls

1 pound ground beef
1 envelope taco seasoning mix
1/4 cup water
1 large (12-count) package egg roll wrappers

1 (20-ounce) can refried beans
2 cups shredded Cheddar cheese
Vegetable oil for frying

❧ Cook the beef in a large skillet over medium-high heat until browned, stirring often to crumble; drain. Add the taco seasoning and water. Simmer for 5 minutes. Let cool. Fill each egg roll wrapper with 1 tablespoon meat mixture, 1 heaping tablespoon refried beans and 1 tablespoon cheese. Moisten the ends of the wrappers with water, fold the ends and roll.

❧ Heat the oil in a deep fryer. Add the egg rolls in small batches. Deep-fry until golden brown; drain on a plate lined with paper towels. Serve with hot sauce or salsa.

Yield: 12 servings

When my mother wanted to eat out, she would always fix something my dad didn't like. When he found out what it was, he'd always say "Okay, get your coat. I'll take you out to the cafeteria."

Marty Curtis

Tomato Basil Santa Fe Pizza

2 teaspoons chopped garlic
2 tomatoes, sliced
2 tablespoons olive oil
Salt and pepper to taste
2 whole wheat tortillas,
    pierced with a fork

6 ounces mozzarella cheese,
    sliced
2 tablespoons minced fresh
    basil
1/2 cup grated Parmesan
    cheese

❧ Preheat the oven to 350 degrees. Combine the garlic, tomatoes and olive oil in a small bowl; toss gently. Season with the salt and pepper. Arrange the tortillas on a baking sheet. Top with the mozzarella cheese slices and tomato slices. Sprinkle the basil and Parmesan cheese over the tomatoes. Bake for 8 minutes or until the cheese is melted. Cut into wedges.

Yield: 2 servings

Party Meatballs with Sweet-Sour Sauce

1 egg
1/2 cup water
1 pound ground chuck or
    sausage
1/2 cup fresh bread crumbs
1 cup water chestnuts, finely
    chopped

2 teaspoons horseradish
1/2 cup orange marmalade
1 clove of garlic, minced
1/4 cup soy sauce
2 teaspoons lemon juice
1/3 cup water

❧ Beat the egg and water together in a large bowl. Mix in the ground chuck, bread crumbs, water chestnuts and horseradish. Shape into 1-inch meatballs, and arrange in a shallow baking dish. Bake at 350 degrees for 30 minutes. Combine the orange marmalade, garlic, soy sauce, lemon juice and water in a small saucepan; warm over low heat until blended, stirring often. Pour over the meatballs.

Yield: 12 servings

Corn and Crab Fritters

3 tablespoons butter or
   margarine
1½ cups frozen corn
⅓ cup chopped red bell
   pepper
3 green onions, chopr
2 eggs
1 cup ricotta c'
½ cup butt'
1 tables·

M
th

a.
mix.
in cra.

Pour th
over medium-
3 minutes on ea
Cook the remainii.

Yield: 10 servings

1

1

. Fold

,4 inch; heat
. patties for 2 to
.d with paper towels.

A Thyme to
Remember

I entered medical school at

the directive of my surgeon

'ther, and with the

ent of my mother,

.rse. I chose to be a

spinal surgeon because of

my exposure to several

outstanding mentors.

Spinal surgery offers the

opportunity to dramatically

improve the quality

of a patient's life.

Craig C. Callewart, M.D.,

Orthopedic Surgeon

Crabmeat Cheesecake with Pecan Crust

3/4 cup pecans
1 cup flour
1/2 teaspoon salt
5 tablespoons cold butter
3 tablespoons ice water
1 tablespoon butter
1/2 small onion, minced
4 ounces crabmeat,
   shelled
8 ounces cream cheese,
   softened

1/3 cup Creole cream cheese or
   2 1/2 tablespoons
   plain yogurt plus
   2 1/2 tablespoons sour
   cream
2 eggs
Salt and white pepper to
   taste
Hot sauce to taste
Crab Claw Fingers with
   Sauce (page 21)

❧ Combine the pecans, flour and salt in the bowl of a food processor; process at medium speed until the pecans are finely ground and evenly distributed, pulsing as often as necessary. Remove to a bowl. Cut in 5 tablespoons butter, using a pastry blender or two knives, until it forms coarse crumbs. Add the water, tossing the dough with your fingers to evenly distribute; the dough will be fairly crumbly. Press into a 9-inch tart pan, starting with the side and ending with the bottom. Bake at 350 degrees for 20 minutes.

❧ Melt the 1 tablespoon butter in a skillet over medium heat; add the onion. Sauté until translucent. Add the crabmeat; stir to mix. Cook just until heated through, stirring occasionally.

❧ Cream the cream cheese in a large bowl, using a wooden spoon, or in the mixer bowl of an electric mixer until smooth. Beat in the Creole cream cheese and the eggs, one at a time. Fold in the crabmeat mixture, and season with the salt, white pepper and hot sauce. Spoon the mixture into the prepared pecan crust. Bake at 300 degrees for 30 minutes or until set and firm to the touch. Top each serving with 3 crab claw fingers and 2 tablespoons sauce.

Yield: 8 servings

Crab Claw Fingers with Sauce

1 tablespoon unsalted butter
2 tablespoons chopped
    shallots
4 ounces sliced mixed wild
    mushrooms
1 tablespoon lemon juice
1 ounce hot sauce

3 ounces Worcestershire sauce
3 tablespoons whipping cream
3 tablespoons unsalted butter,
    softened
24 crab claw fingers
Salt and pepper to taste

❧ Warm the 1 tablespoon butter in a skillet over medium heat; add the shallots. Sauté until translucent. Add the mushrooms. Cook until the mushrooms begin to sweat, stirring. Stir in the lemon juice, hot sauce and Worcestershire sauce. Cook until reduced by three quarters. Stir in the cream. Cook until reduced by 1/2, stirring. Whisk in the 3 tablespoons butter.

❧ Arrange the crab claw fingers in another skillet; season with the salt and pepper. Pour the shallot mixture over the crab fingers.

Salmon Mousse

9 ounces cream cheese,
    softened
1/4 teaspoon salt
1 tablespoon prepared
    horseradish
1 tablespoon lemon juice

1 tablespoon minced onion
1 tablespoon liquid smoke
1 (16-ounce) can red salmon,
    boned, skinned, flaked
Capers, rinsed, drained
Chopped fresh parsley

❧ Combine the cream cheese, salt, horseradish, lemon juice, onion and liquid smoke in a food processor container; process at medium speed until smooth and creamy. Stir in the salmon. Chill, covered, in the refrigerator for 12 hours. Remove to a serving bowl. Top with the capers and parsley.

Yield: 12 servings

May use chive cream cheese for a different flavor.

Shrimp Cocktail Mold

1/2 cup chili sauce
1/4 cup ketchup
1 tablespoon unflavored
   gelatin
5 ounces shrimp
1 tablespoon minced onion

1/2 teaspoon Worcestershire
   sauce
1/2 teaspoon horseradish
1 1/2 tablespoons lemon juice
Tabasco sauce to taste
1/2 teaspoon sugar

Combine the chili sauce and ketchup in the top of a double boiler, stirring to blend. Sprinkle the gelatin over the mixture; stir. Let soften for 5 minutes. Stir in the shrimp, onion, Worcestershire sauce, horseradish, lemon juice, Tabasco sauce and sugar. Cook over simmering water until heated through, stirring constantly. Grease a 1 cup mold. Pour in the shrimp mixture. Chill, covered, in the refrigerator until firm. Serve with crackers.

Yield: 6 servings

Your guests don't come

for gourmet food. They

come to see you. They come

for good conversation.

Donna Beavers

Syrian Grand Fromage

8 teaspoons minced garlic
1/2 cup lemon juice
1 1/2 cups vegetable oil
1/3 cup dried mint

4 teaspoons Greek seasoning
2 teaspoons garlic pepper
4 tomatoes, chopped
8 ounces goat cheese, sliced

Combine garlic, lemon juice, oil, mint, Greek seasoning and garlic pepper in a bowl, whisking vigorously until well mixed. Stir in tomatoes. Pour mixture over goat cheese. Serve with crackers or toast points.

Yield: 12 servings

Smoked Catfish Pâté

½ cup water
½ cup vermouth
1 pound catfish fillets
16 ounces cream cheese,
  softened

1 clove of garlic, minced
2 tablespoons lemon juice
2 teaspoons Creole seasoning
½ to 1 teaspoon liquid smoke
Salt and pepper to taste

❧ Combine the water and vermouth in a skillet or shallow saucepan, stirring to blend. Bring to a simmer; add the catfish. Poach, covered, until the fish flakes easily when probed with a fork; drain. Let cool. Combine the catfish, cream cheese, garlic, lemon juice, Creole seasoning and liquid smoke in a food processor or blender container; process at medium speed until smooth and creamy. Season with salt and pepper. Chill, covered, in the refrigerator for 12 to 24 hours. Serve with assorted crackers or toast.

Yield: 20 servings

Last of the Red Hot Hams

3 cups finely chopped or
  ground ham, cooked
8 ounces cream cheese,
  softened
⅔ cups chutney

2 teaspoons Tabasco sauce
1 cup chopped pecans
Strips of pimento
Chopped fresh parsley

❧ Combine the ham, cream cheese, chutney and Tabasco sauce in a medium bowl; mix until well blended. Stir in ⅔ cup pecans. Line a 4-cup mold or bowl with plastic wrap; firmly pack in the ham mixture. Chill, covered, for 2 hours. Invert the pâté onto a serving plate and remove the plastic wrap. Press the remaining nuts into the top and sides. Decorate with the pimento and parsley.

Yield: 12 servings

The ham pâté at left may be

decorated to look like a gift

box. Simply shape the pâté in

a square mold or baking pan,

and arrange the pimento and

parsley so they appear to

be a ribbon and bow.

Roquefort Timbales

2 tablespoons unsalted butter,
   softened
2 ounces cream cheese,
   softened
3 ounces Roquefort cheese, at
   room temperature
White pepper to taste
1/16 teaspoon cayenne
3 eggs

1/4 cup whipping cream
2 tablespoons white burgundy
Salt and white pepper to
   taste
1/2 cup whipping cream
2 tablespoons chopped fresh
   chives
4 slices French bread, toasted

❧ Combine the butter, cream cheese and Roquefort cheese in a food processor container; process at medium speed until blended and creamy, scraping the bowl as necessary. Season with the white pepper and cayenne.

❧ Beat the eggs in a medium bowl until blended. Whisk in the 1/4 cup whipping cream. Stir in the Roquefort cheese mixture and mix well. Strain through a sieve.

❧ Butter 4 round or oval timbale molds. Divide the Roquefort cheese mixture among the molds, and arrange in a large pan filled with 1-inch hot water. Bake at 325 degrees for 45 minutes.

❧ Combine the burgundy, salt and pepper in a small saucepan; stir to mix. Cook over medium-high heat until reduced to 1 teaspoon liquid. Stir in the 1/2 cup cream and chives. Boil for 5 minutes.

❧ Arrange the toast on 4 plates. Unmold the Roquefort cheese timbales, and place on the toast. Top with the burgundy sauce.

Yield: 4 servings

Bleu Cheese and Spiced Walnut Terrine

1/2 teaspoon salt
1/2 teaspoon ground cumin
1/4 teaspoon ground
  cardamom
1/4 teaspoon pepper
1 tablespoon olive oil
1 cup walnuts
3 tablespoons sugar
2 1/2 ounces soft fresh goat
  cheese, such as
  Montrachet

16 ounces bleu cheese,
  crumbled
2 1/2 ounces cream cheese,
  softened
1/4 cup butter, softened
1/2 cup chopped green onions
2 tablespoons brandy
2 tablespoons chopped fresh
  parsley
1 tablespoon chopped chives
Red leaf lettuce

❧ Combine the salt, cumin, cardamom and pepper in a medium bowl; whisk lightly to blend. Warm the olive oil in a medium heavy skillet over medium heat; add the walnuts. Sauté for 5 minutes or until light brown. Sprinkle sugar over the nuts. Sauté for 4 minutes or until the sugar melts and turns pale amber, stirring frequently. Remove to the bowl with the cumin mixture; toss to coat well. Let cool. Coarsely chop the nuts. Combine the goat cheese, 12 ounces bleu cheese, cream cheese and butter in a food processor container; process until smooth and creamy. Remove the mixture to a large bowl. Stir in the green onions and brandy. Mix the parsley and chives in a small bowl.

❧ Lightly oil a 4 x 8-inch loaf pan. Line with plastic wrap so the wrap extends over the sides. Spoon 1/3 of the cheese mixture into the bottom of the pan, spreading evenly with the back of a spoon. Layer 1/3 of the remaining crumbled blue cheese and the walnuts. Sprinkle with 1 tablespoon of the parsley mixture. Repeat layering. Spread the remaining cheese mixture evenly over the top. Fold the plastic over the cheese to cover. Chill for 12 hours. Chill, in separate containers and covered, the remaining crumbled bleu cheese and parsley mixture. Store the remaining walnuts at room temperature. Line a serving platter with lettuce. Invert the bleu cheese mold onto the platter; remove the plastic wrap. Sprinkle with the remaining bleu cheese, walnuts, and parsley mixture.

Yield: 12 servings

Bleu Cheese Mousse on Endive with Apple and Walnuts

3 ounces cream cheese,
  softened
2 tablespoons whipping cream
Tabasco sauce to taste
30 endive spears

6 ounces bleu cheese
15 walnut halves, toasted,
  split in half
Sliced Granny Smith apple

☙ Combine the cream cheese, heavy cream and Tabasco sauce in a food processor container; process at medium speed until smooth and well blended. Divide the cream cheese mixture among the endive spears; top with some crumbled bleu cheese and a walnut half. Serve with apple slices.

Yield: 30 servings

For best flavor, this torte

may be made several days in

advance. To fill a 9-inch

springform pan, make

1½ times the recipe.

Pecan Cheddar Cheese Torte

12 ounces sharp Cheddar
  cheese, shredded
1 cup chopped red onion
¼ cup chopped fresh parsley
1½ cups chopped pecans

½ teaspoon pepper
1 to 3 tablespoons
  mayonnaise
8 ounces jalapeño jelly

☙ Combine the Cheddar cheese, onion, parsley, pecans and pepper in a bowl, tossing lightly. Add the mayonnaise, 1 tablespoon at a time, just until the mixture holds together; mix well. Oil a 7-inch springform pan. Press the cheese mixture into the pan. Chill, covered, in the refrigerator until very cold.

☙ Remove the pan side, and spread the jalapeño jelly over the cheese torte. Serve with assorted crisp crackers.

Yield 10 servings

Mushroom Strudels

1 pound mushrooms, minced
3/4 cup butter
1 tablespoon vegetable oil
1/2 cup minced yellow onion
1 cup minced green onions
1/4 teaspoon Tabasco sauce
1/2 cup sour cream

2 tablespoons minced fresh
   dill or 1 tablespoon dried
   dillweed
1/2 teaspoon salt
1/4 teaspoon pepper
6 to 8 sheets of phyllo

❧ Preheat the oven to 350 degrees; butter a baking sheet. Place the mushrooms, a handful at a time, in a tea towel and squeeze out the moisture. Melt 3 tablespoons butter with the oil in a skillet over medium-high heat; add the mushrooms and onions. Sauté for 15 minutes or until the moisture has evaporated. Remove the skillet from the heat, and stir in the Tabasco sauce, sour cream, dill, salt and pepper. Let cool.

❧ Place the phyllo sheets under plastic wrap and a damp tea towel to keep them moist. Melt the remaining butter in a small saucepan. Place 1 phyllo sheet on a sheet of waxed paper; brush gently with butter. Place a second sheet directly over the first; brush with butter. Spread a 1-inch-wide strip of the mushroom mixture along one long side of the stacked sheets; roll up jelly-roll fashion. Place, seam side down, on the baking sheet. Stack, butter and fill the remaining phyllo sheets. Brush butter over all the phyllo rolls.

❧ Bake for 45 minutes or until crisp and golden brown. Allow the phyllo rolls to cool for 5 minutes on a wire rack. Bias cut into 1-inch slices.

Yield: 24 servings

To make triangular strudels,

spoon the mushroom filling

onto small phyllo squares;

fold to form triangles. The

strudels may be frozen.

Cheddar Cream Cheese Chutney

8 ounces cream cheese,
softened
8 ounces sharp Cheddar
cheese, shredded

1/8 teaspoon curry powder
3/4 to 1 cup toasted almonds
1 (16-ounce) jar chutney

❧ Combine the cream cheese, Cheddar cheese, curry powder, 1/2 cup almonds and 2 tablespoons chutney in a food processor container; process at medium speed until smooth, scraping the bowl as necessary. Line a bowl with plastic wrap; spoon in the cheese mixture. Chill, covered, in the refrigerator until firm.

❧ Remove from the refrigerator and place on a serving plate 2 hours before serving. Spoon the remaining chutney over the cheese mixture and top with the remaining almonds just before serving.

Yield: 12 servings

I hate to cook unless I'm

cooking for a big crew.

Betty Hayes

Mexican Cheese Ball

8 ounces cream cheese,
softened
8 ounces shredded Cheddar
cheese
1/4 teaspoon garlic powder
1/4 teaspoon onion powder

1/2 teaspoon chili powder
1/4 teaspoon ground cumin
1 tablespoon minced pickled
jalapeño
2 tablespoons snipped
cilantro

❧ Combine the cream cheese, Cheddar cheese, garlic powder, onion powder, chili powder, cumin, pepperoncini and 1 tablespoon of the cilantro in a bowl; mix well. Chill, covered, in the refrigerator for 12 hours.

❧ Form into a ball, and coat with the remaining cilantro. Serve with tortilla chips or assorted crackers.

Yield: 8 servings

Hill Country Cheese Pecan Spread

8 ounces cream cheese,
  softened
2 tablespoons milk
2 ounces chipped dried beef
1/4 cup chopped green bell
  pepper
2 tablespoons minced onion

1/2 cup sour cream
1/2 teaspoon minced garlic
1 to 2 tablespoons chopped
  pickled jalapeño
1/4 teaspoon pepper
1/2 cup chopped pecans
2 tablespoons butter

❧ Preheat the oven to 350 degrees. Blend the cream cheese and milk in the mixer bowl of an electric mixer at medium speed. Stir in the dried beef, bell pepper, onion, sour cream, garlic, pepperoncini, and black pepper; blend well. Spoon into a 1-quart baking dish; smooth with the back of a spoon. Sauté pecans in butter in small skillet over medium heat until light brown. Sprinkle over the cheese mixture. Bake for 20 minutes.

Yield: 12 servings

Pecan Spread with Chipped Beef

2 teaspoons butter
1/2 cup chopped pecans
1/2 teaspoon salt
8 ounces cream cheese,
  softened
2 tablespoons milk
1 (2 1/2-ounce) jar chipped
  dried beef

1/4 cup finely chopped green
  bell pepper
2 teaspoons minced dried
  onions
1/2 teaspoon garlic salt
1/4 teaspoon pepper
1/2 cup sour cream

❧ Melt the butter in a small skillet over medium heat; add the pecans and salt. Sauté until toasted. Cream the cream cheese and milk in a bowl. Stir in the remaining ingredients. Spoon into a baking dish and top with the pecans. Bake at 350 degrees for 20 minutes. Serve with melba toast.

Yield: 12 servings

When I look in my recipe

box, I find recipes from my

aunts. I can see them

cooking that good food.

Cooking is a tie to my past.

Nancy Shelton

Spicy Peanut Dip

1/2 cup peanut butter
2 tablespoons water
1/4 cup soy sauce
1/4 cup dark sesame oil
2 tablespoons sherry
4 teaspoons rice wine vinegar

1/4 cup honey
4 cloves of garlic, minced
3 teaspoons minced
   gingerroot
2 tablespoons hot-pepper oil
Chopped peanuts (optional)

❧ Combine the peanut butter, water, soy sauce, sesame oil, sherry, vinegar, honey, garlic, gingerroot and hot-pepper oil in a food processor container; process at medium speed until smooth, scraping the bowl occasionally. Thin with hot water, 1 tablespoon at a time, if necessary. Pour into a serving bowl. Top with peanuts if desired.

Yield: 16 servings

The immediate world was

at our house for dinner. The

mailman would come for pie.

The breadman would sell his

wares, finish his run, and

then end up at my mother's

house for a piece of her cake.

Mary Ann Blome

Ancho Chile Salsa

8 ancho chiles, seeded,
   deveined
8 to 10 sun-dried tomatoes
   (not oil-packed), chopped
1 medium sweet onion,
   chopped
2 to 4 cloves of garlic, finely
   chopped

1/2 cup olive oil
1/2 cup red wine vinegar
1 teaspoon dried oregano,
   crushed
2 (3-ounce) rounds Texas
   goat cheese
Tortilla chips

❧ Roast the ancho chiles in an iron skillet over medium-high heat for 5 minutes; the skin will blister somewhat. Chop into 1/4- to 1/2-inch pieces. Soak briefly in hot water to cover in a small bowl; drain. Soak the sun-dried tomatoes briefly in hot water to cover in a small bowl; drain. Combine the ancho chiles, sun-dried tomatoes, onion, garlic, olive oil and vinegar in a medium bowl; mix well. Marinate for 2 hours at room temperature. Remove to a serving bowl; top with the goat cheese rounds. Serve with tortilla chips.

Yield: 6 to 8 servings

Authentic Mexican Green Sauce

2 pounds tomatillos, husks
    removed
1 teaspoon chicken base or
    chicken bouillon
1/8 teaspoon oregano
1 clove of garlic, finely
    chopped

2 bunches cilantro, chopped
1 teaspoon Worcestershire
    sauce
2 serranos, seeded, chopped
1/4 cup chopped onions
1 tablespoon sugar, or
    to taste

❧ Soak the tomatillos in warm water to cover in a large bowl for 30 minutes. Chop and place in a saucepan; pour in water to cover. Cook for 10 minutes or until tender; drain. Combine the chicken base, oregano, garlic, cilantro, Worcestershire sauce, serranos, onions and tomatillos in a food processor or blender container; process until smooth. Remove to a saucepan; stir in the sugar. Simmer over medium heat for 30 minutes. Serve with tortilla chips.

Yield: 12 servings

Tuscan Tomato Bruschetta

14 plum tomatoes
4 tablespoons minced garlic
3/4 cup chopped fresh basil
1/4 cup chopped fresh Italian
    parsley
2 tablespoons lemon juice

1/16 teaspoon crushed red
    pepper flakes
Salt and pepper to taste
30 (1/4-inch-thick) slices
    French bread
6 cloves of garlic, halved

❧ Combine the tomatoes, minced garlic, basil, parsley, lemon juice, red pepper flakes in a bowl; mix well. Season with salt and pepper. Marinate, covered, in the refrigerator for 4 to 5 hours. Toast the bread slices just before serving. Rub with the garlic cloves. Arrange around the edge of a serving platter. Fill a bowl with the tomato mixture; place in the center of the platter.

Yield: 15 servings

The tomato mixture

also makes a tasty filling

for omelettes.

Hot Onion Dip

1 (12- to 16-ounce) package
  frozen chopped onions,
  thawed
24 ounces cream cheese,
  softened

2 cups grated Parmesan
  cheese
1/2 cup mayonnaise

❧ Squeeze the onions dry a handful at a time. Combine the onions, cream cheese, Parmesan cheese and mayonnaise in a large bowl. Pour into a 2-quart baking dish. Bake at 425 degrees for 15 minutes. Serve with corn chips.

Yield: 24 servings

One of my husband's

patients was the famed

gourmet Helen Corbit.

She inscribed her *Green*

House Cookbook with

the following: "Good luck!

It's never too late to start."

Elizabeth Gunby

Easy and Elegant Shrimp Dip

1 pound shrimp, cooked,
  peeled, deveined
9 ounces cream cheese,
  softened
3 tablespoons chili sauce

1/2 teaspoon onion juice or
  minced onion
2 teaspoons lemon juice
1/4 teaspoon Worcestershire
  sauce

❧ Chop the shrimp coarsely. Combine the shrimp, cream cheese, chili sauce, onion juice, lemon juice and Worcestershire sauce in a large bowl. Serve with assorted crackers.

Yield: 16 servings

Almond Tea

2 cups boiling water
3 large tea bags
4 cups water
¾ to 1 cup sugar, or
    to taste

⅓ cup lemon juice
1 tablespoon almond extract
1 tablespoon vanilla extract

🌱 Pour the boiling water over the tea bags in a large heat-proof pitcher and let steep for 5 minutes. Discard the tea bags. Combine the 4 cups water, sugar, lemon juice, almond extract and vanilla extract in a saucepan. Bring to a boil over high heat and pour into the tea mixture. Serve hot.

Yield: 6 servings

Kentucky Mint Tea

4 tea bags
1 tablespoon dried mint
4 cups boiling water
⅔ cup lemon juice

⅓ cup orange juice
3 cups hot water
1¼ cups sugar

🌱 Combine the tea bags and mint in a heat-proof pitcher. Pour in the boiling water and let steep for 5 minutes. Discard the tea bags. Combine the lemon juice, orange juice, hot water and sugar in another pitcher or saucepan. Pour into the tea mixture. Serve cold over ice with a sprig of fresh mint for garnish.

Yield: 16 servings

A Thyme to
Remember

The recipe may be multiplied

by 5 to serve 25 people. Use

proportionally less sugar

when increasing the recipe.

❧❧❧

Superfine sugar is

available in most

supermarkets, or it may

be made by grinding

regular granulated sugar

in a food processor.

❧❧❧

Honey Mint Lemonade

2 cups water
1/2 cup honey
4 large sprigs of mint
1 cup lemon juice

1 tablespoon superfine sugar,
   or to taste
Ice cubes

❧ Combine the water and honey in a saucepan. Bring to a boil over high heat, stirring frequently. Remove from the heat; add the mint and let cool.

❧ Pour the honey mixture into a glass container, add the lemon juice and superfine sugar. Chill, covered, in the refrigerator. Place the ice cubes in a pitcher or glasses. Pour the lemonade through a strainer into the pitcher or glasses.

Yield: 8 servings

Fiesta Sangria

1 (750-milliliter) bottle
   burgundy
1 jigger (about 1 1/2 ounces or
   3 tablespoons) brandy
1 (7-ounce) bottle sparkling
   water

1 orange, sliced
1 lemon or 2 limes, sliced
1 peach, sliced
2 plums, sliced
1/2 cup sliced strawberries
Sugar to taste

❧ Combine the burgundy, brandy and sparkling water in a large pitcher. Stir in the orange, lemon, peach, plums and strawberries. Stir in sugar until dissolved.

Yield: 8 servings

James' Champagne Party Punch

1 (750-milliliter) bottle
  champagne
1 (750-milliliter) bottle
  sauterne

1 quart sparkling water
1/2 cup bourbon
Ice ring

❧ Combine the champagne, sauterne, sparkling water and bourbon in a large punch bowl. Float the ice ring in the punch.

Yield: 20 servings

Hot Cranberry Punch

2 teaspoons whole allspice
2 sticks cinnamon
2 teaspoons whole cloves
2 cups cranberry juice cocktail

2 1/2 cups pineapple juice
1/2 cup water
1/3 cup packed brown sugar

❧ Arrange the allspice, cinnamon and cloves in the basket of a percolator-style coffee pot. Combine the cranberry juice, pineapple juice and water in the pot. Percolate until hot. Discard the allspice, cinnamon and cloves. Add the brown sugar to the hot juice mixture, stirring until dissolved.

Yield: 10 servings

A Thyme to Remember

This recipe is great for

holiday parties and may be

doubled or tripled.

The grapefruit mixture

may be made ahead and

stored, covered, in the

refrigerator for 12 hours.

Vintage Grapefruit Punch

3½ cups grapefruit juice
2 tablespoons sugar
6 tablespoons lemon juice

6 sprigs of mint
3½ cups ginger ale

Combine the grapefruit juice, sugar, lemon juice and mint in a large pitcher or punch bowl. Stir in the ginger ale just before serving. May garnish each serving with additional mint leaves.
Yield: 16 servings

Frozen Cappuccinos

1 cup espresso, at room
    temperature
2 cups ice cubes
¼ cup half-and-half or milk

3 tablespoons superfine sugar
¼ teaspoon cinnamon
¼ cup coffee-flavored liqueur
    (optional)

Combine the espresso, ice, half-and-half, superfine sugar, cinnamon and liqueur in a blender container; process until smooth but still thick. Divide the mixture immediately between 2 tall glasses. Dust with a little cinnamon.

Yield: 2 servings

A Handful of Herbs

SALADS

"I became a doctor
because I felt that my
calling was to
become a better servant
and help others."
—*Kimberly J. Yamanouchi, M.D.,*
Anesthesiologist

Asparagus with Sweet and Savory Dressing

1 pound asparagus, trimmed
1 teaspoon vegetable oil
1/2 teaspoon salt
Sweet and Savory Dressing
    (below)

1/4 cup chopped toasted
    walnuts

❧ Cut the asparagus diagonally into 1 1/2-inch slices. Fill a large saucepan with water. Bring to a boil over high heat; add the asparagus, oil and salt. Cook for 1 to 2 minutes or until the asparagus is tender-crisp. Drain in a colander and rinse briefly under cold water to halt cooking. Drain and pat dry with paper towels.

❧ Add the Sweet and Savory Dressing; toss to coat. Arrange on a serving plate and top with walnuts.

Yield: 4 servings

Sweet and Savory Dressing

2 tablespoons plum sauce
2 tablespoons rice vinegar
2 tablespoons soy sauce
1 tablespoon sesame oil

1 teaspoon chili oil
2 teaspoons sugar or honey
1/2 teaspoon dry mustard

❧ Combine the plum sauce, rice vinegar, soy sauce, sesame oil, chili oil, sugar and dry mustard in a small bowl; mix well.

For *Purple Basil Vinaigrette*,

whisk 1½ tablespoons red

wine vinegar, ⅓ cup olive oil,

½ teaspoon herbes de

Provence, juice of 1 lemon,

½ cup minced purple basil and

2 minced shallots in a small

bowl until well blended.

Season with salt and pepper

to taste; whisk to combine.

Tomato and Grilled Eggplant with Purple Basil Vinaigrette

1 medium eggplant	Purple Basil Vinaigrette (at left)
⅓ cup olive oil	¼ cup shaved Parmesan
Salt and pepper to taste	cheese
2 large tomatoes, sliced	½ cup black olives

❧ Cut the eggplant into ½-inch slices. Brush both sides with the olive oil and season with salt and pepper. Preheat the grill. Coat the grill rack with nonstick cooking spray; place on the grill. Arrange the eggplant on the rack. Grill for 3 minutes on each side; remove to a serving platter. Arrange the tomatoes with the eggplant. Pour the Purple Basil Vinaigrette over the eggplant and tomatoes. Top with the Parmesan cheese and olives.

Yield: 4 servings

Marinated Dill Carrots

2 (16-ounce) jars whole small	1 teaspoon Beau Monde
carrots	seasonsing
½ cup white wine vinegar	¾ cup sugar
1 teaspoon dillweed	

❧ Drain the carrots, reserving ½ cup of the liquid. Remove the carrots to a bowl. Whisk the wine vinegar, dillweed, Beau Monde seasoning, sugar and reserved carrot liquid in a small saucepan until blended. Bring to a boil over medium-high heat; pour over the carrots and toss to coat. Chill, covered, in the refrigerator for 12 hours before serving.

Yield: 8 servings

Walnut Sauce for Green Beans

1/4 cup walnuts, chopped
1/4 cup chopped fresh parsley
2 green onions, chopped
1/4 teaspoon salt
1/8 teaspoon pepper
1/3 cup mayonnaise

2 tablespoons lemon juice
1/4 cup vegetable oil
2 tablespoons chopped
    pimento
Green beans

☙ Combine the walnuts, parsley, onions, salt, pepper, mayonnaise, lemon juice, oil and pimentos in a small bowl; mix well. Pour over hot or chilled cooked green beans; toss to coat.

Yield: 6 servings

Broccoli with Bacon and Parmesan

2 heads broccoli florets
1 small onion, finely chopped
1 1/2 cups golden raisins
10 slices crisp-fried bacon,
    crumbled

1 cup mayonnaise
1 1/2 cups Parmesan cheese
1/3 cup sugar
1 tablespoon white wine
    vinegar

☙ Fill a large saucepan with water. Bring to a boil over high heat; add the broccoli. Cook for 2 minutes. Drain in a colander; rinse with cold water to halt cooking. Combine the broccoli, onion and raisins in a large bowl, tossing gently.

☙ Combine the bacon, mayonnaise, Parmesan cheese, sugar and wine vinegar in a small bowl; mix well. Pour over the broccoli mixture and toss to coat. Chill, covered, in the refrigerator before serving.

Yield: 8 servings

Fusilli Salad with Sun-Dried Tomatoes and Peas

1 pound fusilli or shells
1 (10-ounce) package frozen
  peas
3 ounces sun-dried tomatoes
  (not oil-packed)
2 green bell peppers, julienned

½ cup plus 2 tablespoons
  Reduced-Fat Italian
  Salad Dressing (below)
Salt and pepper to taste

❧ Cook the fusilli according to package directions; drain in a colander and rinse briefly under cold water to halt cooking. Cook the peas according to package directions; drain well. Pour enough boiling water over the sun-dried tomatoes to cover in a small bowl. Let stand for 20 minutes; drain well and pat dry.

❧ Combine the fusilli, peas, tomatoes, bell peppers and Reduced-Fat Italian Salad Dressing in a large bowl; toss to mix. Chill, covered, for 1 hour.

Yield: 6 servings

Reduced-Fat Italian Salad Dressing

½ cup balsamic vinegar
¼ cup red wine vinegar
2 cloves of garlic, minced, or
  to taste
¼ teaspoon dried oregano

¼ teaspoon dried basil
Salt and pepper to taste
2 tablespoons olive oil
2 tablespoons chicken broth

❧ Whisk the balsamic vinegar, red wine vinegar, garlic, oregano and basil in a small bowl until combined. Whisk in the olive oil and chicken broth until well blended.

Asian Noodle Salad with Ginger Sesame Vinaigrette

1 pound fresh or dried thin
    Asian wheat noodles or
    spaghettini
Ginger Sesame Vinaigrette
    (below)
8 ounces snow peas

1 cup finely chopped green
    onions
1 cup coarsely chopped
    unsalted dry-roasted
    peanuts
1/2 cup chopped cilantro

❧ Cook the Asian noodles according to package directions; drain in a colander and rinse briefly under cold water to halt cooking. Remove to a large bowl. Pour in half the Ginger Sesame Vinaigrette and toss to coat. Let cool to room temperature, stirring occasionally to keep the noodles from sticking together. Cut snow peas diagonally. Cook in boiling water in a saucepan for 1 minute or until tender-crisp. Drain in a colander and plunge quickly into ice water to halt cooking. Drain well.

❧ Add the snow peas, green onions, peanuts, cilantro and the remaining Ginger Sesame Vinaigrette to the noodle mixture; toss gently to combine. Serve at room temperature.

Yield: 8 servings

Ginger Sesame Vinaigrette

1/3 cup rice wine vinegar
1/4 cup soy sauce
1 tablespoon minced
    gingerroot

1 teaspoon minced garlic
1/3 cup sesame oil
1/3 cup (total) vegetable oil
    plus hot chili oil

❧ Whisk the rice wine vinegar, soy sauce, gingerroot and garlic until combined. Whisk the sesame oil and vegetable oil mixture in gradually until well blended.

For a main dish salad, add bite-size pieces of cooked chicken, duck, scallops, shrimp, or turkey. To make the salad a day ahead, reserve the snow peas until right before serving. Chill, covered, in the refrigerator. Bring to room temperature before adding the snow peas.

A Thyme to Remember

❦ ❦ ❦

This salad may be served immediately but is better when chilled, covered, in the refrigerator for several hours. To serve as a side salad, omit the chicken.

❦ ❦ ❦

Bow Ties with Tomatoes

1 pound bow tie pasta
1 green bell pepper, chopped
1 red bell pepper, chopped
1 yellow bell pepper, chopped
3 ounces oil-packed sun-dried
   tomatoes, chopped

1 medium red onion, chopped
3 ounces pine nuts
8 ounces red wine dressing
2 teaspoons sugar
3 grilled boneless, skinless
   chicken breasts (optional)

❧ Cook the bow tie pasta according to package directions; drain in a colander and rinse briefly under cold water to halt cooking. Mix the pasta, bell peppers, sun-dried tomatoes, red onion and pine nuts in a large bowl. Whisk the red wine dressing and sugar in a small bowl until well blended. Pour over the pasta mixture and toss to coat. Add the chicken and toss to combine.

Yield: 8 servings

Vermicelli Chicken Salad

1 cup quartered cherry
   tomatoes
1 cup snow peas
8 ounces mushrooms, sliced
1 cup quartered, drained
   canned artichoke hearts
3 cups cubed cooked chicken

1/4 cup chopped fresh parsley
3/4 cup pine nuts or sliced
   almonds
3 teaspoons dried basil
1 1/2 cups Italian dressing
12 ounces vermicelli
Parmesan cheese

❧ Combine the cherry tomatoes, snow peas, mushrooms, artichokes, chicken, parsley, pine nuts and basil in a large bowl; toss gently. Pour in 1 cup Italian dressing and toss to coat. Chill, covered, for 12 hours. Cook the vermicelli according to package directions; drain. Pour in 1/2 cup Italian dressing; toss to coat. Chill, covered, for 12 hours. Combine the tomato mixture and vermicelli just before serving; toss lightly. Sprinkle Parmesan cheese over the salad.

Yield: 10 servings

Rosemary Chicken Fettucini Salad

1 (14-ounce) can chicken
    broth
4 whole chicken breasts
2 pounds fettucini
Rosemary Salad Dressing
    (below)
1½ cups snow peas

4 zucchini, thinly sliced
1 cup chopped green onions
1½ cup chopped fresh parsley
Lettuce leaves
½ cup grated Parmesan
    cheese

❧ Pour the chicken broth into a saucepan. Bring to a simmer; add the chicken. Simmer, covered, until cooked through and tender. Let cool in the broth; discard the broth. Skin, bone, and slice the chicken. Break the fettucini strands into thirds. Cook the fettucini according to package directions; drain in a colander and rinse briefly under cold water to halt cooking. Mix in the chicken.

❧ Reserve ⅓ cup Rosemary Salad Dressing. Pour the remaining dressing over the fettucini mixture. Chill, covered, in the refrigerator for 12 hours. Fill a large saucepan with water 2 hours before serving. Bring to a boil over high heat; add the snow peas. Blanch for 1 minute. Drain in a colander and rinse under cold water to halt cooking. Drain and slice in half lengthwise. Add the snow peas, zucchini, green onions, parsley and reserved ⅓ cup Rosemary Salad Dressing to the fettucini mixture; toss gently to combine. Serve on lettuce, and sprinkle the Parmesan cheese over the salad. Chill, covered, in the refrigerator until serving time if desired.

Yield: 16 servings

Rosemary Salad Dressing

1½ cups olive oil
¾ cup lemon juice
2 cloves of garlic, minced
5 teaspoons sugar, or to taste

2½ teaspoons dry mustard
4 to 6 tablespoons chopped
    fresh rosemary
1¼ teaspoons salt

❧ Whisk the olive oil, lemon juice, garlic, sugar, dry mustard, rosemary and salt in a small bowl until well blended.

A Thyme to
Remember

❧❧❧

When my mother would

come in late from a meeting,

she would head for the

kitchen and, still in her suit

and heels, she would start

frying onions. It gave my

father hope that there would

be dinner that evening.

Marty Curtis

❧❧❧

Chicken and Roast Corn Salad with Cilantro Pesto Dressing

Lime Jalapeño Marinade
(page 47)
4 (6- to 8-ounce) skinless
boneless chicken breasts
2 ears of corn
1 medium red onion, sliced
into thin wedges
1 medium jicama, julienned
1 red bell pepper, julienned

1 yellow bell pepper, julienned
1 green bell pepper, julienned
1 Granny Smith apple,
peeled, julienned
Cilantro Pesto Dressing (page 47)
6 corn tortillas, cut into
1/4x2-inch strips
Juice of 1 lime
Salt to taste

❧ Combine the Lime Jalapeño Marinade and chicken in a self-sealing plastic bag, turning to coat well. Marinate in the refrigerator for 3 to 12 hours.

❧ Preheat the grill. Coat the grill rack with nonstick cooking spray; place on the grill. Arrange the chicken on the rack. Grill until cooked through and a meat thermometer registers 160 degrees. Let cool slightly; julienne while warm.

❧ Pull back the corn husks, keeping them attached at the stalk end, and remove the silk. Reposition the husks over the kernels. Roast at 350 degrees for 20 to 25 minutes. Let cool. Remove the husks and cut off the kernels.

❧ Combine the corn, red onion, jicama, bell peppers, apple and chicken in a large bowl; toss gently. Add the Cilantro Pesto Dressing and tortilla strips; toss to combine. Season with the lime juice and salt. Serve with sour cream and diced tomatoes.

Yield: 4 servings

Lime Jalapeño Marinade

Juice of 2 limes
3 cloves of garlic, minced
2 jalapeños, seeded, minced

¼ cup canola oil
½ bunch cilantro, chopped
Salt to taste

❧ Combine the lime juice, garlic, jalapeños, canola oil and cilantro in a small bowl; whisk until well blended. Season with salt.

Cilantro Pesto Dressing

1 bunch cilantro, chopped
¼ cup toasted pumpkin seeds
Juice of 2 limes
3 cloves of garlic

¼ cup grated Romano cheese
¼ cup olive oil
2 tablespoons mayonnaise
Salt to taste

❧ Combine the cilantro, pumpkin seeds, lime juice, garlic and Romano cheese in a blender container; process at high speed until smooth. Add the olive oil in a thin stream, processing at high speed until emulsified and smooth. Scrape the jar sides as needed. Fold in the mayonnaise. Season with salt.

A Thyme to Remember

"Fortunately, I always

knew that I wanted to

go into medicine."

Allen Jones, M.D.,

Internal Medicine

Asian Chicken Salad

1 head cabbage, shredded
6 green onions, sliced
1 bunch cilantro, chopped
4 cooked chicken breasts,
   chopped
Asian-Seasoned Salad
   Dressing (at left)

½ cup slivered almonds,
   toasted
½ cup sunflower seeds
2 (3-ounce) packages
   Oriental-flavor ramen
   soup mix

Combine the cabbage, green onions, cilantro and chicken in a large bowl; toss gently. Pour in the Asian-Seasoned Salad Dressing; toss gently to combine. Add the almonds and sunflower seeds; toss to combine. Crumble uncooked ramen noodles over the salad just before serving.

Yield: 6 servings

For *Asian-Seasoned Salad Dressing*, whisk ½ cup vegetable oil, ½ teaspoon salt, 6 tablespoons rice wine vinegar, ½ teaspoon pepper, 4 teaspoons sugar and 2 envelopes seasoning from ramen soup mix in a small bowl until blended.

Dried Cherry Chicken Salad

1 cup dried tart red cherries
4 cooked chicken breast
   halves, cut into bite-size
   pieces
3 ribs celery, coarsely chopped
2 cups Granny Smith apples,
   coarsely chopped
1 cup coarsely chopped
   pecans

1¼ cups mayonnaise
½ cup chopped fresh parsley
1 tablespoon raspberry
   vinegar
Salt and pepper to taste
Red leaf lettuce
Dried tart red cherries
   to taste

Combine 1 cup cherries, chicken, celery, apples and pecans in a large bowl; toss lightly. Whisk the mayonnaise, parsley and raspberry vinegar in a small bowl until thoroughly combined. Pour over the chicken mixture and toss gently to coat well. Season with salt and pepper. Chill, covered, in the refrigerator for 2 hours or longer. Serve on a bed of red leaf lettuce. Top with the remaining dried cherries.

Yield: 6 servings

Cilantro Chicken Salad

4 cups chicken broth
6 skinless chicken breasts
1/2 cup lime juice
2 tablespoons red wine vinegar
2 tablespoons vegetable oil
2 teaspoons salt
1 tablespoon sugar
2 tablespoons minced garlic
1/2 cup chopped cilantro

1/2 cup chopped red onion
3 small tomatoes, peeled,
    seeded, chopped
2 to 3 small Anaheim chiles,
    chopped
1 cup cooked black beans
2 small avocados, cut into
    bite-size pieces
Leaf lettuce

❧ Bring the broth to a simmer; add the chicken. Simmer, covered,
until the chicken is tender. Cool in the broth. Remove the chicken
and cut into bite-size pieces. Chill the broth, covered. Skim the
fat. Reserve 1/2 cup broth. Combine the next 10 ingredients and
reserved broth in a large bowl, tossing gently. Add the chicken and
black beans; toss to combine. Marinate, covered, in the refrigerator
for 4 to 12 hours. Add the avocados just before serving; toss lightly
to combine. Serve on leaf lettuce.

Yield: 8 servings

Chicken and Artichoke Rice Salad

6 cooked skinless boneless
    chicken breasts, cut into
    bite-size pieces
1 (7-ounce) box chicken
    Rice-A-Roni mix, cooked
2 (12-ounce) jars marinated
    artichoke hearts

2 (4 1/2-ounce) cans chopped
    black olives
4 to 5 large green onions,
    chopped
2 cups mayonnaise
1/4 teaspoon curry powder
1/2 teaspoon garlic powder

❧ Combine the chicken and Rice-A-Roni in a bowl, tossing gently.
Drain and chop the artichokes, reserving half the marinade. Add the
artichokes, olives and onions to the chicken mixture; toss lightly.
Blend the reserved artichoke marinade and remaining ingredients
in a small bowl. Spoon over the chicken mixture; mix well.

Yield: 6 servings

❧❧❧

For *Castillian Vinaigrette*,

whisk 2 tablespoons tarragon

vinegar, 1/3 cup olive oil,

1 teaspoon seasoned salt,

1 teaspoon Greek seasoning,

and 1/4 teaspoon dry

mustard in a small bowl

until thoroughly blended.

❧❧❧

Paella Salad

1 (7-ounce) package yellow
   saffron rice, cooked,
   cooled
Castillian Vinaigrette (at left)
1 large tomato, chopped
1/2 cup finely chopped onion
1/2 green bell pepper, chopped

1/3 cup thinly sliced celery
1 tablespoon chopped pimento
2 cups cubed cooked chicken
   breasts
1 cup (about 8 ounces) peeled
   cooked shrimp
1 cup peas

❧ Combine the rice and Castillian Vinaigrette in a medium bowl; toss to coat. Chill, covered, in the refrigerator. Add the tomato, onion, bell pepper, celery, pimento, chicken, shrimp and peas; toss gently to combine.

Yield: 8 servings

Wild Rice Salad

1 cup wild rice
Seasoned salt (optional)
2 cups diced cooked chicken
1 cup drained sliced water
   chestnuts

1 1/2 cups halved green grapes
3/4 cup light mayonnaise
1 cup toasted pecan pieces
Lettuce leaves

❧ Cook the rice according to package directions, substituting the seasoned salt for salt. Let cool to room temperature.

❧ Remove to a large bowl. Add the chicken, water chestnuts, grapes and mayonnaise; toss gently to combine. Chill, covered, in the refrigerator. Add the pecans just before serving, tossing lightly. Serve on lettuce leaves.

Yield: 6 servings

West Indies Crabmeat Salad

1 pound cooked crabmeat
3 tablespoons white balsamic
   vinegar
½ cup olive oil

1 minced medium onion
1 tablespoon minced fresh dill
½ cup ice water
Salt and pepper to taste

❧ Combine the crabmeat, vinegar, olive oil, onion, dill and ice water in a medium bowl; mix well. Season with salt and pepper. Chill, covered, in the refrigerator for 1 to 6 hours.

Yield: 4 servings

Exotic Curried Shrimp Salad

2 pounds peeled, cooked
   shrimp
1 cup mayonnaise
2 teaspoons soy sauce
2 teaspoons curry powder

1 cup sliced water chestnuts
¼ cup chopped green onions
¼ cup chopped celery
Shredded lettuce

❧ Combine the shrimp, mayonnaise, soy sauce and curry powder in a medium bowl; mix well. Add the water chestnuts, green onions and celery; toss gently to combine. Serve on shredded lettuce and with assorted crackers.

Yield: 6 servings

A Thyme to
Remember

❧❧❧

For *Caviar Dressing*,

whisk 1 cup sour cream,

2 tablespoons

prepared horseradish,

1 cup mayonnaise and

4 tablespoons caviar

in a small bowl until

thoroughly blended.

❧❧❧

Bouillabaisse Salad with Caviar Dressing

1 head Boston lettuce
1 head romaine lettuce
1 bunch watercress
1 cup crab meat
1 lobster tail, cooked, cut into bite-size pieces
8 ounces cooked shrimp
2 tomatoes, peeled, quartered
½ cup thinly sliced celery
1 hard-cooked egg, chopped
1 tablespoon chopped fresh chives
1 small red onion, thinly sliced
Caviar Dressing (at left)

❧ Tear the Boston lettuce, romaine lettuce and watercress into a bowl. Arrange the crab meat, lobster, shrimp, tomatoes and celery on top of the greens. Sprinkle with the egg and chives. Top with onion slices. Toss with the Caviar Dressing.

Yield: 8 servings

Crunchy Pea Salad

1 (10-ounce) package frozen petite peas
1 cup peanuts
1 cup coarsely shredded carrots
2 ribs celery, sliced
2 tablespoons vegetable oil
2 tablespoons white wine vinegar
1 tablespoon soy sauce
4 chopped green onions
4 tablespoons mayonnaise
Lettuce leaves

❧ Place the peas in a strainer or colander. Fill a saucepan with water. Bring to a boil; pour over the peas. Combine the drained peas, peanuts, carrots, celery, oil, white wine vinegar, soy sauce and green onions in a large bowl; toss lightly. Let stand for 30 minutes; drain. Add the mayonnaise and toss gently to coat. Serve on lettuce leaves.

Yield: 8 servings

Ham and Pea Salad with Dill Mustard Dressing

2 (10-ounce) packages frozen
   petite peas
1/4 cup chopped pimento
1 cup chopped ham

1 cup shredded Swiss cheese
Dill Mustard Dressing
   (at right)

❧ Combine the peas, pimento, ham and Swiss cheese in a large bowl; toss lightly. Pour in the Dill Mustard Dressing; toss gently to coat. Let stand for 45 minutes to thaw the peas before serving. This salad is tastiest when made 24 hours ahead; store, covered, in the refrigerator.

Yield: 8 servings

Botswana Bean and Banana Salad

2 tablespoons vegetable oil
2 onions, sliced
1 teaspoon curry powder
2 (15-ounce) cans butter
   beans, drained

1/2 cup chutney
2 bananas, sliced
Parsley

❧ Warm the oil in a large skillet over medium-high heat; add the onions. Sauté until translucent. Stir in the curry powder; let cool. Add the butter beans, bananas and chutney; toss gently to combine. Garnish with the parsley.

Yield: 6 servings

A Thyme to Remember

❧ ❧ ❧

For *Dill Mustard Dressing,* whisk 2 tablespoons minced onion, 1/2 cup sour cream, 1/4 cup mayonnaise, 1 teaspoon Dijon mustard and 1/2 teaspoon dillweed in a small bowl until blended. Season with salt and pepper to taste.

❧ ❧ ❧

For *Avocado Dressing*,

combine 4 ripe avocados,

peeled and mashed,

1 teaspoon sugar,

1 teaspoon chili powder,

2 tablespoons lemon juice,

½ teaspoon Tabasco sauce,

1 teaspoon seasoned salt,

1 teaspoon garlic powder

and ⅔ cup vegetable oil

in a food processor or

blender container. Process

at medium speed until

smooth. Chill, covered,

in the refrigerator.

Spanish Salad with Avocado Dressing

1 head iceberg lettuce, torn
4 tomatoes, chopped
½ cup sliced black olives
1 cup chopped green onions
2 cups corn chips

Avocado Salad Dressing
   (at left)
1 cup shredded Cheddar
   cheese or Monterey Jack
   cheese

❧ Combine the lettuce, tomatoes, olives, green onions and corn chips in a large bowl, tossing lightly. Pour in the Avocado Dressing and toss gently to coat. Add the Cheddar cheese and toss gently to combine. Serve with a Mexican or Southwestern menu.

Yield: 8 servings

White Corn Salad

2 (11-ounce) cans white
   shoe peg corn
3 green onions, chopped
2 tomatoes, chopped
½ cup chopped cilantro

Juice of a small lime
1 to 2 tablespoons
   mayonnaise
Salt and pepper to taste

❧ Combine the white corn, green onions, tomatoes, cilantro and lime juice in a medium bowl; toss lightly. Stir in enough mayonnaise to moisten; season with salt and pepper. For a unique presentation, serve this salad in a hollowed pumpkin.

Yield: 6 servings

Spicy Black Bean and Corn Salad

2 cups cooked, or canned,
    black beans
3 cups corn
1/2 cup minced red onion
1/2 cup minced green onions
1/2 cup chopped cilantro

2 cups chopped peeled
    tomatoes
1 tablespoon cumin seeds
1 tablespoon salt
Smoked Chile Vinaigrette
    (below)

Rinse and drain the black beans, if canned. Combine the beans, corn, onions, cilantro and tomatoes in a bowl, tossing lightly. Season with the cumin seeds and salt. Pour in the Smoked Chile Vinaigrette and toss gently to coat.

Yield: 6 servings

Smoked Chile Vinaigrette

1/3 cup red wine vinegar
2/3 cup vegetable oil
1/2 teaspoon salt
1/2 teaspoon pepper

2 tablespoons minced
    chipoltes in sauce
1 tablespoon sugar (optional)

Whisk the red wine vinegar, oil, salt, pepper, chipoltes and sugar in a small bowl until thoroughly blended.

If people want to help

in the kitchen, give

them something to do.

Donna Beavers

Corn Bread Salad with Lime Juice and Cilantro

3 cups coarsely crumbled
   dried corn bread
1/2 red bell pepper, diced
1/2 green bell pepper, diced
1/2 small red onion, chopped
1/4 cup chopped fresh parsley
2 tablespoons chopped
   cilantro
2 green onions, chopped
2 cloves of garlic, minced

1 (4-ounce) can diced green
   chiles, drained
1 tablespoon cumin seeds
Salt and cracked black pepper
   to taste
3 tablespoons olive oil
1 tablespoon white vinegar
6 tablespoons (about 3 limes)
   lime juice

This salad goes well with pork, sausage and Mexican dishes. The corn bread crumbs should be a mixture of coarsely crumbled pieces and 1/2-inch chunks.

Spread the corn bread in a jelly roll pan. Bake at 250 degrees for 1 1/2 hours or until crisp. Combine the corn bread, bell peppers, red onion, parsley, cilantro, green onions, garlic and green chiles in a large bowl, tossing lightly. Season with the cumin seeds, salt and cracked black pepper.

Whisk the olive oil, white vinegar and lime juice in a small bowl until thoroughly blended. Pour over the corn bread mixture; toss gently to coat.

Yield: 4 servings

Cranberry Cashew Green Salad

8 cups European blend mixed
   greens
12 slices crisp-fried bacon,
   crumbled
1/2 cup dried cranberries
6 green onions chopped
1 (10-ounce) package frozen
   peas, thawed

1 cup crumbled bleu cheese
1 cup honey-roasted cashews
   or other candied nuts
1/2 cup Balsamic Maple
   Salad Dressing (below)

🌱 Toss the greens, bacon, dried cranberries, green onions and peas in a large bowl. Add the bleu cheese and honey-roasted cashews; toss to combine. Drizzle in 1/2 cup Balsamic Maple Salad Dressing and toss gently to coat well.

Yield: 8 servings

Balsamic Maple Salad Dressing

1 cup balsamic vinegar
1/2 cup maple syrup
1/4 cup minced shallots
3 cups olive oil

2 teaspoons seasoned salt
1 teaspoon pepper
1/2 teaspoon garlic powder

🌱 Combine the balsamic vinegar, maple syrup, shallots, olive oil, seasoned salt, pepper and garlic powder in a jar with a tightfitting lid; shake until thoroughly blended. This make a large amount of dressing which will keep for weeks in the refrigerator.

A Thyme to
Remember

🌱 🌱 🌱

To make candied nuts, cook

1/2 cup brown sugar in a

saucepan over medium heat

until melted. Stir in 1 cup

nuts (any type) and 1/4 cup

water. Cook until well

coated, stirring constantly.

Spread on waxed paper to

cool and dry.

🌱 🌱 🌱

For *Soy Sauce Dressing*,

combine ½ cup sugar, ¾ cup

vegetable oil, 1 teaspoon salt,

½ cup cider vinegar and

2 teaspoons soy sauce in

a jar with a tightfitting lid.

Shake until thoroughly

blended. Let stand for

several hours. Shake before

pouring over the salad.

Asian Water Chestnut and Cashew Salad

1 head leaf lettuce
1 (8-ounce) can sliced water
 chestnuts, drained
2 tablespoons toasted sesame
 seeds

½ cup cashews
1 (8-ounce) can Chinese
 noodles
Soy Sauce Dressing
 (at left)

❧ Combine the leaf lettuce, water chestnuts, sesame seeds, cashews and Chinese noodles in a large bowl, tossing lightly. Drizzle the Soy Sauce Dressing over the salad; toss gently to coat.

Yield: 6 servings

Atomic Salad

3 cloves of garlic, crushed
⅛ teaspoon dry mustard to
 taste
½ teaspoon salt
½ teaspoon pepper
2 tablespoons lemon juice

2 tablespoons Parmesan
 cheese
½ cup vegetable oil
3 cups torn fresh spinach
6 cups torn fresh assorted
 greens

❧ Place the garlic in the bottom of a large salad bowl. Add the dry mustard, salt, pepper, lemon juice, Parmesan cheese and oil; whisk with a fork until well blended. Layer the spinach and greens in the bowl. Chill, covered with foil, in the refrigerator until serving time. Toss and serve.

Yield: 8 servings

Molded Spinach Salad

1 (3-ounce) package lemon
    gelatin
3/4 cup hot water
1 teaspoon lemon juice
1/16 teaspoon salt
1 cup mayonnaise
8 ounces small curd cottage
    cheese

1 cup chopped celery
1/2 cup chopped green bell
    pepper
1/4 cup chopped onion
1 (10-ounce) package frozen
    spinach, thawed

❧ Dissolve the lemon gelatin in the hot water in a large bowl and let cool. Stir in the lemon juice and salt. Chill, covered in the refrigerator until partially set.

❧ Combine the mayonnaise and cottage cheese in a medium bowl, mixing to blend well. Mix in the celery, bell pepper and onion. Squeeze the spinach dry a handful at a time; separate with a fork. Add to the cottage cheese mixture; toss gently to mix well.

❧ Fold the cottage cheese mixture into the partially set gelatin. Spoon into a mold. Chill, covered, in the refrigerator until completely set. Dip the bottom of the mold briefly into hot water, and invert onto a serving plate.

Yield: 10 servings

I like to cook because it

is a creative outlet.

Marty Curtis

Warm Spinach Toss

1 tablespoon margarine or
   butter
1 tablespoon olive or vegetable
   oil
1 clove of garlic, minced
1/4 teaspoon salt
1/8 teaspoon cayenne
1/4 cup raisins

2 tablespoons pine nuts or
   chopped walnuts or
   pecans
12 cups torn fresh spinach,
   about 10 ounces
1 tablespoon shredded
   Parmesan cheese

❧ Melt the margarine in a small microwave-safe bowl in the microwave on High. Combine the olive oil, garlic, salt and cayenne in a 3-quart microwave-safe baking dish; mix well. Stir in the raisins and nuts.

❧ Microwave, covered, on High for 1 minute, stirring once. Add the spinach; tossing to mix well. Spoon the margarine over the spinach mixture; toss to coat.

❧ Microwave, covered, on High for 2 to 3 minutes or just until the spinach is wilted and heated through. Sprinkle the Parmesan cheese over the spinach mixture.

Yield: 4 servings

Wheat Berry Salad with Spinach

1½ cups wheat berries
10 sun-dried tomato halves
  (not oil-packed)
3 tablespoons olive oil
2 tablespoons red wine
  vinegar
1 teaspoon salt
½ teaspoon sugar

½ teaspoon prepared
  mustard
¼ teaspoon coarsely ground
  pepper
1 cup golden raisins
1 pound spinach, coarsely
  chopped
1 medium tomato, diced

❧ Soak the wheat berries in enough water to cover by 2 inches in a large bowl for 12 hours; drain. Pour 7 cups water into a 4-quart saucepan. Bring to a boil over high heat; add the wheat berries. Return to a boil; reduce heat to low. Simmer, covered, for 2 hours or until tender; drain.

❧ Place the dried tomatoes in a small bowl; pour in 1 cup boiling water. Let stand for 5 minutes or until softened; drain. Chop coarsely.

❧ Whisk the olive oil, red wine vinegar, salt, sugar, mustard and pepper in a large bowl until well blended. Add the raisins, tomato, sun-dried tomatoes, spinach and wheat berries; toss to mix well.

Yield: 4 servings

Couscous, which takes

about 5 minutes to cook,

may be substituted for

the wheat berries. Simply

cook one 10-ounce package

couscous according to

package directions,

omitting the margarine

or butter.

Apple and Walnut Salad with Feta

3 tablespoons butter
1 cup walnuts
1/2 cup sugar
1 tablespoon medium grind
    black pepper
2 green apples, thinly sliced
3/4 cup crumbled feta cheese

8 cups torn assorted greens,
    such as red leaf lettuce,
    romaine lettuce,
    butterhead lettuce,
    radicchio
Garlic Vinaigrette (below)

❧ Preheat the oven to 350 degrees. Melt the butter in a baking dish in the oven; add the walnuts. Bake for 20 minutes, stirring every 5 minutes; drain.

❧ Combine the sugar and pepper in a medium bowl, mixing to distribute the pepper evenly. Add the walnuts and toss to coat well. Discard the excess sugar mixture. Toss the apples, walnuts, feta cheese and greens in a large salad bowl. Pour in the Garlic Vinaigrette; toss to coat.

Yield: 8 servings

Garlic Vinaigrette

1 teaspoon sugar
2 cloves of garlic
1/2 teaspoon dried oregano
1/4 medium onion
1/4 teaspoon salt

1/4 teaspoon pepper
1/4 cup red wine vinegar
1 teaspoon dried parsley
1 1/2 cups olive oil

❧ Combine the sugar, garlic, oregano, onion, salt, pepper, red wine vinegar and parsley in a blender or food processor container; process at low speed until well blended. Add the oil in a steady stream, processing constantly at high speed until smooth.

Raspberry Applesauce Salad

2 (3-ounce) packages
 raspberry gelatin
2¼ cup boiling water
1 (10-ounce) package frozen
 unsweetened raspberries,
 thawed, crushed

1 (20-ounce) can
 applesauce
Lettuce leaves
Sour cream

Dissolve the raspberry gelatin in the boiling water in a large bowl, stirring constantly. Let cool slightly. Add raspberries to the gelatin, stirring gently to mix. Stir in the applesauce. Pour into 8 individual molds. Chill, covered, in the refrigerator until set. Dip the bottom of each mold briefly into hot water, and invert onto a plate lined with lettuce leaves. Serve with sour cream.

Yield: 8 servings

Mango Salad

3 (3-ounce) packages lemon
 gelatin
1 (29-ounce) can mangoes
8 ounces cream cheese

Juice of 1 lime
2 cups sour cream
1 tablespoon brown sugar
Grated coconut to taste

Place the lemon gelatin in a large bowl. Drain the mangoes, reserving the liquid. Combine liquid with enough water to equal 3 cups liquid. Pour into a saucepan. Bring to a boil and pour over the gelatin. Dissolve, stirring constantly; let cool slightly.

Combine the mangoes and cream cheese in a food processor or blender container; process at medium speed until smooth and creamy. Add to the gelatin, mixing gently. Stir in the lime juice. Pour into a ring mold. Chill, covered, in the refrigerator for 4 to 6 hours or until set. Combine the sour cream, brown sugar and coconut, stirring until well blended. Dip the bottom of the mold briefly into hot water, and invert onto a serving plate. Spoon the sour cream mixture over the mango gelatin.

Yield: 8 servings

It was a particularly busy period in my life. One day I picked my daughter up from school and she announced that she had worked extra hard through her study halls so she could help me cook.

Barbara Hickey

Orange Mandarin Salad

1 (3-ounce) package orange
   gelatin
1 cup hot water
6 ounces orange juice
   concentrate, thawed
1 (11-ounce) can mandarin
   orange sections

1 (8-ounce) can crushed
   pineapple
1/2 cup whipping cream
1/2 (6-ounce) package lemon
   instant pudding mix
1/2 cup milk

❧ Dissolve the orange gelatin in the hot water in a large bowl,
stirring constantly. Add the orange juice concentrate, stirring
gently to combine. Stir in the undrained mandarin oranges and
undrained pineapple until evenly distributed. Chill, covered, in the
refrigerator until set. Whisk the whipping cream, pudding mix and
milk until smooth and slightly thickened. Spread over the gelatin.
Chill, covered, in the refrigerator until set.

Yield: 8 servings

New Wave Waldorf Salad

1 red delicious apple, chopped
1 large Granny Smith apple,
   chopped
1 large pear, chopped
1 tablespoon lemon juice
1/4 cup golden raisins
1 rib celery, sliced diagonally

1/2 cup mayonnaise or plain
   yogurt
1/2 cup sour cream
1 tablespoon honey
1 teaspoon crated orange peel
1/4 cup slivered almonds,
   toasted

❧ Combine the apples, pear and lemon juice in a medium bowl,
tossing to coat all pieces with the lemon juice. Add the golden
raisins and celery; toss gently. Whisk the mayonnaise, sour cream,
honey and orange peel in a small bowl until well blended. Pour
1/4 cup mayonnaise mixture into the fruit mixture, tossing to coat.
Remove to a serving bowl, and sprinkle the almonds over the top.
Serve with the remaining mayonnaise mixture.

Yield: 6 servings

Apple-Orange-Avocado Salad with Crème Fraîche

8 leaves of romaine lettuce
8 leaves of red leaf lettuce
8 leaves of green leaf lettuce
4 oranges, sectioned

2 avocados, cut into wedges
2 apples, sliced
Crème Fraîche Raspberry
    Vinaigrette (below)

❧ Arrange the romaine lettuce, red leaf lettuce and green leaf lettuce on individual salad plates. Top attractively with the orange sections, avocado wedges and apple slices. Drizzle the Crème Fraîche Raspberry Vinaigrette over the salads just before serving.

Yield: 6 servings

Crème Fraîche Raspberry Vinaigrette

1/2 cup vegetable oil
3 tablespoons raspberry
    vinegar

2 teaspoons Dijon mustard
1/2 teaspoon sherry or port
3 tablespoons crème fraîche

❧ Whisk the oil, raspberry vinegar, Dijon mustard and sherry in a small bowl until well combined and smooth. Whisk in the crème fraîche until well blended.

If preparing the salad ahead, dip the avocado wedges and apple slices in lemon or orange juice to slow browning.

Orange Kiwi Salad

1 head romaine lettuce, torn
3 kiwi, sliced
1 (11-ounce) can mandarin
    orange sections, drained

1 large red onion, sliced
3 ounces bleu cheese,
    crumbled
Orange Lime Vinaigrette (at left)

❧ Arrange the romaine lettuce on individual serving plates. Top attractively with the kiwi, mandarin orange sections and red onion rings. Sprinkle the bleu cheese over each serving. Drizzle with the Orange Lime Vinaigrette.

Yield: 4 servings

For *Orange Lime*

Vinaigrette, whisk ½ cup

olive oil, 3 tablespoons red

wine vinegar, 3 tablespoons

orange marmalade, ⅓ cup

lime juice, 1 teaspoon salt

and 1 teaspoon freshly

ground pepper in a small

bowl until well mixed.

Apple Pineapple Salad

1 (20-ounce) can
    unsweetened pineapple
    chunks
½ cup butter
2 tablespoons lemon juice
1 tablespoon cornstarch
2 tablespoons orange juice
2 tablespoons sugar

3 cups chopped red delicious
    apples
2 cups green grapes
2 teaspoons poppy seeds
¾ cup chopped pecans,
    toasted

❧ Drain the pineapple, reserving the juice. Combine the butter, lemon juice and reserved pineapple juice in a small saucepan; mix well. Dissolve the cornstarch in the orange juice in a small bowl, stirring constantly, and pour into the pineapple juice mixture. Bring to a boil over medium-high heat, stirring constantly. Cook, continuing to stir constantly for 2 minutes; do not overcook or the mixture will not thicken. Stir in the sugar and remove from the heat. Let cool for 30 minutes or to room temperature.

❧ Combine the pineapple, apple, grapes and poppy seeds in a large bowl, tossing lightly. Pour in the pineapple juice mixture; toss to coat. Chill, covered, in the refrigerator until serving time. Add the pecans just before serving, and toss gently.

Yield: 8 servings

Five Fruit Salad with Peanut Butter Dressing

1 cup drained pineapple
    chunks
1 cup frozen unsweetened
    peach slices, thawed, or
    one (8-ounce) can peach
    slices (juice pack)

1/4 medium cantaloupe, cut
    into thin wedges
1/2 cup seedless green grapes,
    halved
1/2 cup strawberries, halved
Peanut Butter Dressing (at right)

Arrange the pineapple chunks, peach slices, cantaloupe wedges, grape halves and strawberry halves on individual serving plates. Drizzle the Peanut Butter Dressing over the fruit.

Yield: 8 servings

Refreshing Cranberry Sauce

2 tart apples, unpeeled, cored,
    chopped
1 orange, unpeeled, quartered

1 cup crushed pineapple
2 (16-ounce) cans whole
    cranberry sauce

Combine the apples and orange in a food processor container; process at medium speed until blended, pulsing and scraping the sides as necessary. Stir in the pineapple and whole cranberry sauce. Serve with meats or poultry.

Yield: 12 servings

For *Peanut Butter Dressing*, combine 1/3 cup thawed frozen pineapple juice concentrate and 2 tablespoons creamy peanut butter in a blender container. Process at high speed until smooth. Add 1/3 cup vegetable oil in a steady stream, processing constantly at high speed until smooth. Store in a container with a tightfitting lid. Chill in the refrigerator.

Baked Fruit Salad

1 (17-ounce) can apricot
  halves, drained
1 (15-ounce) can peach
  halves, drained
2 (8½-ounce) cans pear
  halves, drained
1 (15¼-ounce) pineapple
  chunks, drained

1 (6-ounce) jar maraschino
  cherries, drained
1 cup orange juice
⅓ cup brown sugar
4 cinnamon sticks
8 whole cloves
1 tablespoon lemon juice
¼ teaspoon mace

❧ Cut the apricot halves, peach halves and pear halves in half lengthwise. Arrange in a single layer in a baking dish. Combine the pineapple chunks, maraschino cherries, orange juice, brown sugar, cinnamon, cloves, lemon juice and mace in a saucepan. Bring to a boil over medium-high heat. Reduce the heat to low. Simmer for 2 minutes and pour over the fruit mixture. Bake, uncovered, at 350 degrees for 30 minutes. Let cool on a wire rack. Chill, covered, in the refrigerator for up to 2 days before serving.

Yield: 10 servings

Frozen Fruit Salad

1 cup sour cream
2 tablespoons lemon
  juice
½ cup sugar
1/16 teaspoon salt
4 canned apricot halves,
  mashed

1 (8-ounce) can crushed
  pineapple
¼ cup sliced maraschino
  cherries
¼ cup pecan pieces, toasted
1 banana, sliced
Lettuce leaves

❧ Whisk the first 5 ingredients in a large bowl until smooth and blended. Add the undrained pineapple, maraschino cherries, pecans, and banana, tossing well. Pour into 6 individual molds. Freeze, covered, until firm. Remove from the freezer 15 minutes before serving. Invert onto plates lined with lettuce.

Yield: 6 servings

Cranberry Horseradish Mousse

1 cup sugar
½ cup water
2 cups whole cranberries
1 cup sour cream
5 tablespoons prepared
    horseradish

1 tablespoon lemon juice
½ cup cold water
1 envelope unflavored gelatin

❧ Combine the sugar and ½ cup water in a large saucepan; stir to blend. Bring to a boil over medium-high heat, stirring often. Boil for 5 minutes, stirring often. Add the cranberries; stir. Cook for 5 minutes or until the cranberries pop, stirring frequently. Remove from the heat and let cool slightly. Pour into a large bowl. Add the sour cream, horseradish and lemon juice, mixing to blend well.

❧ Pour ½ cup cold water into a small saucepan. Sprinkle with the gelatin; let stand until softened. Cook over medium heat until dissolved, stirring constantly. Add to the cranberry mixture; mix gently until well blended. Lightly oil a 4-cup mold and spoon in the cranberry mixture. Chill, covered, in the refrigerator for 6 hours or until set. Dip the bottom of the mold briefly into hot water, and invert onto a serving plate.

Yield: 8 servings

Honey Mustard Salad Dressing

⅓ cup each honey and vinegar
1 tablespoon lemon juice
½ cup sugar
1 teaspoon dry mustard

1 teaspoon paprika
1 teaspoon celery seeds
¼ teaspoon salt
1 cup oil

❧ Whisk the honey, vinegar and lemon juice in a medium bowl until well mixed. Add the sugar, dry mustard, paprika, celery seeds and salt; whisk until combined. Add the oil in a fine stream, whisking until smooth. Serve over fruit or vegetable salads.

Yield: 8 servings

❧❧❧

I was trying to make my mother's recipe for aspic. Beside the ingredients I could find at the store—a can of tomato soup, onions, green peppers, etc.—the recipe called for a can of water. That one stumped me. I didn't know where a can of water was on the grocery shelves.

Carol Bywaters

❧❧❧

Caesar Salad Dressing

3 cloves of garlic
2 teaspoons dry mustard
6 anchovies
2 egg yolks
2 tablespoons Worcestershire
    sauce

1 tablespoon Dijon mustard
1/4 cup red wine vinegar
1 1/3 cups vegetable oil
1 cup Parmesan cheese
Salt and pepper to taste

❧ Combine the garlic, dry mustard, anchovies, egg yolks and Worcestershire sauce in a blender container; process at medium speed until blended. Combine the mustard and red wine vinegar in a small cup, whisking briskly until thoroughly blended. Add to the anchovy mixture gradually, processing at high speed until blended.

❧ Add the oil in a fine stream, processing at high speed until thick and smooth. Add the Parmesan cheese and process at medium speed until blended. Season with salt and pepper.

Yield: 4 servings

Sesame Dressing

3/4 cup corn oil
1/2 cup rice vinegar
1/4 cup sesame oil
1 tablespoon salt
1 tablespoon sugar
2 tablespoons grated orange
    peel

1 teaspoon pepper
1 teaspoon minced gingerroot
1 teaspoon soy sauce
1/2 teaspoon minced garlic
1/4 teaspoon crushed red
    pepper flakes

❧ Combine the corn oil, rice vinegar, sesame oil, salt, sugar, orange peel, pepper, gingerroot, soy sauce, garlic and red pepper flakes in a food processor or blender container; process at high speed until smooth, stopping once to scrape down the sides.

Yield: 10 servings

A Handful of Flour

HEARTY BREADS AND SOUPS

❧ ❧ ❧

"My father was a kind,
helpful, efficient person.
As a urologist and
administrator at Scott and
White Hospital in Temple,
I saw how he helped
people. I wanted to be able
to do the same."

—*John S. Bradfield, M.D.,*
Radiation Oncology

❧ ❧ ❧

Homespun Bran Rolls

1 cup bran flakes
1 cup water
1 cup shortening
½ cup sugar
1½ teaspoons salt

1 cup boiling water
2 envelopes dry yeast
2 eggs
5 to 6 cups flour

❧ Combine the bran flakes and 1 cup water in a small bowl; mix to moisten the flakes.

❧ Combine the shortening, sugar and salt in a large bowl; mix well. Pour in the 1 cup boiling water; let cool to lukewarm. Stir in the yeast. Beat in the eggs and bran flakes mixture. Add 5 cups flour; beat to combine well. Mix in enough remaining flour to form a soft dough.

❧ Turn out onto a floured work surface. Knead for 10 minutes or until smooth and elastic. Oil a large bowl. Place the dough in the bowl, turning once to oil both sides. Let rise, covered, in a warm place (80 to 90 degrees) for about 1 hour or until doubled in bulk. Punch the dough down.

❧ Grease two 9-inch round baking pans. Turn dough out onto a floured work surface; divide into 2 portions. Divide each portion into 12 equal pieces; shape into balls. Arrange in the pans. Let rise, lightly covered, for 45 minutes or until doubled in bulk.

❧ Preheat the oven to 375 degrees. Bake for 20 minutes. Remove from pans and let cool on wire racks. Serve warm or at room temperature.

Yield: 24 servings

A Thyme to Remember

I like to cook meals for

my family as that is a

special time for us to be

together and visit.

Janet Nylund

My aunt was a terrible

cook. She could screw up a

baloney sandwich. She'd

forget to add the baloney.

Mary Ann Blome

Dilly Bread

1 envelope dry yeast
1/4 cup warm water
1 cup cream-style cottage
   cheese
2 tablespoons sugar
1 teaspoon minced dried onion

1 tablespoon butter
1 teaspoon salt
1 egg
2 teaspoons dillseeds
1/4 teaspoon baking soda
2 1/4 to 2 1/2 cups flour

Dissolve the yeast in the water in a small bowl. Combine the cottage cheese, sugar, onion, butter and salt in a saucepan over medium-high heat; mix well. Bring to a boil, stirring frequently. Let cool to room temperature. Remove to a large bowl. Beat the egg, dillseeds and baking soda into the cottage cheese mixture. Stir in the yeast mixture. Beat in 2 1/4 cups flour. Mix in enough remaining flour to form a soft dough. Let rise, covered, in a warm place for about 1 hour or until doubled in bulk. Preheat the oven to 350 degrees. Place the dough in a large greased loaf pan or 2 small loaf pans. Bake for 40 to 50 minutes or until the bread tests done. Remove from the pan and let cool on a wire rack.

Yield: 12 servings

Easy Cheese Bread

2 1/2 cups baking mix
2 teaspoons dry mustard
1 1/2 cups shredded extra
   sharp Cheddar cheese

2 eggs, beaten
3/4 cup water
2 tablespoons butter

Preheat the oven to 350 degrees. Grease a large loaf pan or two small loaf pans. Combine the baking mix, dry mustard and Cheddar cheese in a medium bowl. Blend the eggs and water in a large bowl. Add the Cheddar cheese mixture, stirring just until mixed. Pour into the loaf pan. Dot with the butter. Bake for 45 minutes. Let cool in the pan for 10 to 15 minutes; remove to a wire rack to cool completely.

Yield: 8 servings

Aunt Effie's Monkey Bread

2 envelopes dry yeast
1 cup warm water
1 cup shortening
1½ teaspoons salt
¾ cup sugar

1 cup boiling water
2 eggs, beaten
2 cups whole wheat flour
4 cups all-purpose flour
¾ cup butter

❧ Dissolve the yeast in the warm water in a small bowl. Combine the shortening, salt and sugar in a large bowl, mixing well. Pour in the boiling water. Let cool to room temperature. Add the eggs, beating well. Beat in the yeast mixture, whole wheat flour and all-purpose flour.

❧ Turn out onto a floured work surface. Knead for 10 minutes or until smooth and elastic. Oil a large bowl. Place the dough in the bowl, turning it once to oil both sides. Let rise, covered, in a warm place (80 to 90 degrees) for about 1 hour or until doubled in bulk. Punch the dough down.

❧ Turn the dough out onto a floured work surface. Divide into 3 portions. Roll each portion ¼ inch thick; cut into varying shapes and sizes.

❧ Melt the butter in a small saucepan. Dip each piece of dough into the butter. Arrange in a round or square baking pan. Let rise, lightly covered, for about 30 minutes or until doubled in bulk.

❧ Preheat the oven to 350 degrees. Bake for 20 to 30 minutes. Remove to a wire rack to cool.

Yield: 36 servings

❧❧❧

My mother was a great cook. She used to cook for the priests. They would give her a bottle of wine for her gifts of pies, a loaf of bread, a meal. She was not a drinker and the bottles accumulated in the basement. At her death, we found cases and cases of wine.

Mary Ann Blome

❧❧❧

Parmesan Wine Bread

1/3 cup melted butter or margarine
1/4 cup dry white wine
1 egg, beaten
1/2 cup milk
2 cups baking mix

1 tablespoon sugar
1 teaspoon minced dried onion
1/2 teaspoon dried oregano
1/4 cup shredded Parmesan cheese

❧ Preheat the oven to 400 degrees. Grease an 8-inch round baking pan. Combine the butter, wine, egg and milk in a medium bowl, whisking to blend well.

❧ Combine the baking mix, sugar, onion and oregano in a large bowl; mix well. Add the butter mixture; stir just until blended. Pour into the baking pan. Sprinkle the Parmesan cheese over the top. Bake for 20 to 25 minutes or until bread tests done. Cut into wedges and serve warm.

Yield: 8 servings

Italian Flat Bread

1/4 cup mayonnaise
2/3 cup grated Parmesan cheese
1/4 teaspoon dried basil leaves
1/4 teaspoon dried oregano

3 green onions, chopped
1 clove of garlic, minced, or 1/8 teaspoon garlic powder
1 (10-count) can refrigerated flaky biscuits

❧ Preheat the oven to 400 degrees. Combine the mayonnaise, Parmesan cheese, basil, oregano, green onions and garlic in a bowl; stir to mix thoroughly. Separate the dough into 10 biscuits. Stretch or roll each biscuit into a 4-inch circle on a baking sheet. Spread 1 tablespoon of the Parmesan cheese mixture over each biscuit to within 1/4 inch of the edge. Bake for 10 to 13 minutes or until golden brown. Serve warm.

Yield: 10 servings

Orange Oatmeal Bread

2 envelopes dry yeast
1/4 cup warm water
2 cups milk
2 cups rolled oats
1/4 cup butter
2 eggs

2 cups orange juice
1/2 cup molasses
2/3 cup sugar
1 tablespoon salt
2 cups raisins
1 to 2 cups flour

❧ Dissolve the yeast in the water in a small bowl. Place the oats in a large bowl. Combine the butter and milk in a heavy saucepan. Scald the milk over high heat, taking care not to scorch; stir. Pour over the oats; mix well. Let stand for 30 minutes. Beat in the next 5 ingredients. Stir in the raisins. Beat in enough flour to make a soft dough. Place the dough in a greased bowl, turning it once to oil both sides. Let rise, covered, in a warm place (80 to 90 degrees) for about 1 hour or until doubled in bulk. Punch the dough down. Turn the dough out onto a floured work surface. Knead for 10 minutes or until smooth and elastic. Shape into 3 loaves. Place on a greased baking sheet. Let rise, lightly covered, until doubled in bulk. Preheat the oven to 350 degrees. Bake for 1 hour. Remove to a wire rack to cool.

Yield: 24 servings

Pizza Loaf

1/2 cup process cheese spread
2/3 cup milk
1 egg, lightly beaten
2 cups baking mix

2 tablespoons chopped green
   onions
1 teaspoon Italian seasoning
2/3 cup chopped pepperoni

❧ Preheat the oven to 375 degrees. Blend the cheese, milk and egg in a medium bowl. Mix the baking mix, green onions and Italian seasoning in a large bowl. Pour in the cheese mixture; stir just until mixed. Stir in the pepperoni. Spoon into a small greased loaf pan. Bake for 30 to 40 minutes or until golden brown. Let cool in the pan for 5 minutes. Cool on a wire rack for 20 minutes.

Yield: 8 servings

My aunt announced

at one dinner that people

are dying today that have

never died before.

Mary Ann Blome

🌿🌿🌿

"I saw how much pleasure

my Dad derived from his

interaction with his patients.

My Dad is an OB/GYN in

Houston. It is challenging,

rewarding and stimulating."

Clay Alexander, M.D.,

Obstetrician/Gynecologist

🌿🌿🌿

Featherbeds

1 large potato	1 envelope dry yeast
1½ cups water	¼ cup warm water
⅓ cup sugar or honey	1 egg
1 teaspoon salt	4½ cups flour
½ cup butter or margarine	Melted butter

🌿 Cook the potato in 1½ cups water in a covered saucepan until tender; drain, reserving the liquid and mashing the potato. Combine the sugar, salt, butter and ¾ cup of the hot reserved liquid in a small bowl. Let cool to lukewarm.

🌿 Dissolve the yeast in ¼ cup warm water in a large bowl. Add the sugar mixture, ½ cup of the mashed potato, egg and 2 cups of the flour; beat until smooth. Stir in enough of the remaining flour to form a soft dough.

🌿 Turn out onto a floured work surface. Knead for 8 to 10 minutes or until smooth and elastic. Oil a large bowl. Place the dough in the bowl, turning once to oil both sides. Let rise, covered, in a warm place (80 to 90 degrees) for about 1 hour or until doubled in bulk. Punch the dough down.

🌿 Grease two 9-inch round baking pans. Turn dough out onto a floured work surface; divide into 2 portions. Divide each portion into 12 equal pieces; shape into balls. Arrange in the pans. Let rise, lightly covered, for 45 minutes or until doubled in bulk.

🌿 Preheat the oven to 375 degrees. Bake for 45 minutes or until done. Brush immediately with melted butter.

Yield: 24 servings

Jalapeño Blue Corn Muffins

6 tablespoons shortening
9 tablespoons butter
1/4 cup finely chopped red bell
    pepper
1/4 cup finely chopped green
    bell pepper
4 teaspoons finely chopped
    seeded jalapeño or serrano
    pepper
1 tablespoon finely minced
    garlic

1 cup buttermilk
1/8 teaspoon baking soda
2 eggs, lightly beaten
1 cup flour
1 1/4 cups blue cornmeal
2 tablespoons sugar
1 teaspoon salt
1 tablespoon baking powder

❧ Preheat the oven to 400 degrees; grease 12 muffin cups with butter. Melt the shortening in a skillet; pour into a medium bowl. Melt the butter in the skillet; add 6 tablespoons of the melted butter to the shortening. Let the mixture cool to lukewarm.

❧ Add the red and green bell peppers, jalapeño and garlic to the butter remaining in the skillet. Cook for 2 minutes, stirring frequently; remove from the heat.

❧ Combine the buttermilk and baking soda in a measuring cup; stir. Add the eggs to the shortening mixture; beat well. Stir in the buttermilk mixture.

❧ Sift the flour, cornmeal, sugar, salt and baking powder into a large bowl. Stir in the egg mixture. Add the pepper mixture and mix well. Fill the muffin cups 2/3 full. Bake for 20 to 25 minutes or until golden brown. Let cool on wire racks.

Yield: 12 muffins

"I chose to be a pediatrician

because I have always

liked children."

Pochin H. Yin, M.D.,

Pediatrician

❧❧❧

My mother was not a cook. She only taught me how to line up TV dinners on a cookie sheet. When I was a sixth grader, I became the main cook in the family. I began to cook the family dinner alone. Since that experience, I have always had a special place in my heart for that time of day.

Tammy Vines

❧❧❧

Ball Park Soft Pretzels

1 envelope dry yeast
1½ cups warm water
1 teaspoon salt
1 tablespoon sugar

4 cups flour
1 egg, beaten
Coarse salt or
    cinnamon-sugar

❧ Dissolve the yeast in the 1½ cups warm water in a large bowl. Add the salt, sugar and flour; mix until a soft dough forms.

❧ Turn out onto a floured work surface. Knead for 10 minutes or until smooth and elastic. Break off pieces of dough and form pretzel shapes. Arrange on baking sheets. Brush with the egg and sprinkle with the coarse salt or cinnamon-sugar.

❧ Let rise, lightly covered, in a warm place (80 to 90 degrees) for 1 hour. Preheat the oven to 425 degrees. Bake for 12 to 15 minutes or until lightly browned. Remove to wire racks and cool.

Yield: 12 servings

French Bread Spread

½ cup butter or margarine,
    softened
1 cup mayonnaise
2 cups mozzarella cheese
⅔ cup chopped black olives

6 green onions, minced
1 teaspoon garlic powder
1 loaf French or sour dough
    bread, sliced

❧ Combine the butter, mayonnaise, mozzarella cheese, black olives, green onions and garlic powder in a small bowl; mix well. Spread the butter mixture on the bread slices. Arrange the bread on a baking sheet. Bake at 350 degrees for 8 to 10 minutes.

Yield: 12 servings

Chunky Gazpacho

1 (10½-ounce) can tomato
   soup
1 cup plus 2 tablespoons
   water
3 tablespoons olive oil
2 tablespoons wine vinegar
1 teaspoon garlic salt

Tabasco sauce to taste
12 pitted black olives, halved
3 tablespoons chopped green
   onions
½ cucumber, chopped
1 tomato, chopped
1 avocado, chopped

❧ Combine the tomato soup, water, olive oil, wine vinegar, garlic salt and Tabasco sauce in a large bowl, whisking until smooth. Stir in the black olives, green onions, cucumber, tomato and avocado. Chill, covered, for 8 hours. Serve in chilled bowls.

Yield: 4 servings

Carrot Coriander Soup

2 tablespoons butter
2 onions, finely chopped
3 tablespoons flour
1 quart milk
1 quart water

1½ pounds carrots, grated
Juice and peel of 2 oranges
1 tablespoon ground coriander
1 chicken bouillon cube
Salt and pepper to taste

❧ Melt the butter in a large saucepan over medium-high heat; add the onions. Sauté until tender. Add the flour and mix well. Add the milk and water gradually, stirring constantly.

❧ Stir in the carrots, orange juice, orange peel, coriander and bouillon. Season with salt and pepper. Bring the mixture to a boil. Simmer until the carrots are tender, stirring frequently. Let stand until cool. Remove the soup to a blender container; process on medium speed until smooth. Cook until heated through. Garnish each serving with cream and parsley.

Yield: 10 servings

"I chose to be a pediatrician

because I have always

liked children."

Pochin H. Yin, M.D.,

Pediatrician

Creamy Vegetable Soup

2 tablespoons butter
1 medium onion, chopped
1 teaspoon curry powder
6 cups chicken broth
2 cups sliced celery

1 medium potato, peeled,
  diced
1 tart apple, peeled, diced
½ medium banana, sliced
1 cup sour cream

❧ Melt the butter in a large saucepan over medium-high heat; add the onion. Sauté until brown. Stir in the curry powder. Cook for 1 minute, stirring constantly. Stir in the chicken broth, celery, potato, apple and banana. Bring to a boil; reduce heat. Simmer, covered, for 30 minutes or until the vegetables are very tender. Let cool slightly. Pour into a blender container and add the sour cream. Process on medium speed until puréed. Serve hot or cold. Garnish with minced chives.

Yield: 6 servings

Cooking is fun, creative,

relaxing. It is not a chore.

Lynn Hamilton

Spinach and Cucumber Soup

1 tablespoon butter
¾ cup chopped onion
2½ cups chicken broth
4 cups diced, seeded
  cucumbers
½ cup sliced peeled potato

½ teaspoon salt
Cayenne or Tabasco sauce to
  taste
1 tablespoon lemon juice
2 cups packed fresh spinach
1 cup whipping cream

❧ Melt the butter in a large saucepan over medium-high heat; add the onion. Sauté until tender. Stir in the chicken broth, cucumbers and potatoes; season with the salt, cayenne and lemon juice. Bring to a boil. Reduce the heat to medium-low. Simmer for 15 to 20 minutes or until the potato slices are tender. Stir in the spinach. Remove from the heat and let cool. Process in a blender on medium speed until smooth. Add the cream; mix well. Chill, covered, in the refrigerator for up to 24 hours. Adjust the seasonings.

Yield: 6 servings

Mushroom Brie Soup

1/4 cup butter
2 yellow onions, chopped
1 clove of garlic, crushed
12 ounces mushrooms
1 1/4 teaspoons lemon juice
2 tablespoons flour

5 cups chicken stock
4 ounces Brie cheese, cut in
  half
1 1/3 cups half-and-half
2 teaspoons sherry
Salt and pepper to taste

❧ Melt the butter in a large saucepan over medium-high heat; add the onions and garlic. Sauté for 4 to 5 minutes or until the onions are tender. Add the mushrooms and lemon juice, stirring to mix. Cook for 10 minutes, stirring occasionally. Let cool slightly. Remove to a food processor or blender container; process on medium speed until the mushrooms are coarsely chopped. Remove to the saucepan.

❧ Add the flour. Cook for 3 minutes, stirring frequently. Add the stock gradually, stirring constantly. Cook over low heat until slightly thickened; do not boil.

❧ Chop 2 ounces of the Brie and place in a small saucepan. Melt over low heat, stirring constantly. Add the melted Brie and half-and-half to the onion mixture; mix well. Cook until heated through, stirring occasionally.

❧ Divide the soup evenly among 6 heatproof bowls. Thinly slice the remaining Brie. Top each serving with the Brie slices. Broil until the Brie melts.

Yield: 6 servings

This soup may be stored, covered, in the refrigerator. Reheat, add the cheese slices and broil just before serving.

Roasted Potato and Garlic Soup

4 medium potatoes
1 teaspoon dried rosemary,
    crushed
1 large onion, coarsely
    chopped
1 garlic bulb, chopped
1 tablespoon olive oil
Chopped carrots to taste

1 tablespoon water
1 (14-ounce) can chicken
    broth
1 tablespoon flour
1/4 teaspoon pepper
1 cup half-and-half or light
    cream

Peel 2 of the potatoes. Chop the peeled and unpeeled potatoes separately. Arrange the peeled potatoes on 1 side of a 9-inch square baking pan; arrange the unpeeled potatoes on the other side. Sprinkle the rosemary, onion and garlic evenly over the potatoes. Drizzle with the olive oil. Bake, covered, at 400 degrees for 50 minutes. Let cool slightly.

Place the carrots and water in a microwave-safe bowl. Microwave, covered, on High until the carrots are tender. Drain.

Combine the peeled potatoes, half the chicken broth, flour and pepper in a food processor or blender container; process on medium speed until smooth. Pour into a medium saucepan.

Stir in the unpeeled potatoes, carrots, remaining broth and half-and-half. Cook over medium heat until slightly thickened and bubbly, stirring frequently. Cook for 1 minute longer, stirring constantly. Stir in additional half-and-half if necessary for the desired consistency. Ladle into soup bowls. Garnish each serving with croutons or grated cheese.

Yield: 4 servings

Wild Rice Soup

1 tablespoon minced onion
2 tablespoons butter
¼ cup cake flour
4 cups chicken broth
2 cups cooked wild rice
¼ teaspoon salt

½ cup minced ham
⅓ cup finely grated carrots
3 tablespoons slivered
 almonds
1 cup half-and-half
2 tablespoons dry sherry

🌿 Sauté the onion in the butter in a large saucepan until tender. Add the cake flour; mix well Whisk in the chicken broth gradually. Cook until slightly thickened, stirring constantly. Stir in the wild rice, salt, ham, carrots and almonds. Simmer, covered, for 5 minutes. Stir in the half-and-half and sherry. Heat to serving temperature. Garnish with minced parsley or chives.

Yield: 6 servings

Minestrone

1 pound sweet Italian
 sausage, sliced
1 tablespoon vegetable oil
1 cup diced onion
1 clove of garlic, minced
1 cup sliced carrots
1 teaspoon basil
2 small zucchini, sliced

2 (14-ounce) cans beef broth
1 can pear tomatoes, chopped
2 cups finely shredded
 cabbage
1 teaspoon salt
¼ teaspoon pepper
1 (16-ounce) can Navy beans

🌿 Brown the sausage in the oil in a large heavy saucepan, stirring frequently; drain on paper towels. Drain excess grease. Cook the next 5 ingredients in the saucepan for 5 minutes, stirring frequently. Stir in the sausage. Add the broth and undrained tomatoes, stirring gently. Bring to a boil; reduce the heat. Stir in the cabbage. Season with the salt and pepper. Simmer, covered, for 1 hour. Stir in the undrained Navy beans. Cook, covered, for 20 minutes, stirring occasionally. Garnish each serving with parsley.

Yield: 8 servings

I learned to cook, because

it was time to eat.

Lynn Hamilton

Cold Curried Crabmeat Soup

2 tablespoons butter
1 tablespoon chopped chives
   or green onion tops
2 teaspoons curry powder
2 tablespoons flour

3 cups milk
2 cups crabmeat
1/4 cup sherry
2 cups light cream

❧ Melt the butter in a saucepan over medium heat; add the chives. Sauté for 1 minute. Add the curry and flour; mix well. Add the milk gradually, whisking constantly. Cook until thickened, stirring constantly. Combine the crabmeat and sherry in a saucepan; mix well. Cook over medium heat until warm; add the cream. Bring to a boil. Add the curry mixture; mix well. Chill, covered, in the refrigerator. Serve very cold.

Yield: 10 servings

Crawfish and Corn Soup

4 cups chicken stock
1/2 cup chopped green onions
1 cup butter
1/2 cup flour
1 (15-ounce) can corn,
   drained, or 1 1/2 (10-
   ounce) packages frozen

1 pound crawfish tails,
   cooked, peeled
2 cups half-and-half
Salt to taste
White pepper to taste

❧ Heat the stock to a simmer in a saucepan over medium-high heat. Sauté the green onions in the butter in a large saucepan over medium-high heat until tender. Add the flour; mix well. Add the heated stock gradually, whisking constantly. Bring to a simmer. Add the green onions, corn and crawfish tails; mix well. Return to a simmer; add the half-and-half. Cook for 8 to 10 minutes or until slightly thickened and reduced in volume, stirring frequently. Season with salt and white pepper. Garnish each serving with parsley.

Yield: 4 to 6 servings

Post Thanksgiving Turkey Soup

8 cups turkey broth
1 (16-ounce) can chopped
   tomatoes
2 cups each diced zucchini,
   carrots and celery
1 1/2 cups chopped leeks
1/2 cup chopped onion
1 tablespoon minced garlic

2 ounces linguini
1 (15 1/4-ounce) can whole
   kernel corn
3 cups chopped turkey
1/2 cup chopped fresh parsley
1/2 cup grated Parmesan
   cheese
Pepper to taste

❧ Mix the first 8 ingredients in a large pot. Bring to a boil; reduce the heat. Simmer, covered, for 10 minutes. Stir in the linguini. Cook, uncovered, for 5 minutes, stirring once or twice. Stir in the corn, turkey, parsley and Parmesan cheese; season with the pepper. Simmer, covered, for 15 minutes.

Yield: 20 servings

Mulligatawny Soup

1 whole chicken breast
3 cups chicken broth
2 tablespoons olive oil
1 medium onion, chopped
1 rib celery, chopped
1/2 green bell pepper, chopped
1/2 teaspoon powdered
   cardamom

1 1/2 teaspoons curry powder
1 large tomato, peeled,
   chopped
Salt to taste
1 medium Granny Smith
   apple, chopped
1 1/2 cups cooked rice

❧ Cook the chicken in the broth in a covered saucepan over medium-high heat until tender. Let cool slightly. Remove chicken from broth; cut into bite-size pieces, discarding the skin and bones. Pour the broth into a bowl. Chill, covered; skim the fat. Add the olive oil to the saucepan; add the next 5 ingredients. Sauté until tender. Stir in the tomato, chicken and broth. Simmer, covered, for 1 hour. Season with salt. Stir in the apple and rice just before serving. Cook until heated through, stirring occasionally.

Yield: 10 servings

A Thyme to
Remember

❧❧❧

When Phil was in medical

school, we had no money.

We would get together

in the kitchen, treat cooking

like chemistry class, and

have a great time.

Wendy Hansen

❧❧❧

White Chili

1 pound boneless skinless chicken breasts, chopped	1 teaspoon garlic powder
1 tablespoon olive oil	1/2 teaspoon dried oregano
1/4 cup chopped onion	1 teaspoon ground cumin
1 cup chicken broth	1/2 teaspoon coriander
1 (4-ounce) can chopped green chiles	1/8 to 1/4 teaspoon cayenne
	1 (19-ounce) can white kidney beans

❧ Sauté chicken in olive oil in a saucepan over medium-high heat for 4 to 5 minutes or until cooked through. Remove to a bowl, using a slotted spoon; keep warm. Add onion to the saucepan. Cook for 2 minutes, stirring frequently. Stir in broth, green chiles and spices. Simmer, covered, for 30 minutes. Stir in the chicken and undrained kidney beans. Simmer, covered, for 10 minutes. Garnish with Monterey Jack cheese and green onions.

Yield: 4 servings

Acapulco Chili

1 small onion, chopped	1 1/2 to 2 tablespoons chili powder
1 1/2 teaspoons minced garlic	2 teaspoons ground cumin
1 pound ground turkey breast	1 (14 1/2-ounce) can Rotel tomatoes
2 tablespoons flour	1 (16-ounce) can black beans, rinsed, drained
1/4 teaspoon salt	
1/2 teaspoon dried cilantro leaves	

May substitute 2 tablespoons fresh cilantro for the 1/2 teaspoon dried cilantro leaves.

❧ Sauté the onion in a nonstick saucepan coated with nonstick cooking spray over medium-high heat for 4 to 5 minutes or until translucent. Stir in the garlic. Sauté for 1 minute. Add the ground turkey. Cook until brown and crumbly, stirring frequently. Stir in the next 5 ingredients. Stir in the tomatoes and black beans. Simmer, covered, for 5 minutes or until heated through, stirring occasionally. Serve with jalapeños, fat-free sour cream, fresh cilantro and chopped fresh onions.

Yield: 4 servings

A Handful of Sunshine

SWEET BREADS AND BRUNCH

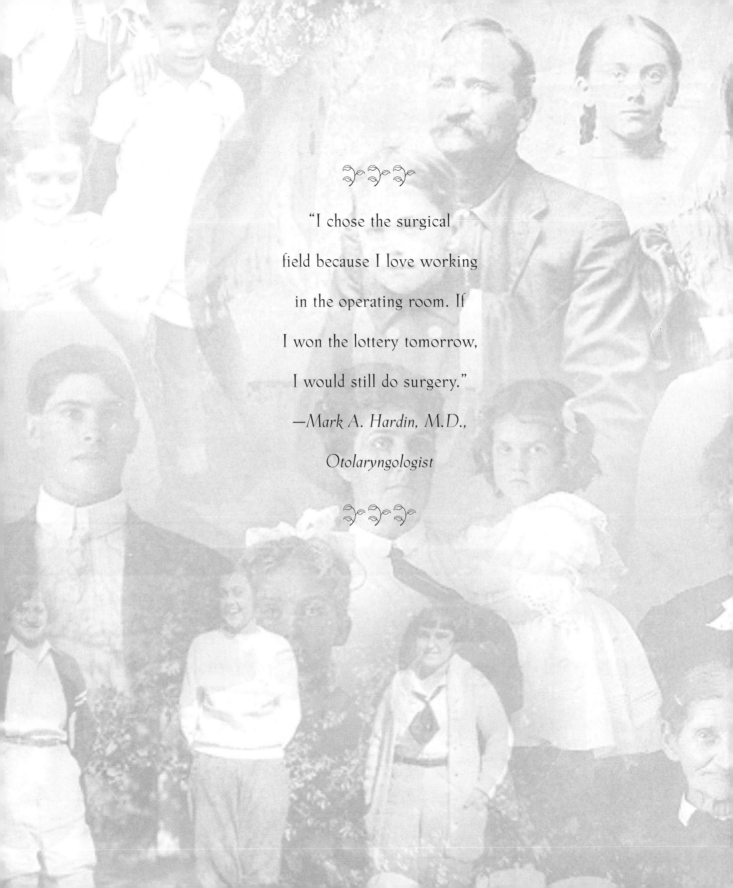

"I chose the surgical field because I love working in the operating room. If I won the lottery tomorrow, I would still do surgery."
—*Mark A. Hardin, M.D.,*
Otolaryngologist

Apricot Almond Coffee Cake

1 cup butter, softened
2 cups sugar
2 eggs
1 teaspoon almond extract
2 (scant) cups cake flour
1 teaspoon baking powder

1/4 teaspoon salt
1 cup sour cream
1 cup sliced almonds
1 (12-ounce) jar apricot
   preserves

❧ Preheat the oven to 350 degrees; grease and flour a bundt pan. Cream the butter in the large bowl of an electric mixer set at medium speed until soft and fluffy. Add the sugar gradually, beating at medium speed for 6 to 7 minutes or until well combined. Add the eggs, one at a time, beating just until the mixture is pale yellow. Stir in the almond extract.

❧ Combine the flour, baking powder and salt in a medium bowl; mix well. Beat in the egg mixture, a small amount at a time, alternating with the sour cream.

❧ Spoon about 1/3 of the batter into the bundt pan, smoothing lightly with the back of a spoon. Sprinkle half the almonds over the batter, and dot with half the apricot preserves. Top with the remaining batter, almonds and preserves.

❧ Bake for 50 to 55 minutes or until a toothpick or cake tester inserted in the center comes out clean. Cool in the pan on a wire rack for 10 to 15 minutes. Remove from the pan and let cool completely on the rack.

Yield: 12 servings

My mother always told me to

get up in the morning with

my husband, put a smile on

my face and fix him a hot

breakfast before he goes to

work. She never thought I'd

marry a doctor who would

get up in the middle of the

night to go to the hospital.

Sarah Hardin

Blueberry Coffee Cake

1 cup butter, softened
2 cups sugar
2 eggs
1 cup sour cream
1/2 teaspoon vanilla extract
1 1/2 cups plus 2 tablespoons
   flour
1 teaspoon baking powder

1/4 teaspoon salt
1/2 to 1 cup fresh or frozen
   (thawed) blueberries
1/2 cup brown sugar
1 teaspoon cinnamon
1 cup chopped pecans
Confectioners' sugar

⊱ Preheat the oven to 350 degrees; grease and flour a bundt pan. Cream the butter and sugar in a large bowl until soft, fluffy and well blended. Beat in the eggs, one at a time, the sour cream and the vanilla extract.

⊱ Combine the flour, baking powder and salt in a medium bowl; mix well. Add to the sour cream mixture; mix well. Fold in the blueberries.

⊱ Combine the brown sugar, cinnamon and pecans in a small bowl; mix well. Spoon half the batter into the bundt pan, smoothing it lightly with the back of a spoon. Top with the pecan mixture. Spoon in the remaining batter, smoothing it.

⊱ Bake for 50 to 60 minutes or until a toothpick or cake tester inserted in the center comes out clean. Cool in the pan on a wire rack for 10 to 15 minutes. Remove from the pan. Sift confectioners' sugar over the top.

Yield: 12 servings

Chocolate-Raspberry Coffee Cake

1 cup butter or margarine,
    softened
1 cup sugar
3 eggs
1 teaspoon vanilla extract
1/2 teaspoon almond extract
    (optional)
2 1/2 cups flour
2 teaspoons baking powder

1 teaspoon baking soda
1 teaspoon salt
1 cup sour cream
1/2 cup mini semisweet
    chocolate chips
1/2 cup slivered almonds,
    toasted
1/2 cup seedless raspberry
    jam, stirred until smooth

Preheat the oven to 350 degrees; grease and flour a 10-inch bundt pan. Cream the butter in the large bowl of an electric mixer set at high speed for 45 seconds or until soft and fluffy. Add the sugar; beat for 1 minute or until well blended. Add the eggs, vanilla and almond extract; beat for 2 minutes or until light and well blended.

Whisk the flour, baking powder, baking soda and salt in a medium bowl until blended. Add gradually to the butter mixture, mixing at low speed until well combined. Beat on high speed for 30 seconds or until well blended. Beat in the sour cream.

Reserve 2 tablespoons of chocolate chips and 2 tablespoons of almonds. Sprinkle the remaining chocolate chips and almonds in the bottom of the bundt pan. Spoon in half the batter, smoothing it lightly with the back of a spoon. Drizzle the jam over the batter; sprinkle with the remaining chocolate chips and almonds. Top with the remaining batter, smoothing it lightly.

Bake for 50 minutes or until a cake tester inserted in the center comes out clean. Cool in the pan on a wire rack for 30 minutes. Remove from the pan and let cool completely on the rack.

Yield: 12 servings

A Thyme to Remember

To toast the almonds, spread them in a cold nonstick skillet. Cook over medium heat, stirring constantly until the almonds are slightly browned.

Gift of the Magi Bread

½ cup margarine
1 cup sugar
2 eggs
1 teaspoon vanilla extract
2 cups flour
1 teaspoon baking soda
1 teaspoon baking powder
Salt to taste
1 cup mashed bananas
1 cup semisweet chocolate
   chips

1 (11-ounce) can mandarin
   orange segments, drained
1 cup shredded coconut
¾ cup chopped pecans
½ cup chopped maraschino
   cherries
½ cup chopped dates or
   raisins
Confectioners' sugar

❧ Preheat the oven to 350 degrees; grease two small loaf pans.
Cream the margarine and sugar in a large bowl until soft, fluffy
and well blended. Add the eggs, one at a time, and the vanilla; beat
until well combined.

❧ Combine the flour, baking soda, baking powder and salt
in a medium bowl; mix well. Add to the margarine mixture,
beating alternately with the bananas until well blended. Stir in
the chocolate chips, mandarin oranges, coconut, ½ cup of the
pecans, and all the cherries and dates. Pour into the prepared pans.

❧ Sprinkle the remaining pecans over the batter. Bake for 1 hour.
Cool on a wire rack; sprinkle with confectioners' sugar.

Yield: 12 servings

My father, at age 91, still

bakes bread once a week.

Jean Bremner

Mother's Cinnamon Bread

¼ cup melted shortening
1 cup milk, scalded
1 envelope dry yeast
¼ cup lukewarm water
¼ cup sugar
1 teaspoon salt
1 egg, beaten

3½ cups flour
Milk
¼ cup sugar
½ teaspoon cinnamon
Melted butter
1½ tablespoons sugar
1 teaspoon cinnamon

Grease a large loaf pan. Let the melted shortening and 1 cup scalded milk cool to lukewarm. Dissolve the yeast in the lukewarm water in a small bowl. Combine ¼ cup sugar, the salt and egg in a large bowl; mix well. Add the shortening, milk and yeast mixture; mix well. Stir in the flour until combined.

Turn out onto a floured work surface. Knead for 10 minutes or until smooth and elastic. Oil a large bowl. Place the dough in the bowl, turning once to oil both sides. Let rise, covered with a tea towel, in a warm place (80 to 90 degrees) for about 1 hour or until doubled in bulk. Punch the dough down.

Turn out onto the floured work surface; roll or stretch into a rectangle; brush with milk. Combine ¼ cup sugar and ½ teaspoon cinnamon in a small bowl, stirring until mixed; sprinkle over the dough. Roll up jelly-roll fashion; tuck under the ends. Place in the loaf pan, seam side down. Let rise, lightly covered with a tea towel, until slightly more than doubled in bulk.

Preheat the oven to 350 degrees. Brush the top of the loaf with melted butter. Combine the 1½ tablespoons sugar and 1 teaspoon cinnamon in a small bowl; stir until mixed. Sprinkle over the loaf. Bake for 45 minutes.

Yield: 12 servings

Mother was like the "Bread Santa Claus," baking bread for friends all over town. When we were young, we loved to be "Mother's elves," delivering smiles to everyone who received Mother's beautiful and fragrant cinnamon bread.

Sarah Hardin

Waldorf Salad Bread

2 eggs
1/3 cup unsweetened apple
    juice
1/2 cup mayonnaise
1 teaspoon vanilla extract
2 1/2 cups flour
1 tablespoon baking powder

1/4 teaspoon salt
3/4 cup sugar
1 cup diced red apple
1/4 cup finely diced celery
3/4 cup coarsely broken
    walnuts

I had two wonderful teachers

in the kitchen—my mother

and our maid, Ruby, who is

like my second mother.

Marty Curtis

❧ Preheat the oven to 350 degrees; grease and flour 2 small loaf pans. Beat the eggs lightly in a small bowl. Add the apple juice, mayonnaise and vanilla; beat until blended.

❧ Mix the flour, baking powder, salt and sugar in a large bowl. Add the egg mixture; stir just until moistened. Stir in the apple, celery and walnuts. Pour into the prepared loaf pans.

❧ Bake for 50 minutes or until a cake tester inserted in the center comes out clean. Cool in the pans on a wire rack for 10 minutes. Loosen the edges and turn out onto the rack. Let cool completely.

❧ Store, wrapped tightly in plastic wrap, for 12 hours before cutting. Store leftovers, wrapped in plastic wrap, in the refrigerator.

Yield: 24 servings

Apricot Bread

1 pound dried apricots, chopped
2 cups sugar
2 cups apricot nectar
¾ cup shortening
1 teaspoon salt

2 eggs, beaten
4 cups flour
2 teaspoons baking soda
½ cup chopped pecans, toasted (optional)

❧ Preheat the oven to 325 degrees; grease and flour 2 large loaf pans. Combine the apricots, sugar, apricot nectar, shortening and salt in a saucepan; mix well. Bring to a boil over medium-high heat, stirring occasionally. Boil for 5 minutes, stirring occasionally. Strain, reserving the apricot liquid in a large bowl to cool. Set the apricots aside.

❧ Stir the eggs into the cooled apricot liquid; mix well. Combine the flour, baking soda and pecans in a small bowl; mix well. Add to the egg mixture; beat just until moistened. Stir in the apricots and pour into the prepared loaf pans.

❧ Bake for 1 hour or until a cake tester inserted in the center comes out clean. Cool in the pans on a wire rack for 10 minutes. Loosen the edges and turn out onto the rack. Let cool completely.

Yield: 24 servings

Chocolate Chip Banana Nut Bread

1/4 cup butter, softened
1/2 cup shortening
1 1/2 cups sugar
2 eggs
1 teaspoon vanilla extract
1 teaspoon baking soda
1/4 cup sour cream

1 1/2 cups flour
1/4 teaspoon salt
1 cup (about 3) mashed
   bananas
1 cup chocolate chips
   (optional)
1 cup pecans, broken

This bread freezes

beautifully.

❧ Preheat the oven to 350 degrees; grease and flour one large loaf pan or two medium loaf pans.

❧ Cream the butter and shortening in a large bowl until soft, fluffy and well blended. Add the sugar; beat until light and fluffy. Beat in the eggs, one at a time, and the vanilla. Stir the baking soda into the sour cream in a small bowl. Stir into the egg mixture.

❧ Whisk the flour and salt in a medium bowl until combined. Add to the egg mixture; beat just until moistened. Mix in the bananas, chocolate chips and pecans. Pour into the loaf pan.

❧ Bake for 1 hour or until a cake tester inserted in the center comes out clean. Cool in the pan on a wire rack for 10 to 15 minutes. Remove from the pan and let cool completely on the rack.

Yield: 12 servings

Cream Cheese Carrot Bread

2 cups flour
1 1/2 teaspoons baking soda
1 1/2 teaspoons baking powder
1 teaspoon cinnamon
1/4 teaspoon salt
1 cup vegetable oil
1 1/2 cups sugar

3 eggs, beaten
1 1/2 cups grated carrots
1 cup pecans, chopped
1/2 cup golden raisins
8 ounces cream cheese, softened
1/4 cup butter, softened

❧ Preheat the oven to 350 degrees; grease and flour two 1-pound coffee cans. Sift the flour, baking soda, baking powder, cinnamon and salt into a medium bowl.

❧ Combine the oil and sugar in a large bowl; mix well. Beat in the flour mixture, a little at a time, alternating with the eggs. Stir in the carrots, pecans and raisins; mix well. Pour into the coffee cans.

❧ Bake for 1 hour or until a cake tester inserted in the center comes out clean. Cool in the cans on a wire rack for 10 minutes. Remove from the cans and let cool completely on the rack. Wrap in foil and store in the refrigerator or freezer. Slice just before serving.

❧ Blend the cream cheese and butter in a medium bowl. Spread on the bread slices.

Yield: 24 servings

A Thyme to Remember

"I knew I wanted to be a doctor in 10th grade when I was a Medical Explorer in Boy Scouts. I loved my Boy Scout volunteer work at Baylor Hospital. In 11th grade I visited the Dean of Southwestern Medical School and told him I wanted to go to school there. I never lost sight of my goal."

Paul P. Rodriquez, M.D.,

General Surgeon

Cranberry Bread

Juice of 2 oranges
Water
2 tablespoons grated orange
   peel
6 tablespoons margarine
3 cups (or more) all-purpose
   flour
1 cup whole wheat flour
1 teaspoon salt
1 teaspoon baking soda
1 1/2 teaspoons baking powder

2 cups sugar
1 teaspoon cinnamon
1 teaspoon nutmeg
1/2 teaspoon ground allspice
1/2 teaspoon powdered ginger
2 eggs, beaten
3 cups fresh or dried
   cranberries
2 cups chopped walnuts
1/2 cup all-purpose flour

You may add or eliminate

spices as desired.

❧ Preheat the oven to 350 degrees; line two large loaf pans with foil and grease well.

❧ Combine the orange juice and enough water to equal 1 3/4 cups liquid in a measuring cup; pour into a saucepan. Bring to a boil over high heat. Stir in the orange peel and margarine. Remove from the heat and let cool.

❧ Whisk the 3 cups all-purpose flour, the whole wheat flour, salt, baking soda, baking powder, sugar, cinnamon, nutmeg, allspice and ginger in a large bowl. Create a well in the center. Pour in the orange juice mixture and stir just until moistened. Add the eggs; stir gently.

❧ Toss the cranberries, walnuts and 1/2 cup flour in another large bowl until coated. Stir gently into the batter. Stir in additional flour if needed to make a stiff dough. Divide batter between the loaf pans.

❧ Bake for 1 1/2 hours or until a cake tester inserted in the center comes out clean, covering the pans with foil during the last 30 minutes of baking. Cool in the pans on a wire rack for 10 to 15 minutes. Remove from the pans and let cool completely on the rack.

Yield: 24 servings

Plum Bread

3 cups flour
1 teaspoon cream of tartar
1 teaspoon salt
1/2 teaspoon baking soda
3/4 cup plain yogurt
1 teaspoon grated lemon peel
1 cup butter, softened

2 cups sugar
1 teaspoon vanilla extract
4 eggs
2 cups diced purple prune
    plums
1 cup chopped pecans or
    walnuts

❧ Preheat the oven to 350 degrees; grease and flour two large loaf pans. Sift the flour, cream of tartar, salt and baking soda into a medium bowl. Blend the yogurt and lemon peel in a small bowl.

❧ Cream the butter, sugar and vanilla in a large bowl until soft, fluffy and well blended. Add the eggs, one at a time, beating well after each addition. Beat in the flour mixture, alternating with yogurt mixture. Stir in the prune plums and pecans.

❧ Pour the batter into the prepared loaf pans. Bake for 50 to 55 minutes or until a cake tester inserted in the center comes out clean. Cool in the pans on a wire rack for 10 to 15 minutes. Remove from the pans and let cool completely on the rack.

Yield: 24 servings

If prune plums are

unavailable, you may

substitute any other ripe

yet firm plums.

Sometimes in my kitchen I

feel like a juggler. I like to

cook so much food for my

family that there is not

enough counter space to

hold it all. There are times

when I'm stirring the pot

while holding a completed

dish in my other hand.

Gail Loeb

Pumpkin Coconut Bread

2 cups flour
1 teaspoon salt
1 teaspoon cinnamon
1 teaspoon nutmeg
1½ teaspoons baking soda
2 cups sugar
1½ cups vegetable oil

5 eggs
1 (16-ounce) can pumpkin
2 (4-ounce) packages coconut
    pudding and pie filling
    mix
1 cup chopped pecans or
    walnuts

☙ Preheat the oven to 325 degrees; grease and flour two
large loaf pans, four medium loaf pans or eight small loaf pans.
Sift the flour, salt, cinnamon, nutmeg and baking soda into a
medium bowl.

☙ Combine the sugar and oil in a large bowl, stirring vigorously
to mix well. Beat in the eggs, one at a time. Add the flour mixture;
stir just until moistened. Mix in the pumpkin and coconut pudding
mix. Stir in the pecans. Spoon into the loaf pans; smooth gently
with the back of a spoon.

☙ Bake, covered with foil for 30 minutes; uncover. Bake for an
additional 30 to 45 minutes or until a cake tester inserted in the
center comes out clean. Cool in the pans on a wire rack for 10 to
15 minutes. Remove from the pans and let cool completely on the
rack. May use instant pudding mix instead of the pudding and pie
filling mix.

Yield: 24 servings

Quick Little Apricot Sweet Rolls

2 eggs
2 tablespoons water
1/2 cup apricot preserves
1 cup chopped pecans

1 cup sugar
2 teaspoons cinnamon
1 (8-count) can refrigerated
   crescent rolls

Grease a jelly roll pan. Beat the eggs and water in a small bowl. Stir the preserves in a measuring cup, using a fork. Combine the pecans, sugar and cinnamon in a medium bowl, stirring to mix well. Separate the rolls and cut each in half. Spread about 1 teaspoon preserves on each roll. Roll up starting with the wide end and tucking under the ends. Dip into the egg mixture, coat with the pecan mixture, and arrange on the jelly roll pan. Bake using package directions. Remove to wire racks to cool slightly.

Yield: 16 servings

Strawberry Nut Bread

4 eggs, beaten
1 1/4 cups vegetable oil
3 cups flour
1 teaspoon baking soda
1 teaspoon salt

1 tablespoon cinnamon
2 cups sugar
2 cups frozen sliced
   strawberries, thawed
1 1/4 cups chopped pecans

Preheat the oven to 350 degrees; grease six small foil loaf pans or two large loaf pans. Combine the eggs and oil in a medium bowl, beating to blend well. Combine the flour, baking soda, salt, cinnamon and sugar in a large bowl, stirring to mix thoroughly. Make a well in the center of the flour mixture, pour in the egg mixture, and stir just until moistened. Mix in the strawberries and pecans. Pour into the pans. Bake for 40 minutes in the small foil pans or 1 hour in large loaf pans or until a cake tester inserted in the center comes out clean. Cool in the pans on wire racks for 5 minutes. Remove from the pans and let cool completely on the racks.

Yield: 24 servings

Shortly after we married, my husband said, "I wish you could bake bread like my mother." So I got out my new Joy of Cooking and learned how to bake. I am now in my 38th year of making bread.

Pam Edmunds

Chocolate Zucchini Bread

2½ cups flour
1 teaspoon baking soda
2½ teaspoons baking powder
½ cup cocoa
½ teaspoon salt
3 eggs, beaten

1 cup vegetable oil
2 cups sugar
2 cups shredded peeled
  zucchini
2 teaspoons vanilla extract
1 cup chopped pecans

Preheat the oven to 350 degrees; grease two large loaf pans. Combine the flour, baking soda, baking powder, cocoa and salt in a medium bowl, whisking to mix thoroughly. Combine the eggs, oil, sugar, zucchini and vanilla in a large bowl; stir to blend well. Add the flour mixture; beating briefly to blend well. Stir in the pecans. Bake for 45 to 60 minutes or until a cake tester inserted in the center comes out clean. Cool on a wire rack.

Yield: 24 servings

On Sunday mornings—the one day he doesn't have to go in to the hospital—my husband makes the pancakes and biscuits for the family.

Mary Pat Smith

Raisin Bran Muffins

1 cup vegetable oil
4 cups buttermilk
1 (15-ounce) package raisin
  bran cereal

5 cups flour
3 cups sugar
5 teaspoons baking soda
2 teaspoons salt

Preheat the oven to 350 degrees; grease 24 large muffin cups. Combine the oil and buttermilk in a large bowl, whisking to combine well. Combine the bran cereal, flour, sugar, baking soda and salt; mix well. Pour in the buttermilk mixture; stir to blend thoroughly. Spoon into muffin cups, filling them two-thirds full.

Bake for 15 to 20 minutes or until a cake tester inserted in the center of a muffin comes out clean. Cool in the pan on a wire rack. The batter can be stored, covered, in the refrigerator for several days.

Yield: 24 servings

Apple Cheddar Corn Bread

1 cup cornmeal
1 cup flour
½ cup sugar
1 tablespoon baking powder
1 egg
¼ cup melted butter

1 cup milk
2 small tart red apples,
  chopped
½ cup shredded Cheddar
  cheese

❧ Preheat the oven to 425 degrees; grease a 9-inch square baking pan, iron muffin pan or iron skillet. Combine the cornmeal, flour, sugar and baking powder in a large bowl, whisking to mix well. Beat the egg, butter and milk in the large mixer bowl of an electric mixer at medium speed until well blended. Add the flour mixture; stir just until moistened. Stir in the apples and cheese. Pour into the pan. Bake for 20 to 25 minutes or until a cake tester inserted in the center comes out clean. Cool in the pan on a wire rack.

Yield: 9 servings

Baked French Toast

8 slices white bread, crusts
  trimmed, cut into 1-inch
  cubes
4 ounces cream cheese,
  softened
6 eggs

1 cup whipping cream
⅓ cup maple syrup
½ teaspoon maple extract
Warmed maple syrup or
  confectioners' sugar

❧ Grease an 8-inch baking dish; fill with the bread cubes. Beat the cream cheese in the mixer bowl of an electric mixer at medium speed until smooth. Add the eggs, whipping cream, maple syrup and maple extract; beat until blended. Pour over the bread cubes. Chill, covered, in the refrigerator for 8 to 12 hours. Remove from the refrigerator; let stand at room temperature for 30 minutes. Bake at 375 degrees for 20 minutes; cover with foil. Bake for 10 to 15 minutes longer or until set. Serve with maple syrup.

Yield: 4 servings

A Thyme to Remember

Apple Cheddar Corn Bread

has been in my family for

over 100 years. It is an old

Pennsylvania Dutch recipe.

My great grandmother

brought it with her during the

Oklahoma land run of 1889.

Sarah Hardin

Hazelnut Meusli

4 cups rolled oats
1/3 to 1/2 cup wheat, rye or
    barley flakes
1/3 cup bran (optional)
1/2 cup packed dried apricots,
    chopped
1/2 cup packed brown sugar

2/3 cup raisins
2/3 cup golden raisins
1/4 to 1/3 cup hazelnuts,
    walnuts or pecans,
    coarsely chopped

❧ Combine the oats, wheat flakes, bran, apricots, brown sugar, raisins, golden raisins and hazelnuts in a large container with a tight-fitting lid, tossing to mix. Serve with milk, grated apples, sliced bananas and/or stewed fruit.

Yield: 10 servings

Breakfast Bars

1 1/2 cups flour
1 teaspoon baking soda
1 teaspoon cinnamon
1/4 teaspoon nutmeg
6 tablespoons mixed dried
    fruit bits

1 egg
3/4 cup sugar
1 cup applesauce
1/2 cup buttermilk
2 cups toasted whole-grain
    Cheerios

Quick, tasty, low in

fat—and kids love

them. May substitute

honey–nut Cheerios.

❧ Preheat the oven to 350 degrees; grease a 9x13-inch baking pan. Combine the flour, baking soda, cinnamon and nutmeg in a large bowl, whisking briefly. Stir in 4 tablespoons of the dried-fruit bits. Beat the egg and sugar in a mixer bowl at high speed for 1 minute. Stir in the applesauce. Beat in the flour mixture, alternating with the buttermilk. Stir in 1 1/2 cups of the cereal. Pour the batter into the pan. Sprinkle the remaining fruit and cereal over the top. Bake for 15 minutes or until a toothpick inserted in the center comes out clean. Cool on a wire rack.

Yield: 16 servings

Jalapeño and Swiss Cheese Chicken Crêpes

1 (3- to 4-pound) chicken,
   cooked, chopped
1¼ pounds Swiss cheese,
   shredded
2 jalapeños, seeded, finely
   chopped, or to taste

1 teaspoon salt
1 teaspoon pepper
12 Easy Crêpes (below)
2 cups whipping cream

❧ Preheat the oven to 325 degrees. Combine the chicken, 4 cups
of the shredded Swiss cheese and the jalapeños in a bowl, tossing to
mix well. Season with the salt and pepper.

❧ Place large spoonfuls of the mixture down the centers of the
Easy Crêpes; roll up. Arrange in a shallow baking dish; top with
the remaining Swiss cheese and the whipping cream. Bake for
20 to 30 minutes or until heated through.

Yield: 12 servings

Easy Crêpes

3 eggs
1 cup milk
1 tablespoon vegetable oil

1 cup flour
½ teaspoon salt

❧ Grease a crêpe pan or a griddle. Preheat until hot. Combine the
eggs, milk, oil, flour and salt in a blender container; process until
smooth. Pour approximately ⅛ cup batter at a time into the crêpe
pan; swirl to distribute thinly and evenly. Cook until the edges
appear dry; flip to cook the second side. Remove to a platter and
cover with a tea towel to keep warm. Repeat until all the batter has
been used.

Chayote Squash Stuffed with Shrimp

6 chayote squash
3 tablespoons butter
1/2 white onion, chopped
3 green onions, chopped
1/2 green bell pepper, chopped
3 ribs celery, chopped
1 pound shrimp, peeled, chopped

2 cups Italian bread crumbs
1 egg, beaten
Salt and pepper to taste
Grated Parmesan cheese
Seasoned bread crumbs

Chopped turkey or pork

may be substituted for

the shrimp.

❧ Place the squash in a large saucepan; fill with water. Bring to a boil; reduce the heat. Simmer, covered, until tender when probed with a fork; drain. Halve the squash and discard the seeds. Scoop out the pulp and place in a large bowl, leaving a 1/8- to 1/4-inch-thick shell suitable for stuffing. Mash with a potato masher; set aside.

❧ Melt the butter in a skillet over medium-high heat; add the white onion. Sauté until tender. Add the green onions, bell pepper and celery. Sauté until tender. Add the shrimp. Sauté until pink and cooked through.

❧ Add to the mashed squash. Stir in the 2 cups bread crumbs and egg; season with salt and pepper. Spoon into the squash shells. Sprinkle Parmesan cheese and seasoned bread crumbs over the shrimp filling. Place on a baking sheet. Bake at 350 degrees for 25 minutes.

Yield: 12 servings

Brown Sugar Ham Loaf

2 pounds ground ham
1 pound ground pork
1 cup soft bread crumbs
1 cup tomato juice
3 eggs

1/4 teaspoon pepper
1 cup packed brown sugar
1 tablespoon dry mustard
1/4 cup cider vinegar
1/2 cup water

❧ Preheat the oven to 325 degrees. Mix the ham, pork, bread crumbs, tomato juice, eggs and pepper in a large bowl. Shape into a loaf in a baking dish. Whisk the remaining ingredients in a saucepan until well blended. Cook over medium-low heat until the sugar is dissolved, stirring often. Spoon over the ham loaf. Bake for 2 hours.

Yield: 8 servings

Sausage Spinach Bread

1 pound hot pork sausage
1 (10-ounce) package frozen
    chopped spinach, cooked,
    squeezed dry
1 egg, beaten
2 loaves frozen French bread
    dough, thawed

12 ounces mozzarella cheese,
    shredded
12 ounces Parmesan cheese,
    grated

❧ Preheat the oven to 375 degrees. Brown the sausage in a large skillet over medium-high heat, stirring often; drain. Place spinach in a bowl. Add 1/2 of the egg, mixing well. Roll 1 loaf of dough to 9x13 inches. Spread half the spinach mixture, half the sausage and half the mozzarella over the dough. Sprinkle with half the Parmesan cheese. Roll up jelly roll style and tightly seal all the edges so the filling stays inside. Lightly score the top, using a sharp knife. Brush lightly with half of the remaining egg. Repeat filling and shaping the loaf with the remaining ingredients. Bake for 20 minutes or until browned. Remove to a wire rack. Serve hot.

Yield: 16 servings

When I sleep at night I

dream about food.

Linda Eichenwald

Twenty-Four-Hour Wine and Cheese Omelet Casserole

1 large loaf dried French or
    Italian bread, cubed
6 tablespoons unsalted butter,
    melted
3/4 pound Swiss cheese,
    shredded
1/2 pound Monterey Jack
    cheese, shredded
9 thin slices ham or Genoa
    salami, slivered
16 eggs

3 1/4 cups milk
1/2 cup dry white wine
4 large green onions, minced
1 tablespoon Dusseldorf
    German mustard
1/4 teaspoon black pepper
1/8 teaspoon cayenne
1 1/2 cups sour cream
2/3 to 1 cup grated Parmesan
    cheese

Chopped mushrooms

may be added to the shredded

cheeses and slivered ham.

🌱 Grease 2 shallow 3-quart (9x13-inch) baking dishes. Place the bread over the bottom and drizzle with the butter. Sprinkle the Swiss cheese, Monterey Jack cheese and ham over the bread.

🌱 Whisk the eggs, milk, wine, green onions, mustard, black pepper and cayenne in a large bowl until foamy. Pour over the bread-cheese mixture. Chill, covered with foil, in the refrigerator for 12 to 24 hours.

🌱 Remove from the refrigerator 30 minutes before baking. Preheat the oven to 325 degrees. Bake, covered, for 1 hour or until set. Uncover. Spread sour cream over the top; sprinkle with the Parmesan cheese. Bake, uncovered, for 10 minutes.

Yield: 40 servings

Breakfast Blintz Soufflé

6 eggs
1½ cups sour cream
½ cup orange juice
⅓ cup sugar
1 cup butter
2 teaspoons baking powder
2 cups flour
8 ounces cream cheese, cut
    into small pieces

2 cups small curd cottage
    cheese
3 egg yolks, lightly beaten
1 tablespoon sugar
1 teaspoon vanilla
Strawberry Sauce
    (below)

❧ Preheat the oven to 350 degrees. Grease a 9x13-inch baking
dish. Combine the eggs, sour cream, orange juice, sugar, butter and
baking powder; process until mixed. Add the flour; process until
well blended. Pour half the batter into the baking dish.

❧ Combine the cream cheese, cottage cheese, egg yolks, sugar and
vanilla; stir gently. Spoon evenly over the sour cream batter. Top
with the remaining batter. Bake for 55 minutes or until puffed in
the center and golden brown. Cut into squares and serve topped
with Strawberry Sauce.

Yield: 10 servings

Strawberry Sauce

2 pounds (about 1 quart)
    strawberries, sliced

3 tablespoons sugar
3 tablespoons orange juice

❧ Place the strawberries in a saucepan. Cook over medium-low
heat until heated through. Add the sugar and orange juice, stirring.
Cook until thickened, stirring constantly.

Stilton Cheese Soufflé with Chives

8 slices dried bread, cut into
　½-inch cubes
1½ pounds Stilton cheese,
　crumbled
2½ cups milk
6 eggs, lightly beaten
⅛ teaspoon white pepper
¼ teaspoon cayenne
¼ teaspoon paprika

1 tablespoon grated onion
2 tablespoons chopped fresh
　chives
¼ teaspoon dry mustard
½ teaspoon salt
½ teaspoon Worcestershire
　sauce
½ teaspoon sugar

❧ Grease a 9x13-inch baking dish. Layer the bread cubes and
Stilton cheese, half at a time, in the baking dish, starting with the
bread. Combine the milk, eggs, white pepper, cayenne, paprika,
onion, chives, dry mustard, salt, Worcestershire and sugar in a large
bowl; mix well. Pour slowly over the bread and cheese, lightly pressing
down the bread cubes so they remain on the bottom of the baking
dish. Chill, covered, in the refrigerator for 12 hours. Preheat the
oven to 300 degrees. Bake for 1 hour or until browned and bubbly.

Yield: 16 servings

Louisiana Crawfish Tarts

1 cup sliced mushrooms
1 cup chopped green onions
½ cup butter
4 eggs, well beaten
½ cup half-and-half
1 teaspoon salt

½ teaspoon dry mustard
⅛ teaspoon nutmeg
1 cup shredded mozzarella
　cheese
1 pound crawfish tails
12 unbaked tart shells

❧ Sauté mushrooms and green onions in butter in skillet until
tender. Combine the eggs, half-and-half, salt, dry mustard, nutmeg
and mozzarella cheese in a large bowl; mix well. Fold in the crawfish
and the mushroom mixture. Spoon into the tart shells. Bake in
preheated 400-degree oven for 15 minutes. Reduce the oven
temperature to 300 degrees; bake for 30 minutes or until set.

Yield: 12 servings

Autumn Apple Quiche

12 ounces mild sausage
1 large apple, thinly sliced
1 large onion, chopped
1 1/2 cups shredded Cheddar
    cheese
3 tablespoons flour
3 eggs, beaten

1 cup half-and-half
2 tablespoons chopped fresh
    parsley
1/8 teaspoon dry mustard
1/8 teaspoon celery seed
1 (9-inch) unbaked pie crust

❧ Preheat the oven to 375 degrees. Brown the sausage in a large skillet over medium-high heat. Drain on a platter lined with paper towels. Place the apple and onion in the skillet. Cook for 5 to 6 minutes or until browned.

❧ Toss the Cheddar cheese and flour in a medium bowl. Combine the eggs and half-and-half, whisking to blend well. Whisk in the parsley, dry mustard, celery seed. Stir in the Cheddar cheese mixture.

❧ Spread the sausage over the bottom of the pie crust. Top with the apples and onions. Pour in the Cheddar cheese mixture. Bake for 40 minutes or until a knife inserted in the center comes out clean. Cool for 10 minutes before serving.

Yield: 6 servings

I come from a long line of outstanding cooks on both sides of my family. On one side two aunts owned a tea room and a catering business. On the other my grandmother and aunts were always entering competitions and winning blue ribbons. I've always known that I have a family reputation of great cooking to uphold.

Sarah Hardin

Three Cheese Spinach Quiche

½ (17-ounce) package frozen
   puff pastry, thawed
1 (10-ounce) package frozen
   chopped spinach, cooked,
   drained
1 cup cream
¼ teaspoon salt
½ teaspoon pepper

3 eggs, lightly beaten
½ cup finely chopped onion
1½ cups shredded mozzarella
½ cup shredded Cheddar
   cheese
1 (7-ounce) jar roasted red
   peppers, drained, chopped
½ cup crumbled feta cheese

❧ Grease a 9-inch deep-dish pie plate or quiche pan. Unfold the puff pastry on a lightly floured work surface, and roll to a 13-inch square. Place in the pie plate, tuck the edges under, and crimp. Freeze for 15 minutes. Bake at 400 degrees for 12 minutes; let cool on a wire rack. Reduce the oven temperature to 350 degrees.

❧ Squeeze the spinach dry. Combine with the cream, salt, pepper and eggs in a bowl, stirring to mix well. Sprinkle the onion, mozzarella and Cheddar over the baked puff pastry. Pour in the spinach mixture. Top with the roasted peppers; sprinkle with the feta cheese.

❧ Bake, uncovered, for 55 minutes or until set. Cover loosely with foil and let stand 30 minutes before serving.

Yield: 8 servings

I learned to cook reading

my history homework to

my mother while she

cooked dinner every night.

Carol Bywaters

Asparagus Brunch con Queso

1 pound Colby cheese,
     shredded
12 eggs, beaten
2 (15-ounce) cans or 1 pound
     steamed fresh asparagus

1 pound processed cheese
1 (10-ounce) can diced Rotel
     tomatoes
Paprika to taste

❧ Preheat the oven to 325 degrees. Sprinkle the Colby cheese
over the bottom of a greased 9x13-inch baking dish. Pour
in the eggs. Bake for 45 minutes or until the eggs are set. Arrange
the asparagus over the eggs. Melt the processed cheese with the
tomatoes in a saucepan, stirring frequently. Pour over the
asparagus. Bake for 5 minutes or until hot. Sprinkle with paprika.

Yield: 8 servings

Huevos con Esparragos

10 mushrooms, sliced
6 tablespoons unsalted butter
1 tablespoon parsley
1/2 clove of garlic, minced
1/4 cup flour
2 cups milk

1/2 teaspoon salt
2 cups asparagus tips, steamed
6 hard-cook eggs, sliced
2 tablespoons soft bread crumbs
1 cup shredded Monterey
     Jack cheese

❧ Preheat the oven to 350 degrees; grease a 2-quart baking dish.
Sauté mushrooms in 2 tablespoons of the butter in a skillet for
1 minute. Add the parsley and garlic and sauté for 2 minutes
longer. Melt the remaining butter in a saucepan over medium-low
heat; stir in the flour. Cook for 4 minutes, stirring constantly. Add
the milk gradually, stirring constantly to prevent lumping. Season
with the salt. Bring the sauce to a boil. Stir in the asparagus tips,
cover and remove from the heat. Alternate layers of the sauce,
egg slices and mushroom mixture in the baking dish, starting and
ending with the sauce. Sprinkle the bread crumbs and cheese over
the sauce. Bake for 15 minutes or until lightly browned.

Yield: 6 servings

Goat Cheese, Artichoke and Smoked Ham Strata

2 cups milk
1/4 cup olive oil
8 cups cubed sour dough
    bread
1 1/2 cups whipping cream
5 eggs
1 tablespoon chopped garlic
1 1/2 teaspoons salt
3/4 teaspoon pepper
1/2 teaspoon nutmeg
12 ounces goat cheese,
    crumbled
2 tablespoons chopped fresh
    sage

1 tablespoon chopped fresh
    thyme
1 1/2 teaspoons herbes de
    Provence
12 ounces smoked ham,
    chopped
3 (6 1/2-ounce) jars marinated
    artichoke hearts
1 cup shredded fontina cheese
1 1/2 cups grated Parmesan
    cheese

The strata may be made

one day ahead and stored,

covered, in the refrigerator.

Bake right before serving.

❧ Preheat the oven to 350 degrees; butter a 9x13-inch baking dish. Whisk the milk and olive oil in a large bowl until combined. Stir in the bread and let stand for 10 minutes or until the liquid is absorbed. Whisk the whipping cream, eggs, garlic, salt, pepper and nutmeg in another large bowl until well blended. Stir in the goat cheese. Combine the sage, thyme and herbes de Provence in a small bowl, stirring until well mixed.

❧ Layer the bread mixture, ham, artichoke hearts, fontina cheese, Parmesan cheese, herb mixture and cream mixture, half at a time, in the baking dish until all the ingredients are used. Bake, uncovered, for 1 hour or until firm in the center and brown around the edges.

Yield: 8 servings

Ham Roll-Ups with Wine Sauce

2 cups chopped cooked
   chicken
4 green onions, chopped
1 teaspoon dried tarragon

6 tablespoons sour cream
8 thin slices Swiss cheese
8 slices boiled ham
White Wine Sauce (below)

☙ Preheat the oven to 350 degrees. Combine the chicken,
green onions, tarragon and sour cream; mix well. Place the
Swiss cheese slices atop the ham slices. Top with a spoonful of
the chicken mixture. Roll up and secure with toothpicks. Arrange
in a baking dish. Pour the White Wine Sauce over the roll-ups.
Bake for 30 minutes.

Yield: 8 servings

White Wine Sauce

1 cup butter
1 cup flour
1 cup cream
1/2 cup dry white wine
1/2 teaspoon dried tarragon

1/2 teaspoon garlic powder
1/2 teaspoon salt, or to taste
1/2 teaspoon pepper, or
    to taste

☙ Melt the butter in a saucepan over medium-low heat. Whisk
the flour, cream, white wine, tarragon and garlic powder in a small
bowl until well blended. Season with salt and pepper. Add to the
butter, stirring to mix well. Cook until smooth and thick, stirring
constantly. Do not overcook, or the mixture will curdle.

I always thought that boys

dated me because of my

mother's cooking and one

time that proved true. I

answered the doorbell

expecting my current date

only to find an ex-beau. I

was flustered but he was

non-plus. He was hungry

and had come to have

dinner with my mother.

Mary Ann Blome

Marinated Shrimp and Avocado

2 pounds shrimp, peeled,
  cooked, deveined
2 avocados, cut into bite-size
  pieces

2 small onions, sliced
12 mushrooms, sliced
Lemon Thyme Marinade
  (below)

❧ Combine the shrimp, avocados, onions and mushrooms in a bowl; toss lightly. Pour in the Lemon Thyme Marinade and toss gently to coat. Chill, covered, in the refrigerator for 12 to 24 hours. Drain and serve.

Yield: 8 servings

Lemon Thyme Marinade

1 cup white wine vinegar
1/2 cup water
1/2 cup lemon juice
1 cup vegetable oil
1 tablespoon salt

1/4 teaspoon pepper
2 tablespoons sugar
1 teaspoon dried thyme
1 teaspoon dried oregano
1 teaspoon prepared mustard

❧ Whisk the white wine vinegar, water, lemon juice, oil, salt, pepper, sugar, thyme, oregano and mustard in a medium bowl until well combined.

Roquefort Mousse

1 envelope unflavored gelatin
¼ cup lemon juice
1 cup boiling water
¼ pound Roquefort cheese,
    mashed
1 cup grated cucumber
¼ cup minced fresh parsley

2 tablespoons minced pimento
1 tablespoon minced capers
1 teaspoon grated onion
Salt and freshly ground
    pepper to taste
1 cup whipping cream

❧ Soften the gelatin in the lemon juice in a small bowl. Pour in the boiling water, stirring until dissolved.

❧ Combine the Roquefort cheese, cucumber, parsley, pimento, capers and onion in a large bowl; mix well. Season with salt and pepper. Stir in the gelatin mixture. Chill in the refrigerator just until the mixture begins to set.

❧ Beat the whipping cream in another large bowl until soft peaks form. Fold into the gelatin mixture. Spoon into a 6-cup ring mold, and smooth evenly with back of a wooden spoon. Chill, covered, for 4 hours or until completely firm.

❧ Dip the bottom of the mold briefly into hot water, and invert onto a chilled serving platter.

Yield: 6 servings

Fill the center of the

mousse with a seafood salad,

dust with paprika and

garnish with parsley. Or

serve with asparagus and a

vinaigrette dressing.

African Butternut Squash Fritters

Vegetable oil for frying
1½ cups flour
½ teaspoon salt
2 tablespoons sugar
1½ teaspoons baking powder

½ cup mashed cooked
    butternut squash
½ cup milk
1 egg

❧ Heat the oil in a large heavy skillet. Combine the flour, salt, sugar and baking powder in a medium bowl; whisk to mix well. Combine the butternut squash, milk and egg in a large bowl; whisk to blend well. Add the flour mixture; mix just until combined.

❧ Drop the batter by the heaping teaspoonful into the hot oil. Fry until golden brown. Remove and drain on a plate lined with paper towels.

Yield: 8 servings

When they were

little I taught my children to

say, "Ummm good!"

Elizabeth Gunby

Vegetable Spoon Bread

1 (10-ounce) package frozen
    chopped spinach, thawed,
    drained
2 eggs, lightly beaten
1 (8-ounce) can creamed corn

1 cup sour cream
½ cup butter, melted
¼ teaspoon salt
1 (8-ounce) package corn
    muffin mix

❧ Preheat the oven to 350 degrees; grease an 8-inch round baking dish. Combine the spinach, corn, eggs, sour cream, butter and salt in a large bowl; mix well. Add the corn muffin mix and stir until thoroughly combined.

❧ Pour the batter into the baking dish. Bake for 30 to 45 minutes or until a toothpick inserted in the center comes out clean. Let cool on a wire rack.

Yield: 8 servings

Old Nellie's Grits

1 cup hot cooked grits
1 (8-ounce) package garlic
   processed cheese
2 eggs, beaten

1 (4-ounce) can chopped
   green chiles, drained
1/2 cup margarine or butter

❧ Combine the grits, garlic cheese, eggs, chiles and margarine in a large bowl; mix thoroughly. Pour into a baking dish. Bake at 325 degrees for 45 minutes or until firm.

Yield: 6 servings

Hominy Chile Bake

2 (29-ounce) cans white
   hominy, drained, rinsed
2 (4-ounce) cans chopped
   green chiles
Salt and pepper to taste

1/4 cup sour cream
1/4 cup butter
1 cup shredded Monterey
   Jack cheese
Chili powder

❧ Preheat the oven to 350 degrees. Grease a 2½- or 3-quart baking dish. Alternate layers of hominy, green chiles, salt and pepper, sour cream and butter in the baking dish until all ingredients are used, ending with the hominy.

❧ Sprinkle the Monterey Jack cheese over the hominy. Sprinkle with the chili powder. Bake for 25 to 30 minutes or until heated through.

Yield: 6 servings

Baked Apricots

8 ounces dried apricots, cut
   into halves
6 tablespoons brown sugar
1/4 cup rolled oats

2 tablespoons flour
1/4 cup dark rum
1/4 cup lemon juice
2 tablespoons melted butter

❧ Soak the apricots in water to cover in a small bowl for 12 hours; drain, reserving the soaking liquid in a saucepan. Boil until the liquid is reduced to 1/2 cup. Combine the brown sugar, oats and flour in a food processor; process at medium speed until a coarse mixture forms. Combine the rum and lemon juice in a small bowl. Arrange half the apricots, cut side up, in a 1-quart baking dish. Top with half the brown sugar mixture, 2 tablespoons rum mixture and 1/4 cup reduced soaking liquid. Repeat layering with the remaining apricots, brown sugar mixture, rum mixture and reduced soaking liquid. Pour the butter evenly over the top. Bake at 350 for 1 hour. Serve warm.

Yield: 6 servings

Cranberry Pear Conserve

Peel of 1/3 orange
1 cup sugar
1 pound pears, peeled,
   quartered
2 tablespoons lemon juice

1/8 teaspoon ground cloves
3/4 teaspoon cinnamon
1/2 cup golden raisins
12 ounces cranberries

❧ Combine the orange peel and sugar in a blender container; process for 45 seconds or until the peel is finely chopped. Add the pears, lemon juice, cloves and cinnamon; process at medium speed until coarsely chopped, about 4 pulses. Add the raisins and cranberries; process at medium speed to combine, about 3 pulses. Pour into a large saucepan, scraping the sides of the container. Cook over low heat for 30 to 40 minutes or until thickened, stirring occasionally. Pour into a bowl and let cool slightly. Chill, covered, in the refrigerator for 1 to 10 days.

Yield: 6 servings

A Handful of Flavors

MAIN ENTREES

"I grew up in a family
of physicians. While
growing up, it was a
tremendous thing to see
the satisfaction they
achieved in doing all that
they could to help those
they treated. Therefore,
I strove to emulate."
—James L. Sweatt III, M.D.,
Thoracic Surgeon

Beef au Poivre

1 (4-pound) rib eye of beef
Olive oil
Salt to taste
Garlic powder to taste

¾ cup peppercorns, cracked,
   to taste
1 cup burgundy

Coat the rib eye with the olive oil, salt and garlic powder. Press in the pepper and place in a roasting pan. Roast at 350 degrees for 20 minutes per pound or until done, pouring the burgundy over the roast after 1 hour and basting frequently after that.

Yield: 8 servings

Gingered Beef

1 (3-pound) rib eye of beef
2 tablespoons soy sauce
Garlic powder to taste

¼ cup slivered gingerroot
1 cup sherry

Coat the rib eye with the soy sauce. Rub with the garlic powder and gingerroot. Roast at 350 degrees for 20 minutes per pound or until done, pouring the sherry over the roast after 1 hour and basting frequently after that. Slice and serve with pan juices.

Yield: 6 servings

Enjoy the moment.

Carol Bywaters

Marinated Flank Steak with Chipotle Glaze

3 tablespoons olive oil
3 tablespoons lime juice
1 teaspoon minced garlic
1 teaspoon ground cumin

1 pound flank steak
Salt and pepper to taste
Chipotle Glaze (below)

❧ Combine the olive oil, lime juice, garlic and cumin in a baking dish or self-sealing plastic bag. Add the flank steak; turn to coat both sides. Marinate, covered, for 1 to 24 hours in the refrigerator.

❧ Preheat the grill. Coat the grill rack with nonstick cooking spray; place on the grill. Place the steak on the grill rack. Grill over medium heat for 5 minutes per pound until done. Season with salt and pepper. Brush on the Chipotle Glaze. Let stand for 5 minutes before thinly slicing crosswise.

Yield: 2 servings

The glaze may be made

a day ahead and stored,

covered, in the refrigerator.

Chipotle Glaze

2 tablespoons honey
1 tablespoon Dijon mustard
1 tablespoon hoisin sauce
1 tablespoon lime juice

1 tablespoon minced chipotles
   in adobe sauce
1 teaspoon minced garlic

❧ Combine the honey, Dijon mustard, hoisin sauce, lime juice, chipotles and garlic in a small bowl; stir until well blended.

Chutney Marinade for Steak

⅓ cup soy sauce
⅓ cup vegetable oil
1 tablespoon minced onion
3 tablespoons red wine
    vinegar

2 tablespoons chopped
    chutney
2 cloves of garlic minced

❧ Combine the soy sauce, oil, onion, vinegar, chutney and garlic in a small bowl; stir until well blended. Use to marinate flank or other steaks for at least 4 hours.

Yield: About 1 cup

South African Zulu Bobotie

1 slice white bread
1 cup milk
1 pound ground beef
1 medium onion, finely
    chopped
½ cup raisins
½ cup blanched almonds
1 tablespoon apricot jam

1 tablespoon fruit chutney
2 tablespoons lemon juice
2 teaspoons curry powder
1 teaspoon turmeric
2 teaspoons salt
2 teaspoons butter
3 eggs
2 bay leaves

❧ Soak the bread in ½ cup milk in a small bowl. Squeeze out the milk. Mix the bread, ground beef, onion, raisins, almonds, apricot jam, chutney, lemon juice, curry powder, turmeric and salt in a large bowl.

❧ Melt the butter in a large skillet. Add the ground beef mixture. Cook until browned, stirring to crumble; drain. Spoon into a baking dish.

❧ Combine the eggs and remaining milk in a small bowl; beat until well blended. Pour over the ground beef mixture. Top with the bay leaves. Bake at 350 degrees for 50 minutes. Discard the bay leaves.

Yield: 8 servings

Famous Cincinnati Three-Way Chili

2 pounds lean ground beef
4 cups water
1 (15-ounce) can tomato
    sauce
3/4 teaspoon garlic powder
2 bay leaves
1/4 cup plus 2 tablespoons
    dried minced onions
1 teaspoon cinnamon
1 teaspoon Worcestershire
    sauce

1 1/2 teaspoons salt
1 1/2 teaspoons vinegar
3 teaspoons chili powder
1 1/2 teaspoons allspice
1 teaspoon crushed red
    pepper flakes
2 teaspoons ground cumin
1 pound spaghetti
Chopped onion
Shredded Cheddar cheese

Brown the ground beef in a large skillet or saucepan over medium heat until done, stirring to crumble; drain. Stir in the water, tomato sauce, garlic powder, bay leaves, minced onions, cinnamon, Worcestershire sauce, salt, vinegar, chili powder, allspice, red pepper flakes and cumin. Cook over low heat for 4 hours. Discard the bay leaves.

Fill a large pot with salted water, and bring to a boil over high heat. Add the spaghetti. Cook until al dente; drain. Serve topped with the ground beef mixture. Top with onion and Cheddar cheese.

Yield: 8 servings

As an ex-chemistry teacher I

love to be in the kitchen,

manipulating food.

Lynn Hamilton

Mexican Lasagna

1 pound ground beef
½ cup chopped green bell
   pepper
½ cup chopped onion
1 (8-ounce) can tomato sauce
1 (6-ounce) can tomato paste
1 (1½-ounce) envelope taco
   seasoning mix
1 teaspoon chili powder

¼ cup water
1 cup sour cream
2 eggs, beaten
1 teaspoon pepper
6 (8-inch) flour tortillas
¾ cup shredded Cheddar
   cheese
¾ cup shredded Monterey
   Jack cheese

❧ Preheat the oven to 350 degrees; grease a 9x13-inch baking dish. Cook the ground beef, bell pepper and onion in a large skillet over medium heat until the beef is browned, stirring to crumble the beef; drain.

❧ Combine the tomato sauce, tomato paste, taco seasoning, chili powder and water in a medium bowl, stirring to mix well. Pour into the beef mixture and stir to combine. Simmer for 10 minutes.

❧ Combine the sour cream, eggs and pepper in another bowl. Mix well. Layer the beef mixture and tortillas, ⅓ at a time, in the baking dish, starting and ending with the beef mixture. Top with the sour cream mixture, spreading it evenly. Sprinkle the Cheddar cheese and Monterey Jack cheese over the sour cream mixture. Bake, uncovered, for 30 minutes.

Yield: 8 servings

Bavarian Meat Loaf

1½ pounds lean ground beef
½ pound ground pork
1 onion, finely chopped
½ cup pumpernickel bread
    crumbs
½ cup crushed gingersnaps
2 eggs
3 tablespoons cider vinegar

1½ teaspoons prepared
    mustard
2 teaspoons salt
¼ cup packed brown sugar
3 tablespoons cider vinegar
3 tablespoons catsup
1 tablespoon prepared
    mustard

❧ Preheat the oven to 375 degrees. Combine the ground beef, pork, onion, pumpernickel bread, gingersnaps, eggs, cider vinegar, 1½ teaspoons prepared mustard and salt in a large bowl; mix well. Pack the mixture into a 5x9-inch loaf pan.

❧ Combine the brown sugar, cider vinegar, catsup and 1 tablespoon mustard in a small bowl; mix well. Spoon over the meat loaf. Bake for 1 hour. Transfer to a platter and serve.

Yield: 8 servings

"My father was a doctor and

it was all I ever knew."

Russell Martin, M.D.,

Internal Medicine

Terrific Taco Pie

1 pound lean ground beef
1/2 medium onion, chopped
1 (8-ounce) can tomato sauce
1 (1 1/2-ounce) envelope taco
    seasoning mix
1/3 cup chopped black olives
1 (8-count) can refrigerated
    crescent rolls

2 cups crushed corn chips
1 cup sour cream
1 cup shredded Cheddar
    cheese
Shredded lettuce
Sliced tomato
Sliced avocado
Picante sauce

❧ Preheat the oven to 375 degrees. Cook the ground beef and onion in a large skillet over medium heat until the beef is browned, stirring to crumble; drain. Stir in the tomato sauce, taco seasoning and olives.

❧ Separate the crescent dough and arrange in a 9-inch pie plate, pressing the rolls together to form a pie shell. Sprinkle 1 cup corn chips over the crust and spoon in the beef mixture, spreading it evenly. Spread the sour cream over the beef mixture. Top with the Cheddar cheese and remaining 1 cup corn chips.

❧ Bake for 20 to 25 minutes. Cut into wedges and serve with the lettuce, tomato, avocado and picante sauce.

Yield: 6 servings

Continental Beef Stew

6 slices bacon, cut into pieces
2 pounds round steak or stew meat, cut into 1½-inch cubes
1 cup water
1 cup dry red wine
1 beef bouillon cube
2 cloves of garlic, chopped
1 tablespoon dried minced onion
2 teaspoons salt
1 teaspoon dried thyme
1 teaspoon herbs de Provence

Peel of 1 orange, cut into strips
18 small white onions
1 pound mushrooms, sliced
2 tablespoons cornstarch
2 tablespoons cold water
1 (10-ounce) package frozen peas
1 (15-ounce) can pitted black olives, drained
1 (16-ounce) package potato gnocchi, cooked (optional)

❧ Crisp-fry the bacon in a large heavy saucepan over medium-high heat. Add the round steak; cook until browned. Stir in 1 cup water, red wine, bouillon cube, garlic, minced onion, salt, thyme, herbs de Provence and orange peel. Reduce the heat to low. Simmer, covered, for 1 hour or until the meat is tender.

❧ Cook the white onions in salted boiling water over high heat for 10 minutes. Stir in the mushrooms. Cook for 5 minutes; drain.

❧ Whisk the cornstarch and 2 tablespoons cold water in a small bowl or measuring cup until the cornstarch is dissolved. Pour into the beef mixture. Bring to a boil over medium-high heat, stirring constantly. Cook until thickened, stirring constantly. Stir in the onion mixture, the peas and the olives. Cook for 10 minutes or until the peas are tender. Stir in the gnocchi.

Yield: 8 servings

Saint Patrick's Day Corned Beef Casserole

¼ cup plus 1 tablespoon
   vegetable oil
2 cups chopped cooked potato
1 cup chopped green bell
   pepper
1 cup chopped onion
2 cloves of garlic, minced
2 cups chopped corned beef

½ teaspoon dry mustard
1/16 teaspoon salt
1/16 teaspoon pepper
1 cup sour cream
¾ cup shredded Cheddar
   cheese
⅓ cup soft bread crumbs
1 tablespoon vegetable oil

❧ Preheat the oven to 375 degrees. Warm the ¼ cup plus 1 tablespoon oil in a large skillet over medium-high heat. Add the potato, bell pepper, onion and garlic. Cook until lightly browned, stirring often. Remove from the heat, and stir in the corned beef, dry mustard, salt, pepper and sour cream. Pour into a baking dish.

❧ Combine the Cheddar cheese, bread crumbs and 1 tablespoon oil; stir to mix well. Sprinkle over the corned beef mixture. Bake for 30 minutes or until browned and bubbly.

Yield: 4 servings

A Thyme to Remember

When I got married, I couldn't cook a thing. Furthermore, my husband and I had grown up eating quite differently. I knew a southern kitchen with biscuits and cream gravy; he was from Pennsylvania. My first big attempt at dinner was a pot roast. My husband invited his senior resident to come over. My cooking was a complete failure!

Carol Stevenson

Herb Marinated Leg of Lamb

1 medium onion, chopped
1 large clove of garlic
1 cup dry red wine
1/4 cup olive oil
3 tablespoons prepared
  mustard
3/4 teaspoon dried thyme
1/8 teaspoon pepper

2 teaspoons salt
1/2 teaspoon dried rosemary
8 pounds leg of lamb
1 bunch watercress, chopped
3 tablespoons flour
1/2 teaspoon rosemary
1/4 teaspoon salt

❧ Combine the onion, garlic, red wine, olive oil, prepared mustard, 3/4 teaspoon thyme, pepper and 2 teaspoons salt in a small bowl. Place the lamb in a large bowl and pour the marinade over the lamb, turning to coat. Marinate, covered, in the refrigerator for at least 12 hours, turning occasionally.

❧ Roast at 325 degrees for 25 minutes per pound or until done, covering with the watercress during the last 15 minutes of cooking. Remove to a platter and cover with foil to keep warm. Skim fat from the pan juices. Add the flour, 1/2 teaspoon rosemary and 1/4 teaspoon salt; whisk until smooth. Slice the lamb. Serve topped with the rosemary gravy.

Yield: 20 servings

Pork Chops with Peanut Sauce

1 tablespoon peanut oil
2 cloves of garlic, minced
2 teaspoons minced
    gingerroot
1 (14½-ounce) can reduced-
    salt chicken broth
½ cup peanut butter
1 tablespoon lime juice
½ teaspoon ground coriander
½ teaspoon ground cumin

Crushed red pepper flakes to
    taste
6 (4-ounce) center-cut loin
    pork chops
Salt and freshly ground black
    pepper to taste
Chopped cilantro or green
    onions
Lime wedges (optional)

❧ Preheat the broiler or fire up the grill. Warm the peanut oil in a small saucepan over medium heat; add the garlic and gingerroot. Cook for 30 seconds, stirring. Pour in the chicken broth. Bring to a boil over high heat. Cook until reduced to about 1 cup. Reduce the heat.

❧ Stir in the peanut butter, lime juice, coriander and cumin. Season with the pepper flakes. Simmer for 2 minutes or until thick and smooth, stirring often.

❧ Brush the pork chops lightly with peanut oil. Broil or grill until done, brushing several times with the peanut butter sauce. Season with salt and black pepper. Serve with the peanut butter sauce. Garnish with the cilantro and serve with lime wedges.

Yield: 6 servings

Never cook anything

that takes longer to fix

than it does to eat.

Barbara Munford

Thai Nipa Peanut Dressing

1 (13½-ounce) can coconut
   milk
½ cup chunky peanut butter
1 teaspoon paprika
1 cup milk

¼ cup sugar
¼ cup white wine vinegar
½ cup water
½ cup chopped dry-roasted
   peanuts

✺ Mix the coconut milk, peanut butter, paprika, milk, sugar, white wine vinegar and water in a small saucepan. Cook over low heat for 5 to 8 minutes or until the peanut butter melts and the mixture is creamy, stirring constantly. Remove from the heat and cool to room temperature. Stir in the peanuts.

Yield: 30 servings

The Quintessential Pork Loaf

½ cup applesauce
8 ounces honey nut cream
   cheese
1 cup muesli cereal
1 small onion, chopped
2 eggs, beaten
½ cup half-and-half
1 teaspoon seasoned salt
2 teaspoons minced garlic
2 teaspoons dried thyme

2 teaspoons dried rosemary
½ teaspoon dried oregano
½ teaspoon white pepper
½ teaspoon black pepper
1 teaspoon ground cumin
1 teaspoon nutmeg
1 teaspoon coriander
½ cup golden raisins
½ cup finely chopped pecans
2 pounds ground pork

✺ Preheat the oven to 350 degrees. Combine the applesauce, cream cheese, muesli cereal, onion, eggs and half-and-half in a medium bowl; stir until well blended. Mix the seasoned salt, garlic, thyme, rosemary, oregano, white pepper, black pepper, cumin, nutmeg, coriander, raisins and pecans in a large bowl. Stir in the cream cheese mixture.

✺ Add the pork; mix until well combined. Shape into a loaf and place in a 5x9-inch loaf pan. Bake for 1½ hours.

Yield: 12 servings

Pork Piccata

1/2 cup flour
1/2 teaspoon salt
1/4 teaspoon pepper
2 (12-ounce) pork tenderloins
3 tablespoons olive oil
16 ounces fettuccini
1/2 cup Chablis or other dry
    white wine

1/2 cup lemon juice
3 tablespoons butter or
    margarine
1/4 cup chopped fresh parsley
1 1/2 tablespoons capers
Lemon slices
Fresh parsley sprigs

❧ Mix the flour, salt and pepper in a small bowl. Cut each tenderloin into six 2-inch medallions, and place, cut side down, between 2 sheets of plastic wrap. Flatten to 1/4 inch, using a meat mallet or rolling pin. Coat with the flour mixture.

❧ Heat olive oil in a large skillet over medium heat; add the pork. Cook for 2 minutes on each side or until lightly browned and cooked through. Remove to a platter and keep warm. Fill a large pot with salted water, and bring to a boil over high heat. Add the fettucini. Cook until al dente; drain.

❧ Pour the wine and lemon juice into the skillet, stir to combine. Cook until the mixture is reduced to 1/2 cup, deglazing the pan and stirring occasionally. Stir in the butter, 1/4 cup parsley and the capers. Cook until the mixture is hot and the butter has melted, stirring to blend. Serve the pork over the fettucini. Drizzle the wine-caper sauce over each serving and garnish with the lemon slices and parsley sprigs.

Yield: 8 servings

Everyone who can

read can cook.

Pam Edmunds

Baked Country Pork Ribs

20 pork ribs
1 (15-ounce) bottle catsup
½ cup light corn syrup
¼ cup red wine vinegar
2 tablespoons liquid smoke
1 tablespoon Worcestershire
 sauce

2 tablespoons steak sauce
1 teaspoon salt
2 teaspoons pepper
1/16 teaspoon Tabasco sauce
1 tablespoon dry mustard
2 teaspoons garlic powder

❧ Place the ribs in a large roasting pan. Mix the catsup, corn syrup, red wine vinegar, liquid smoke, Worcestershire sauce, steak sauce, salt, pepper, Tabasco sauce, dry mustard and garlic powder. Pour over the ribs. Bake, covered, at 400 degrees until tender. Uncover. Bake until browned.

Yield: 12 servings

Our guests from all

over the world have been

served *Daddy's Best Texas*

Pork Ribs, and they are

never disappointed.

Daddy's Best Texas Pork Ribs

18 pork ribs, fat trimmed
Garlic powder to taste
Seasoned salt to taste

Pepper to taste
1½ cups honey
½ cup soy sauce

❧ Season both sides of the ribs with the garlic powder, seasoned salt and pepper. Fill the charcoal pan of an upright smoker with charcoal briquettes. Soak 4 or 5 chunks of hickory in water for a few minutes and place around the edge of the charcoal pan. Pour odorless starter fluid on the top of 4 or 5 briquettes. Light. Immediately place a pan of water in its position above the charcoal. Arrange the ribs in the rib racks. Cover with dome lid. Cook for 4 to 5 hours.

❧ Mix honey and soy sauce in a bowl until smooth. Apply the honey sauce to both sides of the ribs with a basting brush. Cook for 20 minutes longer. Do not cook longer than 30 minutes after applying the sauce or the ribs may taste bitter.

Yield: 6 servings

Chinese Risotto with Shiitake Mushrooms

1 tablespoon Oriental
    sesame oil
2 teaspoons minced serrano
2 teaspoons minced garlic
4 teaspoons soy sauce
1 tablespoon rice wine vinegar
1/16 teaspoon sugar
3 tablespoons vegetable oil
1/2 cup chopped shallots

5 ounces shiitake mushrooms
1 cup chopped smoked pork
    or chicken
1 cup arborio rice
3 cups chicken stock
1 cup chopped fresh mustard
    greens
1 cup chopped cilantro

❧ Heat the sesame oil in a large skillet over medium heat; add the serrano. Sauté for 1 minute. Stir in the garlic. Sauté for 1 minute. Remove from the heat. Stir in the soy sauce, rice wine vinegar and sugar. Remove to a bowl.

❧ Heat the 3 tablespoons oil in the same skillet; add the shallots. Sauté for 2 minutes. Add the mushrooms and pork. Sauté for 1 minute. Stir in the rice and 1 cup stock. Cook until the liquid is absorbed, stirring constantly. Stir in additional stock, 1/2 cup at a time, as the liquid is absorbed. Cook until all the stock is absorbed and the rice is tender and creamy, adding additional stock if necessary.

❧ Stir in the mustard greens and cilantro. Cook for 1 minute, stirring constantly. Stir in the soy sauce mixture.

Yield: 4 servings

Pork Roast with Apples and Bourbon

2 tablespoons vegetable oil	1/2 cup bourbon
3 1/2 pounds pork loin roast	1/4 teaspoon salt
2/3 cup Dijon mustard	1/2 teaspoon dried thyme
1/3 cup packed brown sugar	1/4 teaspoon dried sage
2 cups beef broth	3 apples, peeled, sliced

❧ Preheat the oven to 375 degrees. Heat the oil in a skillet over medium-high heat; add the roast. Brown, turning to cook all sides. Spread the mustard over the roast and sprinkle with brown sugar. Brown slowly so the brown sugar does not burn. Remove the pork to a baking dish.

❧ Pour the beef broth, bourbon, salt, thyme and sage into the skillet. Deglaze over medium heat, scraping the pan to loosen browned bits. Simmer for 20 minutes and pour into the baking dish. Bake, covered, for 20 minutes. Arrange the apple slices in the dish around the pork. Bake, covered, for 20 minutes more or until a meat thermometer registers 170 degrees. Serve with noodles.

Yield: 12 servings

For a thick, rich sauce, mix 1/2 cup half-and-half and 1 tablespoon cornstarch in a small bowl; pour into the pan juices. Cook until thickened, stirring constantly.

Marinated Pork Tenderloin Sandwiches

1/2 cup soy sauce
1/2 cup bourbon
1/4 cup packed brown sugar

3 (12-ounce) pork tenderloins
Mustard Sauce (below)
6 biscuits

❧ Mix the soy sauce, bourbon and brown sugar in a small bowl. Place the pork in a shallow baking dish. Pour the soy sauce mixture over the pork, turning the pork to coat. Marinate, covered, in the refrigerator for several hours.

❧ Preheat the oven to 325 degrees. Bake for 45 minutes, basting frequently with the soy sauce mixture. Serve the pork and Mustard Sauce on the biscuits.

Yield: 6 servings

Mustard Sauce

1/2 cup sour cream
1/2 cup mayonnaise
1 tablespoon dry mustard

1 tablespoon chopped onion
1 1/2 tablespoons white wine
   vinegar

❧ Combine the sour cream, mayonnaise, dry mustard, onion and white wine vinegar in a small bowl; stir to mix well. Let stand in the refrigerator for 4 hours before serving.

Sausage Spaghetti Pie

6 ounces spaghetti
2 eggs, beaten
1/4 cup grated Parmesan
cheese
2 tablespoons butter
1/3 cup chopped onion
1 cup sour cream

1 pound Italian sausage,
casing removed, crumbled
1 (6-ounce) can tomato paste
1 cup water
4 ounces mozzarella cheese,
sliced

❧ Preheat the oven to 350 degrees; grease a pie plate. Fill a large pot with salted water, and bring to a boil over high heat. Break the spaghetti strands in half and add to the water. Cook until al dente; drain. Place in a large bowl and add the eggs and Parmesan cheese; toss to coat. Spoon into the pie plate and pat into the bottom and up the side.

❧ Melt the butter in a skillet; add the onions. Sauté until tender but not brown. Stir in the sour cream and spoon over the spaghetti.

❧ Cook the sausage in the skillet over medium-high heat until cooked through, stirring to crumble; drain. Stir in the tomato paste and water. Simmer for 10 minutes. Spread over the sour cream. Bake for 25 minutes. Top with the mozzarella. Bake for 5 minutes or until the cheese melts.

Yield: 6 servings

This recipe may be

doubled to make two

pies. Freeze the extra pie

for another time.

Chicken Niçoise with Latticed Potatoes

4 tablespoons olive oil
8 chicken pieces or 8 boneless
    chicken breasts
2 large onions, thinly sliced
1 cup grape juice
4 medium tomatoes, coarsely
    chopped

12 pitted black olives
3 cloves of garlic, minced
3 tablespoons chopped
    fresh dill
Salt and pepper to taste
3 cups mashed potatoes

☙ Heat the olive oil in a heavy skillet over medium heat; add the chicken. Cook the chicken until browned, turning each piece to brown both sides. Remove from the skillet. Place the onions in the skillet. Cook, covered, until browned, stirring occasionally.

☙ Stir in the grape juice. Cook over medium heat until the liquid is reduced to 1/2 cup. Stir in the tomatoes, olives, garlic and dill. Simmer for 10 minutes. Season with salt and pepper.

☙ Return the chicken to the skillet. Cook, covered, for 40 minutes or until the chicken is cooked through. Turn into a broiler-safe baking dish; top with the mashed potatoes. Broil for 3 minutes or until golden brown.

Yield: 8 servings

I have heard this statement

forever—"Treat your

family like company; your

company like family."

Rosemary Goodman

Cusseta Barbecue Sauce for Chicken

1 cup vegetable oil
2 cups vinegar
1 tablespoon salt

1 tablespoon pepper
2 tablespoons poultry
    seasoning

☙ Whisk the oil, vinegar, salt, pepper and poultry seasoning in a saucepan. Bring to a boil. Simmer for 5 minutes.

Yield: 14 servings

Three of my cousins

were in the Vietnam War.

One time they all came to

our house for dinner. My

mother borrowed all the

platters she could find. They

became the dinner plates for

these hungry soldiers.

Mary Ann Blome

Cherry Chicken

8 chicken breast halves
1/2 cup packed brown sugar
1 (12-ounce) bottle chili sauce
1 (16-ounce) can pitted dark
    cherries, drained
1/2 cup cream sherry

❧ Preheat the oven to 400 degrees. Place the chicken in a deep baking dish. Bake until browned. Mix the brown sugar, chili sauce, dark cherries and sherry in a saucepan. Bring to a boil, stirring constantly; pour evenly over the chicken. Reduce the oven temperature to 350 degrees. Bake for 1 hour.

Yield: 8 servings

Chutney Barbecued Chicken

4 (4-ounce) chicken thighs
4 (4-ounce) chicken breasts
4 (4-ounce) chicken
    drumsticks
2 envelopes onion soup mix
2 large cloves of garlic,
    crushed
1 teaspoon curry powder
1 teaspoon coriander
2 (10-ounce) jars chutney
1 (8-ounce) bottle Russian
    salad dressing

❧ Preheat the oven to 300 degrees. Arrange the chicken in a large baking dish or pan. Combine the soup mix, garlic, curry powder, coriander, chutney and Russian salad dressing in a bowl; mix well. Pour evenly over the chicken. Bake, uncovered, for 2 hours.

Yield: 6 servings

Apricot Chutney Chicken

5 (1-pound) whole chicken
  breasts, halved, boned,
  skinned
3 tablespoons flour
2 tablespoons vegetable oil
2 cups Apricot Chutney
  (below)
½ teaspoon cayenne

2 cloves of garlic, crushed
½ teaspoon salt
½ teaspoon pepper
½ cup dry white wine
½ cup chicken broth
1 teaspoon curry powder
1 teaspoon ground ginger

❧ Preheat the oven to 325 degrees. Coat the chicken lightly with the flour. Heat the oil in a large skillet over medium-high heat; add the chicken. Brown on both sides; drain. Place in a 9x13-inch baking dish. Combine the Apricot Chutney, cayenne, garlic, salt, pepper, white wine, chicken broth, curry powder and ginger in a bowl; mix well. Pour over the chicken. Bake for 30 minutes or until done.

Yield: 8 servings

Apricot Chutney

1 pound dried apricots,
  quartered
8 cloves of garlic
1 (2-inch piece) gingerroot,
  coarsely chopped

1¼ cups red wine vinegar
2 cups sugar
¼ teaspoon salt
½ teaspoon cayenne
¾ cup golden raisins

❧ Soak the apricots in 4 cups boiling water in a large bowl for 2 hours; drain. Combine the garlic, gingerroot, and ¼ cup vinegar in a food processor container; process at medium speed until smooth. Combine apricots and garlic mixture in a heavy enamel or stainless steel saucepan; mix well. Stir in the remaining vinegar, sugar, salt and cayenne. Bring to a boil over medium heat, stirring frequently. Simmer for 45 minutes, stirring frequently. Do not let the mixture stick to the bottom of the pan; lower the heat if necessary. Stir in the raisins. Cook for 30 minutes or until the mixture is thickened and has a shiny appearance.

The *Apricot Chutney* recipe makes a lot— 4 cups. Refrigerate the unused portion to use the next time you make *Apricot Chutney Chicken* or to serve with pork or turkey as an accompaniment.

Shortcut Thai Peanut Chicken

2 tablespoons honey
2 tablespoons soy sauce
1 teaspoon grated gingerroot
1/4 cup orange juice

1/2 cup peanut butter
2 cups picante sauce
1 pound chicken tenders
1 pound pasta (any style)

❧ Mix the honey, soy sauce, gingerroot, orange juice, peanut butter and picante sauce in a saucepan over medium heat. Cook until hot, stirring to blend the peanut butter. Add the chicken; toss to coat.

❧ Fill a large pot with salted water, and bring to a boil over high heat. Add the pasta. Cook until al dente; drain. Top with the chicken and sauce.

Yield: 4 servings

My mother helped me tremendously. My husband proposed after eating a dinner that he thought was my cooking when it was mainly my mother's.

Judy Skinner

Big-D Chicken

3 ounces cream cheese, softened
1/2 cup sliced green onions
1 cup picante sauce
1 teaspoon ground cumin

6 (4-ounce) skinless, boneless chicken breasts
1/3 cup (or more) crushed tortilla chips

❧ Preheat the oven to 350 degrees. Combine the cream cheese, green onions, 1/2 cup picante sauce and cumin in a small bowl; mix until well blended. Spoon the remaining picante sauce into the bottom of a baking dish; spread evenly. Arrange the chicken breasts in the dish, and spread the cheese mixture over the chicken. Sprinkle the tortilla chips over the cheese mixture. Bake for 30 minutes or until the chicken is cooked through.

Yield: 6 servings

Duck Gumbo

3 to 4 ducks, quartered
Salt and pepper to taste
1/2 cup vegetable oil
1/2 cup flour
3 onions, chopped
2 green bell peppers, chopped

2 ribs celery, chopped
Fresh parsley, chopped
3 cloves of garlic, chopped
4 cups water
Tabasco sauce to taste
36 oysters

❧ Season the ducks with the salt and pepper. Warm the oil in a large heavy saucepan over medium-high heat; add the ducks. Brown on both sides. Remove to a platter. Add the flour to the oil. Cook to make a dark roux, stirring constantly. Stir in the onions, bell peppers, celery, parsley and garlic. Add the duck and water. Season with the salt, pepper and Tabasco sauce. Simmer, covered, for 2 hours. Serve over hot rice and topped with oysters.

Yield: 6 servings

New Year's Casserole

4 cups chopped smoked turkey
2 (10-ounce) packages frozen
    chopped spinach, thawed,
    drained
2 (12-ounce) jars marinated
    artichokes
1 cup sour cream
1 (5-ounce) can sliced water
    chestnuts, drained

1 cup mayonnaise
1 (16-ounce) can black-eyed
    peas, drained
1 envelope vegetable soup mix
1 cup Parmesan cheese
2 teaspoons garlic powder
1 teaspoon dried oregano
1/2 cup soft bread crumbs
Paprika

❧ Preheat the oven to 350 degrees. Combine the turkey, spinach, artichokes, sour cream, water chestnuts, mayonnaise, black-eyed peas, vegetable soup mix, Parmesan cheese, garlic powder and oregano in a large bowl; mix well. Spoon into a baking dish. Top with the bread crumbs and paprika. Bake for 30 minutes.

Yield: 12 servings

Indonesian Grilled Turkey

1/3 cup chunky peanut butter
1/4 cup lemon juice
2 teaspoons ground ginger
2 teaspoons onion powder
1/4 to 1/2 teaspoon crushed red
    pepper flakes
1/3 cup teriyaki sauce

1/4 cup vegetable oil
2 teaspoons dried basil
2 teaspoons garlic powder
2 1/2 to 3 pounds boneless
    turkey breast half or
    turkey breast tenders

❧ Combine the peanut butter, lemon juice, ginger, onion powder, red pepper flakes, teriyaki sauce, oil, basil and garlic powder in a food processor or blender container; process at high speed until smooth. Reserve 1/2 cup. Place the turkey and remaining peanut butter mixture in a shallow baking dish, turning the turkey to coat well. Marinate, covered, in the refrigerator for at least 30 minutes.

❧ Preheat the grill. Coat the grill rack with nonstick cooking spray; place on the grill. Arrange the turkey on the rack. Grill, covered, over medium heat for 20 minutes or until a meat thermometer registers 170 degrees, basting occasionally with the peanut butter sauce. To cook the turkey in the oven, preheat to 400 degrees; bake uncovered.

Yield: 8 servings

We would have special

dinners at our house.

Prepared in secret, the meal

and table decorations would

announce to our daughters

where our family vacation

would be spent.

Rosemary Goodman

Sesame Crusted Salmon with Ginger Vinaigrette

1 large cucumber, peeled,
   coarsely chopped
1/2 cup rice wine vinegar
1/8 teaspoon salt
2 tablespoons sugar
1/4 cup water
1/4 cup soy sauce
1 tablespoon honey
1 teaspoon hot sauce

2 tablespoons rice wine
   vinegar
1/2 teaspoon coriander
1/2 teaspoon dark sesame oil
4 (4-ounce) salmon fillets
1 tablespoon toasted sesame
   seeds
1 large cucumber, thinly sliced
Ginger Vinaigrette (at right)

❧ Preheat the oven to 450 degrees; grease a 9x13-inch baking dish. Place the coarsely chopped cucumber in a food processor container; process at medium speed until smooth. Line a strainer with cheesecloth or a coffee filter; strain the cucumber into a bowl. Discard the pulp. Stir in the 1/2 cup rice wine vinegar and the salt.

❧ Combine the sugar and water in a small saucepan over medium-high heat. Bring to a boil, stirring occasionally. Remove from heat. Stir in cucumber mixture; set aside.

❧ Combine soy sauce, honey, hot sauce, 2 tablespoons rice wine vinegar, coriander and sesame oil in a bowl; mix well.

❧ Arrange the salmon in the baking dish. Brush the soy sauce mixture over the salmon. Sprinkle with the sesame seeds. Bake for 10 to 12 minutes.

❧ Remove to individual bowls and arrange the cucumber slices around the salmon. Spoon the cucumber juice mixture over the top; drizzle with the Ginger Vinaigrette.

Yield: 4 servings

A Thyme to Remember

❧ ❧ ❧

For Ginger Vinaigrette, combine one 1/2-inch slice gingerroot and 1 clove of garlic in a food processor or blender container; process at high speed until blended. Add 2 tablespoons rice wine vinegar, 1 tablespoon soy sauce and 1 tablespoon honey; process at high speed until blended. Add 1/4 cup peanut oil and 1/2 teaspoon dark sesame oil in a steady stream, processing constantly at high speed until smooth.

❧ ❧ ❧

Salmon Soy Steak

3/4 cup soy sauce
2 teaspoons garlic powder
2 (8-ounce) salmon fillets,
    about 3/4 inch thick

Garlic pepper to taste
1/2 cup olive oil
Juice of 1 1/2 lemons

❧ Combine the soy sauce and garlic powder in a self-sealing bag; mix well. Add the salmon, turning the bag to coat well. Marinate in the refrigerator for 3 to 12 hours.

❧ Preheat the oven to 475 degrees. Remove the salmon from the soy sauce mixture; discard the mixture. Season with the garlic pepper.

❧ Mix the olive oil and lemon juice. Place the salmon on a broiler pan; brush with the lemon mixture. Broil for 5 minutes. Lower the oven temperature to 425 degrees. Bake, covered, for 25 minutes or until the salmon is done.

Yield: 4 servings

Seafood Mosaic Ballotine

1 teaspoon butter
2 tablespoons minced shallots
8 ounces spinach, chopped
8 ounces fillet of sole
1 egg white
2 tablespoons milk
10 ounces assorted firm fish
   such salmon, shrimp,
   scallops

½ teaspoon dried tarragon
½ teaspoon dried dillweed
1 teaspoon minced chives
⅛ teaspoon pepper
⅛ teaspoon nutmeg
Herbed Butter (at right)

❧ Cut four 6x10-inch rectangles of foil; grease. Melt the butter in a large skillet over medium-high heat; add the shallots. Sauté just until done. Add the spinach; stir. Cook just until wilted. Chill, covered, in the refrigerator.

❧ Place the sole in a food processor or blender container; process until puréed. Blend in the egg white and milk. Pour purée into a large bowl. Cut assorted firm fish into bite-size pieces; stir into purée. Chill, covered, in the refrigerator. Stir the spinach mixture into the seafood mixture. Season with the tarragon, dillweed, chives, pepper and nutmeg.

❧ Fill a large saucepan with 2 to 3 inches of water. Bring to a simmer. Shape seafood-spinach mixture to four 6-inch logs; place each log on the long side of the foil rectangle. Roll up and twist the ends like candy wrappers, sealing tightly. Place the foil logs in the simmering water. Cook for 8 minutes. Remove from saucepan; unwrap and slice. Serve with Herbed Butter.

Yield: 6 servings.

For *Herbed Butter*, combine

1 tablespoon minced shallots,

1½ tablespoons vermouth

and 2½ teaspoons white wine

in a small saucepan. Cook

over medium heat until

reduced to 1 tablespoon,

stirring constantly. Remove

from heat; whisk in ¼ cup

butter. Stir in ½ tablespoon

parsley. Serve warm.

❧ ❧ ❧

My mother worked as a governess in a wealthy section of Pittsburgh. She remembers that food was not freely given there. They really didn't share their bounty. She never ate at that home, preferring to celebrate dining in her more meager quarters.

Mary Ann Blome

❧ ❧ ❧

Parmesan Sauce for Fish

1/4 cup butter
3 tablespoons chopped green
  onions
3 tablespoons mayonnaise
2 tablespoons lemon juice

1/2 cup Parmesan cheese
1/4 teaspoon salt
Freshly ground pepper to
  taste
Tabasco sauce to taste

❧ Melt the butter in a small skillet; add the green onions. Cook just until the onions begin to become translucent.

❧ Combine the mayonnaise, lemon juice, Parmesan cheese, salt, pepper, Tabasco sauce and green onions in a small bowl; mix until well blended. Serve over trout or other fish. Store extras, covered, in the refrigerator. Warm in the microwave before using.

Yield: 8 servings

Grilled Tuna with Oriental Marinade

1/4 cup soy sauce
3 tablespoons rice wine
  vinegar
2 tablespoons sesame oil
3 tablespoons orange juice

1 tablespoon grated orange
  peel
1/3 cup grated gingerroot
1/2 pound tuna or swordfish
  steaks

❧ Combine the soy sauce, rice wine vinegar, sesame oil, orange juice, orange peel and gingerroot in a small bowl; mix until well blended. Place the tuna in a self-sealing plastic bag; add the soy sauce mixture, turning to coat well. Marinate for 30 to 60 minutes in the refrigerator.

❧ Preheat the grill. Coat the grill rack with nonstick cooking spray; place on the grill. Arrange the tuna on the rack. Grill for 4 minutes on each side or until done. The tuna may be sautéed instead of grilled. This recipe may be doubled.

Yield: 2 servings

New Orleans Stuffed Eggplant

1 large eggplant
1 cup water
1/8 teaspoon red wine vinegar
1/2 cup clarified butter
4 tablespoons chopped green
    onions
1 cup chopped cooked shrimp
1 cup jumbo lump crab meat
1 cup Béchamel Sauce
    (at right)

Salt to taste
1/8 teaspoon white pepper
1/16 teaspoon cayenne
3 tablespoons finely chopped
    fresh parsley
2 tablespoons fine bread
    crumbs
1 tablespoon grated Parmesan
    cheese
4 lemon wedges

❧ Preheat the oven to 350 degrees. Cut the stem from the eggplant; cut lengthwise into 4 sections. Place in an 7x11-inch baking dish. Add the water and red wine vinegar. Bake, covered, for 25 minutes or until tender. Remove from the oven and let cool. Scoop out the pulp, keeping the skin intact for stuffing. Chop the pulp.

❧ Place 1/4 cup clarified butter in a saucepan over low heat. Sauté the green onions until tender. Stir in the eggplant pulp, shrimp and crab meat. Simmer, stirring often. Fold in the Béchamel Sauce. Season with the salt, white pepper, cayenne and 2 tablespoons of the parsley. Let cool completely.

❧ Spoon the shrimp mixture into the eggplant shells. Mix the bread crumbs and Parmesan cheese in a small bowl. Sprinkle over the shrimp mixture. Drizzle the remaining clarified butter over the crumbs. Bake for 20 minutes or until golden brown. Garnish with the remaining parsley and lemon wedges.

Yield: 4 servings

A Thyme to Remember

For *Béchamel Sauce*, melt 3 tablespoons butter in a saucepan over low heat; whisk 1/4 cup flour in briskly to prevent lumping. Whisk one 10 1/2-ounce can consommé and 3/4 cup milk in gradually to prevent lumping. Cook over low heat until thickened and smooth, sitrring constantly. Add salt, pepper and paprika to taste.

Pasta Primavera with Scallops

1 large clove of garlic, minced
2 tablespoons olive oil
¼ teaspoon crushed red
    pepper flakes
¼ teaspoon salt
10 large basil leaves, minced
1 large red onion, cut into
    ¼-inch dice

4 ounces fettuccini
2 large carrots, cut into
    ¼-inch slices
15 asparagus spears, cut
    into 1¼-inch slices
6 ounces sea scallops
⅓ cup minced asiago cheese

❧ Mix the first 5 ingredients in a large serving dish. Fill a large pot with salted water. Bring to a boil over high heat; add the onion, fettuccini, carrots and asparagus. Return to a boil. Cook for 5 minutes or until the vegetables are almost tender. Add the scallops. Cook for 1 minute or until they are opaque. Drain, reserving ½ cup cooking liquid. Remove to the serving dish; add the olive oil mixture and toss to coat, adding some of the reserved cooking liquid if necessary. Add the asiago cheese; toss until well combined.

Yield: 2 servings

Greek Pasta with Shrimp

4 teaspoons minced garlic
¼ cup olive oil
1 pound cooked, peeled,
    deveined medium shrimp
1½ cups chopped drained
    artichoke hearts
1½ cups crumbled feta cheese
½ cup chopped tomatoes

¼ cup plus 1 tablespoon
    lemon juice
3 tablespoons chopped fresh
    parsley
1½ teaspoons dried oregano
12 ounces angel hair pasta or
    linguini, cooked

❧ Sauté garlic in olive oil in a large heavy skillet over medium-high heat for 30 seconds. Add the shrimp. Sauté for 1 to 1½ minutes. Add the next 6 ingredients; toss to combine. Sauté for 2 minutes or until the shrimp is hot. Combine hot pasta and shrimp mixture in serving bowl; toss to mix.

Yield: 6 servings

Fettuccini and Spicy Shrimp

6 ounces green fettuccini
1 tablespoon plus 1 teaspoon
  margarine
2 cups sliced mushrooms
2 tablespoons sliced green
  onions
1/2 cup bottled clam juice

1 pound peeled, deveined
  medium shrimp
1/2 cup plain low-fat yogurt
1/4 cup sour cream
Pepper Seasoning Mix (at right)
Grated Parmesan cheese
Sliced green onions

🌿 Fill a large pot with salted water, and bring to a boil over high heat. Add the fettuccini. Cook until al dente; drain. Keep warm in a covered pot. Melt the margarine in a large nonstick skillet over medium-high heat; add the mushrooms and green onions. Cook for 4 to 5 minutes or until tender. Add clam juice and bring to a boil. Add the shrimp. Cook for 3 to 4 minutes or just until pink and cooked through, tossing frequently. Remove from the heat. Stir in the yogurt, sour cream and Pepper Seasoning Mix. Serve over the fettucini. Garnish with Parmesan cheese and remaining green onions.

Yield: 4 servings

Barbecued Shrimp

1 cup butter
1 cup vegetable oil
2 teaspoons minced garlic
4 bay leaves
2 teaspoons dried rosemary
1/2 teaspoon dried basil
1/2 teaspoon oregano

1/2 teaspoon salt
1/2 teaspoon cayenne
1 tablespoon paprika
1/4 teaspoon black pepper
1 teaspoon lemon juice
2 pounds shrimp in shell

🌿 Preheat the oven to 450 degrees. Melt the butter in a heavy skillet over medium-high heat. Stir in the oil, garlic, seasonings and lemon juice. Bring to a boil. Simmer for 8 minutes; let cool for 30 minutes. Discard the bay leaves. Stir the shrimp into the butter-herb mixture. Cook on medium heat for 6 minutes. Pour into a baking dish. Bake for 10 minutes.

Yield: 4 servings

A Thyme to Remember

For *Pepper Seasoning Mix,*

combine 1/4 teaspoon salt,

1/4 teaspoon paprika,

1/8 teaspoon cayenne,

1/8 teaspoon black pepper,

1/8 teaspoon white pepper,

1/8 teaspoon dried thyme,

1/8 teaspoon dried oregano and

1/8 teaspoon onion powder in

a small bowl; mix well.

❧❧❧

Originating in the state of

Kerala, on the southwest

coast of India, this curry has

become popular all over the

country due to its mild and

delicate flavor. Fish fillets

such as catfish or snapper can

be substituted for the shrimp

with equally good results.

Authentic Shrimp Curry

¼ cup vegetable oil
2 medium onions, sliced
3 green chiles, seeded, halved
6 cloves of garlic, finely
   chopped
1 tablespoon finely chopped
   gingerroot
2 medium tomatoes, diced
½ teaspoon cracked pepper
½ teaspoon ground cloves

½ teaspoon ground
   cardamom
1 (14-ounce) can coconut milk
½ teaspoon turmeric powder
Salt to taste
1½ pounds shrimp, peeled,
   deveined
Juice of ½ lime
2 tablespoons chopped fresh
   cilantro

❧ Heat the oil in a large skillet over medium heat; add the onions. Sauté for 1 minute. Stir in the chiles, garlic and gingerroot. Sauté for 10 minutes or until the onions turn light golden. Stir in the tomatoes, pepper, cloves and cardamom. Cook for 2 minutes, stirring constantly. Stir in the coconut milk, turmeric and salt. Simmer over low heat for 10 to 15 minutes or until the mixture is creamy. Stir in the shrimp. Simmer for 2 minutes or until the shrimp turn pink and are cooked through. Top each serving with lime juice and cilantro. Serve with steamed basmati rice.

Yield: 6 servings

❧❧❧

Green Peppercorn Sauce

3 tablespoons butter
3 tablespoons minced shallots
3 tablespoons brandy
1 tablespoon chopped green
   peppercorns

2 teaspoons Dijon mustard
1 bouillon cube, crushed
1 cup whipping cream
1 tablespoon butter, softened

❧ Melt the 3 tablespoons butter in a small saucepan; add the shallots. Sauté until golden. Stir in the brandy. Cook over high heat until the brandy is reduced to about 1½ tablespoons. Stir in the next 4 ingredients. Cook until thickened, stirring constantly. Swirl in the remaining 1 tablespoon butter. Serve over fish or meat.

Yield: 8 servings

A Handful of Seasonings

VEGETABLES

"The field of medicine
provided a wonderful
opportunity to combine my
two favorite interests,
science and people, into a
rewarding career."
—Jennifer Crofford Freeman, M.D.,
Obstetrician/Gynecologist

Cabbage and Sweet Pepper Medley

6 tablespoons white vinegar
2 tablespoons vegetable oil
2 tablespoons water
1 tablespoon brown sugar
1 tablespoon Dijon mustard
1 teaspoon salt
1 teaspoon pepper
4 slices bacon, cut into
    1-inch pieces

1 small red bell pepper, cut
    into thin 2-inch strips
1 small yellow bell pepper, cut
    into thin 2-inch strips
1 small green bell pepper, cut
    into thin 2-inch strips
2 onions, chopped
4 cups shredded cabbage

❧ Combine the white vinegar, oil, water, brown sugar, Dijon mustard, salt and pepper in a jar with a tightfitting lid; shake the jar vigorously to blend well.

❧ Cook the bacon in a large skillet over medium-high heat until almost done, stirring often. Add the bell peppers, onions and cabbage; toss gently to combine. Pour the vinegar mixture over the vegetables; stir gently to coat. Bring to a boil over medium-high heat; reduce the heat. Simmer, covered, for 5 minutes.

Yield: 8 servings

My mother used to say, "All

your taste is in your mouth."

Mary Ann Blome

Braised Red Cabbage with Apples and Wine

2 pounds red cabbage,
　shredded
1 large onion, chopped
2 ribs celery, diced
2 to 3 cloves of garlic, minced
1½ tablespoons olive oil
1 bay leaf
¼ teaspoon dried thyme
Salt and pepper to taste

2 tart green apples, peeled,
　grated
3 tablespoons chopped flat-
　leaf parsley
1¼ cups dry red wine
1½ tablespoons red wine
　vinegar, or 3 tablespoons
　balsamic vinegar
1 tablespoon brown sugar

⅗ Fill a large saucepan with salted water. Bring to a boil over high heat; add the cabbage. Blanch for 2 minutes; drain. Sauté the onion, celery and garlic in the olive oil in a large skillet until the vegetables are tender. Stir in the bay leaf and thyme. Season with salt and pepper. Cook over medium heat until the onion begins to turn pale yellow, stirring frequently. Stir in the cabbage, apples, parsley and wine. Simmer, covered, over low heat for 20 minutes. Stir in the wine vinegar and sugar. Cook, uncovered, for 30 minutes, stirring occasionally. Discard the bay leaf.

Yield: 8 servings

Carrots with Apricot Brandy Sauce

1¼ pounds carrots,
　julienned
¼ cup melted margarine

¼ cup apricot brandy
1 teaspoon sugar
1 teaspoon salt

⅗ Arrange the carrots evenly in an 8-inch square baking dish. Mix the margarine, apricot brandy, sugar and salt in a small bowl. Pour over the carrots. Bake at 375 degrees for 40 minutes or until the carrots are tender, stirring to mix well.

Yield: 4 servings

Carrot Soufflé

1 pound carrots, cooked,
  drained
1/2 cup butter, melted
3 eggs

1/2 cup sugar
3 tablespoons flour
1 teaspoon baking powder
1 teaspoon vanilla extract

❧ Grease a 1-quart baking dish. Combine the carrots and butter in a food processor or blender container; process at medium speed until puréed, scraping the sides as needed. Add the eggs, sugar, flour, baking powder and vanilla extract; process at medium speed until blended. Pour into the baking dish. Bake at 350 degrees for 40 to 45 minutes or until the soufflé is firm in the center.

Yield: 6 servings

Cauliflower and Peas with Ginger

3 tablespoons vegetable oil
1 1/2 teaspoons finely chopped
  gingerroot
1 medium head cauliflower,
  broken into florets

1 1/2 cups frozen peas
1/2 teaspoon ground turmeric
Salt to taste
Chopped cilantro

❧ Heat the oil in a wok or deep skillet over medium-high heat. Add the gingerroot; stir-fry for 1 minute or until fragrant. Add the cauliflower. Stir-fry for 1 minute, tossing the ingredients constantly. Add the peas. Stir-fry for 1 minute, tossing the ingredients constantly. Reduce the heat and stir in the turmeric and salt. Add 2 tablespoons water; stir. Cook, covered, over low heat until the cauliflower is tender.

❧ Cook, uncovered, over medium heat until the remaining liquid has evaporated, stirring as necessary. Top with cilantro. Serve hot or cold.

Yield: 4 servings

Cauliflower and Peas with Ginger is a traditional vegetable dish from the Punjab region of Northeast India. The ginger in this dish brings out the more mellow flavors of cauliflower. Light and tasty, this is a great accompaniment to any curry dish.

Corn and Black Bean Tart with Chili Crust

3 cups canned black beans,
  drained, rinsed
1 bay leaf
1 medium red onion, chopped
2 tablespoons sour cream
1 tablespoon vegetable oil
Salt and pepper to taste
1 (10-ounce) package frozen
  corn, cooked, drained

1 red bell pepper, chopped
½ cup chopped fresh cilantro
1½ cups shredded Monterey
  Jack cheese
2 jalapeños, seeded, minced
½ cup chopped green onions
Chili-Seasoned Crust
  (page 163)
Sour cream

My mother wouldn't let me cook. I grew up in England during the Second World War and we had rationing. She couldn't take the chance that I might spoil the meat.

Jean Bremner

❧ Combine the black beans, bay leaf, onion and ½ cup water in a saucepan. Simmer, covered, over medium heat for 30 minutes or until the onion is tender; drain. Discard the bay leaf. Reserve 2 cups bean mixture and remove 1 cup to a food processor container. Add the sour cream and oil; process at medium speed until the beans are puréed. Season with salt and pepper.

❧ Combine the reserved whole beans, corn, bell pepper, cilantro, Monterey Jack cheese, jalapeños, and green onions in a large bowl, tossing gently to mix well. Season with salt and pepper.

❧ Spread the bean purée over the bottom of the Chili-Seasoned Crust. Top with the bean-corn mixture, pressing slightly to smooth. Bake at 350 degrees for 20 minutes. Let cool for 15 minutes and remove side from tart pan. Serve warm or at room temperature with a dollop of sour cream. May make crust a day ahead and store at room temperature.

Yield: 6 servings

Chili–Seasoned Crust

1¼ cups flour
1 teaspoon ground cumin
1 teaspoon chili powder
1 teaspoon paprika
½ teaspoon salt

½ cup cold butter, cut into
    pieces
2 tablespoons ice water
Rice, beans or pie weights

❧ Combine the flour, cumin, chili, paprika and salt in a food processor container; process until mixed, pulsing several times. Add the butter; process until the mixture resembles coarse meal.

❧ Add the ice water; process until the mixture forms a dough that begins to hold together. Press into a fluted 10-inch tart pan with removable bottom.

❧ Chill for 15 minutes or until firm. Preheat the oven to 350 degrees. Line the crust with foil and fill with rice. Bake for 10 minutes. Remove the rice and foil. Bake for 10 minutes or until golden brown.

Corn Pudding

2 (15-ounce) cans cream-style
    corn
2 (10-ounce) packages frozen
    corn, thawed
½ cup flour

1 teaspoon salt
4 eggs, beaten
1 cup whipping cream
¼ cup sugar, or to taste
½ cup butter, melted

❧ Preheat the oven to 350 degrees; grease a 9x13-inch baking dish. Combine the cream-style corn, corn, flour, salt, eggs, cream, sugar and butter in a large bowl, mixing to blend well. Pour into the baking dish. Bake, uncovered, for 1 hour.

Yield: 6 servings

The eggplant mixture may

be made several hours

ahead and stored, covered,

in the refrigerator. Bake

just before serving.

Spicy Baked Eggplant

1/3 cup finely chopped onion
3/4 cup finely chopped celery
1/3 cup finely chopped green
  bell pepper (optional)
1 tablespoon vegetable oil
1 egg

6 drops of Tabasco sauce
1 medium eggplant, peeled,
  cubed
1/2 cup soft bread crumbs
2 slices bacon

❧ Preheat the oven to 350 degrees; butter a 5x9-inch loaf pan. Sauté the onion, celery and bell pepper in the oil in a large skillet until the onion is translucent but not browned. Combine the egg and Tabasco sauce in a small bowl; beat lightly with a fork to blend. Cook the eggplant in salted water in a saucepan until tender, drain and remove to a large bowl. Mash with a fork. Add the onion mixture and bread crumbs; stir until well mixed. Stir in the egg mixture. Pour into the loaf pan. Arrange bacon slices over the top. Bake for 45 minutes.

Yield: 4 servings

Grilled Portobello Mushrooms with Honey Marinade

1 cup olive oil
2 tablespoons honey
2 teaspoons molasses
6 cloves of garlic

1 teaspoon soy sauce
1/2 cup balsamic vinegar
8 portobello mushrooms

❧ Combine the oil, honey, molasses, garlic, soy sauce and balsamic vinegar in a blender container; process at high speed until well blended. Place the mushrooms in a self-sealing bag or in a baking dish. Pour in the honey mixture and turn gently to coat all the mushrooms evenly. Marinate in the refrigerator for at least 8 hours. Arrange the mushrooms cap side down on a grill rack. Grill for 5 minutes.

Yield: 8 servings

Vidalia Onion Pie

1 cup finely crushed Ritz
    crackers
1/4 cup melted butter
2 cups sliced Vidalia onions
2 tablespoons butter
2 eggs

3/4 cup milk
3/4 teaspoon salt
Pepper to taste
1/4 cup shredded Gruyère
    cheese
Paprika

Preheat the oven to 350 degrees. Combine the cracker crumbs and the 1 cup melted butter in a medium bowl; stir until well mixed. Press into the bottom and up the sides of an 8-inch pie plate. Sauté the onions in 2 tablespoons butter in a skillet until translucent but not browned. Spread the onions over the crust. Beat the eggs, milk, salt and pepper in a medium bowl until well blended. Pour over the onions. Sprinkle the Gruyère cheese and paprika over the egg mixture. Bake for 30 minutes.

Yield: 6 servings

A Thyme to
Remember

This pie may be stored,

covered, in the refrigerator

for a day or two.

Baked Sweet Red Onions

4 red onions, halved from root
    to stem, skin intact
1 1/2 tablespoons olive oil
1/4 cup chicken stock or water
1 teaspoon balsamic vinegar
1 teaspoon sugar

1 teaspoon finely chopped
    fresh rosemary
1 teaspoon finely chopped
    fresh thyme
1/2 teaspoon salt
1/4 teaspoon pepper

Preheat the oven to 350 degrees. Line a large shallow baking dish with enough foil cover the bottom and fold over the top. Coat with cooking spray. Arrange the onions cut sides up in a single layer. Drizzle evenly with a mixture the olive oil, chicken stock and balsamic vinegar. Sprinkle the sugar, rosemary, thyme, salt and pepper over the onions. Fold the foil over the onions, covering them loosely. Bake for 1 hour. Uncover the onions. Bake for 30 to 45 minutes or until the onions are very tender.

Yield: 8 servings

Sake Potatoes

4 medium red potatoes
2 tablespoons unsalted butter

1/2 cup sake
2 tablespoons soy sauce

❧ Cook the potatoes in salted water in a covered saucepan until tender; drain. Melt the butter in a skillet or wok over high heat. Add the potatoes and toss gently to coat. Add the sake, toss gently to coat. Cook, uncovered, on high heat, stirring often until the sake has almost evaporated. Add the soy sauce; toss gently to coat. Lower the heat. Cook for 5 minutes or until the sauce is thick and brown, stirring occasionally.

Yield: 4 servings

Garlic Mashed Potatoes

5 cloves of garlic
1/2 cup olive oil
1 pound Yukon Gold
   potatoes
1/2 cup milk
3 tablespoons butter
2 cups shredded mozzarella
   cheese

1/4 cup shredded white
   Cheddar or smoked
   Cheddar cheese
1/2 cup sour cream
1/8 teaspoon nutmeg
Garlic powder (optional)
Cream
Parmesan cheese

These potatoes may be prepared ahead and stored, covered, in the refrigerator. Bake for 20 minutes before serving.

❧ Bake the garlic in olive oil in a small baking dish at 400 degrees for 30 minutes. Let cool; peel and mince. Cook the potatoes in salted water in a covered saucepan until tender; drain. Add the milk and butter; mash. Let cool. Combine the mozzarella cheese, Cheddar cheese, sour cream, nutmeg and minced garlic in a bowl; stir until well blended. Add to the potatoes. Beat in the large mixer bowl of an electric mixer at low speed until well blended and fluffy; do not overbeat, or the potatoes will become gluey. Season with the garlic powder. Spoon into a baking dish, smoothing with the back of a spoon. Top with cream and Parmesan cheese. Bake at 400 degrees for 20 minutes.

Yield: 10 servings

Sweet Potato Puff

3 cups mashed sweet
    potatoes
1 cup sugar
1/4 cup melted margarine
1 teaspoon vanilla extract

2 eggs, beaten
1 cup packed light brown sugar
1/3 cup flour
1 cup chopped pecans
1/2 cup melted margarine

❧ Grease a baking dish. Combine the sweet potatoes, sugar, 1/4 cup melted margarine, vanilla and eggs in a large bowl; mix until well blended. Spoon into the baking dish, smoothing with the back of a spoon.

❧ Combine the brown sugar, flour, pecans and 1/2 cup margarine in a small bowl, stirring until crumbly. Sprinkle evenly over the sweet potato mixture. Bake, uncovered, at 375 degrees for 30 minutes.

Yield: 8 servings

Golden Squash Patties

2 cups shredded yellow
    squash
2 teaspoons grated onion
2 teaspoons sugar
1/2 teaspoon salt

1/8 teaspoon pepper
1 egg, beaten
1/4 cup plus 2 tablespoons
    flour
2 tablespoons margarine

❧ Combine the squash, onion, sugar, salt and pepper in a medium bowl; stir to mix well. Cover and let stand for 30 minutes. Drain well. Add the egg and flour; stir to mix thoroughtly.

❧ Melt the margarine in a large skillet over medium-high heat; add the squash mixture by the tablespoonful. Cook until golden brown, turning once. Drain on a plate lined with paper towels.

Yield: 4 servings

A Thyme to
Remember

❧❧❧

The casserole may be

assembled the day

before and stored, covered,

in the refrigerator.

❧❧❧

In order to meet the

health needs of our patients,

especially the indigent and

minority populations,

education about health

matters is a key factor."

Ricardo Diaz, M.D.,

Internal Medicine

Tomato Cheese Pie

2 teaspoons dried basil
2 teaspoons dillweed
Salt and pepper to taste
4 tomatoes, peeled, sliced
1 pound Gruyère cheese,
  thinly sliced

1 (9-inch) partially baked pie
  crust
2 tablespoons grated
  Parmesan cheese
2 tablespoons butter

❧ Combine the basil, dillweed, salt and pepper in a small bowl; stir to mix well. Layer the Gruyère cheese, tomatoes, herb mixture and Parmesan cheese in the crust, starting with the Gruyère cheese. Dot with part of the butter. Repeat layering until all the ingredients are used. Bake at 375 degrees for 20 to 30 minutes.

Yield: 6 servings

Mexican Vegetable Casserole

1 (15-ounce) can corn,
  drained
1 (15-ounce) can black
  beans, rinsed, drained
1 (10-ounce) can whole
  tomatoes and green
  chiles, partially drained
1 cup sour cream
1 cup picante sauce
2 cups rice, cooked

8 ounces Cheddar cheese,
  shredded
¼ teaspoon lemon pepper
1 bunch green onions,
  chopped
1 (2-ounce) jar sliced black
  olives
8 ounces Monterey Jack
  cheese, shredded

❧ Grease a 9x13-inch baking dish. Combine the corn, black beans, tomatoes, sour cream, picante sauce, rice, Cheddar cheese and lemon pepper in a large bowl; stir until well mixed. Pour into the baking dish; smooth with the back of a spoon.

❧ Sprinkle the green onions, black olives and Monterey Jack cheese over the top. Bake at 350 degrees for 50 minutes.

Yield: 6 servings

Red Chile Enchiladas

½ cup vegetable oil
12 blue corn tortillas
2 cups Red Chile Sauce
   (below)
1 pound Monterey Jack
   cheese, shredded

1½ cups chopped red onion
Shredded lettuce
Sliced avocado
Chopped tomatoes
Sour cream

Warm the oil in a small skillet over medium-high heat until it sizzles when a cube of bread is dropped in. Soften the tortillas by dipping them, one at a time, into the hot oil for 1 or 2 seconds. Do not allow them to become crisp. Stack on a plate with a paper towel between each tortilla.

Spread 1 tablespoon Red Chile Sauce on each of 4 oven-proof plates. Layer the tortillas, Red Chile Sauce, Monterey Jack cheese and onion, using 2 or 3 tortillas and ending with the sauce topped with some Monterey Jack cheese. Bake at 300 degrees for 10 minutes. Serve with lettuce, avocado, tomatoes and sour cream.

Yield: 4 servings

Red Chile Sauce

2 tablespoons vegetable oil
1 large clove of garlic, minced
¼ teaspoon dried oregano
¼ teaspoon ground cumin

2 tablespoons flour
½ cup chili powder
2½ cups chicken broth
Salt to taste

Warm the oil in a skillet over medium-high heat; add the garlic. Sauté for 3 to 4 minutes or until softened. Add the oregano, cumin and flour; stir constantly to prevent lumping. Cook until lightly browned; remove from the heat.

Combine the chili powder and broth in a bowl; whisk until smooth and well blended. Stir slowly into the garlic mixture. Season with the salt. Return to the heat. Simmer, covered, over low heat for 15 to 20 minutes or until hot and the flavors have blended. Use a premium chili powder for the tastiest sauce.

Before I got married my husband told me he was a good cook. So I'm not too surprised when I find him looking over my shoulder telling me how to cook.

Elizabeth Gunby

Rainbow Vegetable Loaf

6 eggs
1 cup chopped cooked broccoli
   florets
3 tablespoons butter or
   margarine, softened
1 cup shredded Cheddar
   cheese
3/4 teaspoon onion salt
1 cup cooked rice

1/4 cup chopped red bell
   pepper
1/2 cup shredded mozzarella
   cheese
1 cup mashed carrot
Broccoli florets
Carrot curls
Onion rings
Red bell pepper strips

☞ Grease a 4x8-inch loaf pan. Lightly beat 2 of the eggs in a medium bowl. Add the broccoli, 1 tablespoon of the butter, 1/2 cup of the Cheddar cheese and 1/4 teaspoon of the onion salt; mix well. Spoon into the loaf pan and pack firmly.

☞ Lightly beat 2 of the eggs in the same medium bowl. Add the rice, bell pepper, 1 tablespoon of the butter, the mozzarella cheese and 1/4 teaspoon of the onion salt; mix well. Spoon into the loaf pan and spread evenly.

☞ Lightly beat the remaining 2 eggs in the same medium bowl. Add the carrot and the remaining butter, Cheddar cheese and onion salt; mix well. Spread evenly over the rice layer.

☞ Bake at 325 degrees for 1 hour or until a knife inserted in the center comes out clean. Unmold. Garnish with cooked broccoli, carrots, onion and bell pepper.

Yield 6 servings

Vegetable Trio

Whole cloves
8 ounces small white onions
1 pound small new potatoes,
    peeled, quartered
2 cups carrots, julienned
1/8 teaspoon salt
1/8 teaspoon pepper

1/2 teaspoon Accent
1/2 cup butter or margarine,
    melted
1 teaspoon lemon juice
1 teaspoon sugar
2 cloves of garlic, minced
1/2 cup chopped fresh parsley

❧ Preheat the oven to 325 degrees. Insert a whole clove into
each onion. Arrange the onions, potatoes and carrots in a shallow
1½-quart baking dish. Season with salt, pepper and Accent.

❧ Combine the butter, lemon juice, sugar and garlic in a small
bowl, stirring to mix well. Pour over the onion mixture. Bake,
covered, for 1 hour. Stir in the parsley. Bake, uncovered, until the
vegetables are tender. Discard the cloves.

Yield: 6 servings

Old South Corn Bread Dressing

1½ cups finely chopped
    onions
3 cups finely chopped celery
14 cups crumbled corn bread
7 cups crumbled dried bread
8 eggs, beaten

1½ teaspoons pepper
Salt to taste
2 to 3 teaspoons dried sage
    (optional)
8 to 10 cups chicken or
    turkey broth

❧ Preheat the oven to 350 degrees; grease a large iron skillet or a
heavy 3-quart baking pan. Combine the onions, celery, corn bread,
bread, eggs and pepper in a large bowl; toss to mix well. Season
with the salt and sage. Pour in the chicken broth; stir until well
combined. Spoon into the skillet. Bake for 45 minutes or until
browned. This dressing should be very moist, almost "soupy" before
it is baked.

Yield: 8 servings

Cranberry Wild Rice

1 (6-ounce) package long
   grain wild rice
1 cup fresh cranberries
1 cup sliced celery

1/2 cup sugar
1 teaspoon grated orange peel
1/2 cup salted whole cashews

❧ Cook the rice according to package directions in a medium saucepan. Stir in the cranberries. Cook until they begin to pop. Stir in the celery, sugar, orange peel and cashews; spoon into a 1½-quart baking dish. Bake, covered, at 350 degrees for 30 to 40 minutes.

Yield: 6 servings

Fresh Basil Pesto Sauce

3/4 cup pine nuts
2 cups packed fresh basil
1/2 teaspoon salt
1/4 teaspoon pepper
1/2 cup grated Parmesan
   cheese

1/2 cup grated Romano
   cheese
2 large cloves of garlic,
   quartered
1/2 cup olive oil

❧ Combine the pine nuts, basil, salt, pepper, Parmesan cheese, Romano cheese and garlic in a blender container; process at high speed just until smooth, scraping the sides as needed.

❧ Add the oil in a steady stream, processing constantly at high speed until smooth. Use in soups, sauces, dips or spoon over vegetables, pasta or meats.

Yield: 8 servings

This pesto may be stored, covered, in the refrigerator for up to 5 days. For longer storage, freeze for up to 5 months.

Garden Herb Seasoning for Vegetables

2 tablespoons dried marjoram
2 tablespoons dried oregano
2 tablespoons dried rosemary
2 tablespoons dried basil
2 tablespoons dried parsley
1 tablespoon onion powder
1 tablespoon dried thyme
1 tablespoon salt
1 tablespoon garlic powder
1 teaspoon pepper

❧ Combine the marjoram, oregano, rosemary, basil, parsley, onion powder, thyme, salt, garlic powder and pepper in a jar with a tight-fitting lid. Cover and shake until well mixed. Use to season vegetables, such as cauliflower, broccoli, cabbage or turnips.

Yield: 45 servings

Roquefort Sauce

2 tablespoons unsalted butter
1/3 cup minced shallots
3/4 cup dry white wine
2 tablespoons flour
3/4 cup milk
4 ounces Roquefort, crumbled
Tabasco sauce to taste
Freshly ground pepper
   to taste

❧ Melt the butter in a small heavy saucepan over medium-low heat; add the shallots. Cook until softened, stirring often. Add the wine. Cook until the liquid is reduced to about 1 tablespoon, stirring occasionally. Add the flour; whisk briskly to blend and prevent lumping. Add the milk in a thin stream, whisking constantly to prevent lumping. Cook for 2 minutes, continuing to whisk constantly.

❧ Reduce heat to low and add the Roquefort, a little at a time, whisking constantly. Cook until the cheese melts, whisking. Do not let boil to keep it from separating. Stir in the Tabasco sauce and pepper.

Yield: 10 servings

A Thyme to Remember

Store the seasoning in a cool, dry place. May add to melted butter for topping bread or vegetables.

❧❧❧

For *Mango Salsa*, combine

2 cups diced tomatoes,

1 mango, diced, 1 green bell

pepper, diced, 6 green onions,

sliced, 1 jalapeño, seeded,

diced, ¼ cup lime juice,

½ cup chopped cilantro,

1 teaspoon ground cumin,

¼ cup pecan pieces, toasted,

and ½ teaspoon vegetable

oil in a medium bowl;

toss gently.

❧❧❧

Jalapeño Hot Mustard

1 (16-ounce) jar honey
2 (16-ounce) jars prepared
   mustard

12 to 14 jalapeños, seeded,
   minced

❧ Combine the honey and mustard in a large bowl, stirring to blend well. Stir in the jalapeños. Spoon into a jar with a tight-fitting lid. Chill in the refrigerator until serving time. Make ahead of time for best results.

Yield: 96 servings

Bell Pepper Mustard

2 tablespoons olive oil
2 medium red bell peppers,
   julienned
2 medium yellow bell peppers,
   julienned
1 tablespoon tomato paste
1 tablespoon sherry vinegar

Salt and freshly ground
   pepper to taste
2 (4-ounce) jars Dijon
   mustard
Cayenne pepper to taste
2 to 3 drops of lemon juice

❧ Warm the oil in a large saucepan over medium heat. Add the peppers and toss to coat. Add the tomato paste and sherry vinegar; stir to mix well. Season with the salt and pepper. Simmer, covered, for 20 minutes or until the peppers are soft. Uncover. Simmer until the liquid completely evaporates and the peppers are mushy. Strain through a large sieve into a bowl, working the mixture through with the back of a wooden spoon.

❧ Combine the pepper mixture, the mustard, cayenne and lemon juice in a blender container; process at medium speed until blended. Season with salt and pepper.

Yield: 16 servings

A Handful of Sugar

CAKES, COOKIES AND PIES

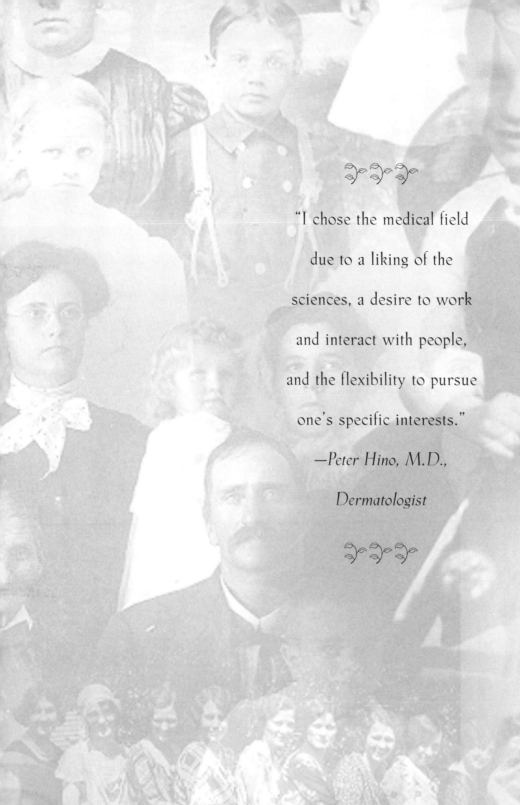

꿏 꿏 꿏

"I chose the medical field
due to a liking of the
sciences, a desire to work
and interact with people,
and the flexibility to pursue
one's specific interests."
—Peter Hino, M.D.,
Dermatologist

꿏 꿏 꿏

Chocolate Carrot Cake

2 cups flour
2 cups sugar
1/3 cup baking cocoa
1 teaspoon salt
1 teaspoon baking powder
1 teaspoon baking soda

4 eggs
1½ cups vegetable oil
4 medium carrots, shredded
Cream Cheese Frosting
   (at right)
Chocolate Glaze (below)

❧ Preheat the oven to 350 degrees; grease and flour two 9-inch round cake pans. Sift the flour, sugar, cocoa, salt, baking powder and baking soda into a medium bowl.

❧ Beat the eggs and oil in the large mixer bowl of an electric mixer at low speed until well combined. Add the flour mixture; beat just until combined. Stir in the carrots. Pour into the prepared cake pans. Bake on the middle oven rack for 50 minutes or until a cake tester inserted into the center comes out clean. Cool in the pans on wire racks for 10 minutes or until cool enough to handle. Remove from the pans and let cool completely on the racks. Spread the Cream Cheese Frosting between the layers. Spread the Chocolate Glaze over the top and side of the cake. Chill for 1 hour or until set.

Yield: 6 servings

Chocolate Glaze

1/2 cup semisweet chocolate
   chips
3 ounces bittersweet chocolate
6 tablespoons whipping cream

1 tablespoon unsalted butter
1/2 teaspoon vanilla extract
1 cup confectioners' sugar

❧ Combine the chocolate chips, bittersweet chocolate, whipping cream, butter, vanilla extract and confectioners' sugar in a small saucepan, stirring to mix well. Cook over medium heat until the chocolate is melted and the glaze smooth, stirring frequently. Remove from the heat; let cool slightly.

For *Cream Cheese Frosting,*

cream 4 ounces softened

cream cheese and

2 tablespoons softened

unsalted butter in the small

mixer bowl of an electric

mixer at medium speed until

fluffy and smooth. Add

1 tablespoon vanilla extract

and ½ cup confectioners'

sugar; beat at high speed

until creamy.

This combination of spices

may be substituted for

the pumpkin pie spice:

1/2 teaspoon allspice,

1/4 teaspoon ground cloves,

1/4 teaspoon nutmeg,

1/4 teaspoon ginger and

1 1/2 teaspoons cinnamon.

Chopped Apple Cake with Caramel Frosting

2 cups flour
2 cups sugar
1/2 teaspoon salt
2 teaspoons baking
    soda
2 teaspoons pumpkin pie
    spice

2 cups canned sliced apples,
    mashed with juice
2 eggs, beaten
1 cup broken walnuts
Caramel Frosting (page 179)

❧ Preheat the oven to 350 degrees; grease and flour three 8-inch round cake pans. Sift the flour, sugar, salt, baking soda and pumpkin pie spice into a large bowl. Stir in the apples and eggs. Stir in the walnuts. Pour the batter into the prepared cake pans.

❧ Bake for 25 to 30 minutes or until a cake tester inserted into the center comes out clean. Cool in the pans on wire racks for 10 to 15 minutes or until the pans are cool enough to handle. Remove from the pans and let cool completely on the racks. Place on a plate.

❧ Spread the Caramel Frosting between the layers and over the cake. Garnish with toasted sliced almonds and confectioners' sugar. Chill until cold.

Yield: 12 servings

Caramel Frosting

3/4 cup packed brown sugar
1/2 cup whipping cream
1 tablespoon light corn syrup

1 cup confectioners' sugar
1/2 cup unsalted butter
1 teaspoon vanilla extract

❧ Mix the first 3 ingredients in a medium heavy saucepan. Cook over medium heat until the mixture comes to a boil, stirring constantly. Boil for 2 minutes, swirling the pan occasionally. Pour the mixture into a small bowl. Chill, covered, in the refrigerator for 1 hour or until thickened, stirring occasionally. Beat sifted confectioners' sugar and softened butter in the large mixer bowl of an electric mixer at medium speed until smooth. Beat in the cooked mixture at medium speed. Beat in the vanilla.

Commander's Carrot Cake

2 cups sifted flour
2 teaspoons baking powder
2 teaspoons baking soda
1 teaspoon salt
2 cups sugar
1 1/2 cups vegetable oil

4 eggs
4 1/2 cups grated carrots
4 cups finely chopped pecans
2 tablespoons vanilla extract
Butter Cream Cheese
    Frosting (at right)

❧ Preheat the oven to 325 degrees; grease three 9-inch round cake pans. Combine the flour, baking powder, baking soda and salt in a medium bowl. Beat the sugar and oil in a large bowl until well blended. Add the eggs, one at a time, beating well after each addition. Stir in the flour mixture. Add the carrots and pecans; mix well. Pour into the prepared cake pans. Bake for 45 minutes or until a cake tester inserted into the center comes out clean. Cool in the pans on wire racks for 10 to 15 minutes. Remove from the pans and cool completely. Frost between the layers and over the top and side with the Butter Cream Cheese Frosting.

Yield: 12 servings

For *Butter Cream Cheese Frosting*, combine 24 ounces confectioners' sugar, 1/2 cup butter, softened, 16 ounces cream cheese, softened, and 2 teaspoons vanilla extract in a medium bowl; beat until the mixture is smooth, fluffy and well blended.

❧❧❧

For Cocoa Butter Cream

Frosting, cream 8 tablespoons

butter, softened, in a

small bowl. Add ¾ cup

baking cocoa and 2⅔ cups

confectioners' sugar

alternately with ⅓ cup

milk or cream, beating until

of a spreading consistency,

adding additional milk

if needed. Beat in

1 teaspoon vanilla extract.

❧❧❧

One-Egg Devil's Food Cake

1½ cups flour
3 tablespoons baking cocoa
1 teaspoon salt
1 cup buttermilk
1 teaspoon baking soda
½ cup shortening

1 cup sugar
1 egg
1 teaspoon vanilla extract
16 to 18 marshmallows
Cocoa Butter Cream Frosting
  (at left)

❧ Preheat the oven to 350 degrees; grease two 8-inch round cake
pans and dust with cocoa. Sift the flour, cocoa and salt together
3 times. Mix the buttermilk and baking soda in a 2-cup measure.

❧ Cream the shortening and sugar in a large bowl until light and
fluffy. Beat in the egg. Add the flour mixture alternately with the
buttermilk, beating well after each addition. Stir in the vanilla.
Pour into the prepared cake pans.

❧ Bake for 25 to 30 minutes or until a cake tester inserted into
the center comes out clean. Cool in the pans on wire racks for
10 minutes. Remove from the pans and let cool completely on
the racks.

❧ Microwave half the marshmallows in a glass bowl until melted.
Spread immediately on top of 1 cake layer; spread with some of the
Cocoa Butter Cream Frosting. Stack the remaining cake layer on
top. Microwave the remaining marshmallows in a glass bowl until
melted. Spread immediately over the top. Frost the top and side
with the remaining Cocoa Butter Cream Frosting. Garnish with
coarsely chopped pecans.

Yield: 12 servings

No-Fat Mocha Cake

1 cup flour
1/3 cup plus 2 tablespoons
    baking cocoa
1 teaspoon instant coffee
1 teaspoon baking powder
1 teaspoon baking soda

6 egg whites
1 1/3 cups packed brown sugar
1 cup plain yogurt
1 teaspoon vanilla extract
Raspberry Sauce (below)

❧ Preheat the oven to 350 degrees. Line a 10-inch round cake pan with waxed paper; coat with cooking spray and dust with flour.

❧ Sift the flour, cocoa, coffee powder, baking powder and baking soda into a bowl. Beat the egg whites, brown sugar, yogurt and vanilla in the large mixer bowl of an electric mixer at medium-high speed for 1 minute or until blended. Mix in the flour mixture. Pour into the prepared cake pan.

❧ Bake for 35 minutes or until a cake tester inserted into the center comes out clean. Cool in the pan on a wire rack for 15 minutes. Loosen the cake by cutting around the pan side. Turn out onto a plate, peel off the waxed paper and let cool completely on the rack. Serve with the Raspberry Sauce.

Yield: 8 servings

Raspberry Sauce

4 cups fresh or frozen
    raspberries

1/2 cup sugar
1/2 cup water

❧ Combine the raspberries, sugar and water in a saucepan, stirring to blend. Bring to a boil, stirring frequently. Pour into a blender container; process at medium speed until puréed. Strain through a sieve into a bowl, pressing the pulp through with the back of a wooden spoon. Chill, covered, in the refrigerator.

❧❧❧

For *Chocolate Ganache*

Frosting, combine 1 cup

whipping cream and 5 ounces

semisweet chocolate, chopped,

in a large bowl. Place over a

pan of simmering water until

the chocolate is melted,

stirring to blend. Stir in 1 cup

whipping cream, ½ teaspoon

almond extract and

½ teaspoon cinnamon. Chill,

covered, for at least 4 hours,

stirring occasionally. Beat at

high speed on the electric

mixer until stiff peaks form.

❧❧❧

Aztec Chocolate Cake

This cake is a perfect dessert for "south-of-the-border" meals or other special occasion dinners.

2 cups cake flour
2 teaspoons baking
   powder
2 teaspoons cinnamon
1 teaspoon salt
¼ cup shortening
2 cups sugar
2 eggs, separated

4 ounces unsweetened
   chocolate, melted, cooled
1½ cups milk
1 teaspoon almond extract
1 cup finely chopped
   almonds, toasted
Chocolate Ganache Frosting
   (at left)

❧ Preheat the oven to 350 degrees; grease and flour two 9-inch round cake pans. Sift the cake flour, baking powder, cinnamon and salt into a medium bowl.

❧ Cream the shortening, 1 cup of the sugar and egg yolks in a large bowl until light and fluffy. Add the chocolate and blend thoroughly. Add the cake flour mixture alternately with the milk, beating well after each addition. Stir in the almond extract and almonds.

❧ Beat the egg whites in a large bowl until frothy. Add the remaining sugar gradually, beating until stiff peaks form. Fold into the chocolate mixture. Pour into the prepared cake pans.

❧ Bake for 30 to 40 minutes or until the cake springs back when pressed lightly in the center. Cool in the pans on wire racks for 10 to 15 minutes or until cool enough to handle. Remove from the pans and let cool completely on the racks. Frost between the layers and on the top and side of cake with the Chocolate Ganache Frosting. Garnish with ground cinnamon and toasted chopped almonds.

Yield: 8 servings

Cranberry Upside-Down Cake

½ cup butter	1 cup sugar
1 cup packed brown sugar	½ cup butter
12 ounces cranberries	2 eggs, separated
½ cup pecans, toasted	1 teaspoon vanilla extract
1½ cups flour	½ cup milk
2 teaspoons baking powder	Cognac Whipped Cream
½ teaspoon salt	(at right)

❧ Preheat the oven to 350 degrees. Melt ½ cup butter in a 9-inch square cake pan. Remove from the oven and stir in the brown sugar. Return the pan to the oven for 2 minutes or until the brown sugar melts and easily spreads across the bottom; stir and swirl to spread. Arrange the cranberries and pecans evenly over the bottom. Let cool.

❧ Combine the flour, baking powder and salt in a medium bowl, stirring to mix. Beat the sugar and remaining ½ cup butter in the large mixer bowl of an electric mixer at medium speed for 30 seconds or until fluffy, smooth and well blended. Add the egg yolks and vanilla; beat for 1 minute, scraping the bowl frequently. Add the flour mixture alternately with the milk, beating well after each addition.

❧ Beat the egg whites in the large mixer bowl of an electric mixer at medium-high speed until soft peaks form. Fold into the flour mixture. Spread the batter over the cranberries and pecans. Bake for 35 to 40 minutes or until a cake tester inserted into the center comes out clean. Cool in the pan on a wire rack for 10 minutes. Loosen the edges using a knife and invert onto a serving plate. Serve the warm cake with the Cognac Whipped Cream.

Yield: 8 servings

For *Cognac Whipped Cream,* combine 2 cups whipping cream, 2½ tablespoons cognac and 2 tablespoons sugar in a large mixer bowl; beat with an electric mixer at medium-high speed until soft peaks form.

Kahlúa Cake

1 (2-layer) package butter
    cake mix
1 (4-ounce) package vanilla
    instant pudding mix
1 cup sour cream
1 teaspoon vanilla extract

4 eggs
3/4 cup margarine
1 cup packed brown sugar
1/3 cup Kahlúa
3/4 cup pecans, finely chopped
Kahlúa Glaze (below)

❧ Preheat the oven to 350 degrees; grease a bundt pan. Combine the cake mix, instant pudding mix, sour cream, vanilla, eggs and margarine in a large bowl; beat until smooth and well blended. Pour half the batter into the bundt pan, smoothing lightly with the back of a spoon.

❧ Combine the brown sugar, Kahlúa, pecans and the remaining batter in a bowl; stir until blended. Pour into the prepared bundt pan, smoothing lightly.

❧ Bake for 1 hour or until a cake tester inserted into the center comes out clean. Cool in the pan on a wire rack for 10 to 15 minutes or until cool enough to handle. Remove from the pan and let cool completely on the rack. Place on a serving plate. Pour the Kahlúa Glaze over the cake.

Yield: 12 servings

Kahlúa Glaze

1/2 cup margarine
1/2 cup Kahlúa

1/2 cup sugar
1 teaspoon vanilla extract

❧ Combine the margarine, Kahlúa, sugar and vanilla in a small saucepan, stirring to mix well. Bring to a boil over medium heat, stirring constantly. Boil until thickened, stirring constantly.

Mother's Lazy Daisy Cake

1/2 cup milk
1 teaspoon butter
1 cup flour
1 teaspoon baking powder

1/4 teaspoon salt
2 eggs, beaten
1 cup sugar
Broiled Coconut Icing (below)

❧ Preheat the oven to 375 degrees; grease a 7x11-inch cake pan. Combine the milk and butter in a small saucepan. Scald over medium heat and let cool to lukewarm. Combine the flour, baking powder and salt in a medium bowl, stirring to mix well.

❧ Combine the eggs and sugar in a large bowl, beating until well combined. Add the flour mixture alternately with the scalded milk mixture, beating well after each addition. Pour into the prepared cake pan.

❧ Bake for 25 minutes or until a cake tester inserted into the center comes out clean. Top with the Broiled Coconut Icing while the cake is still hot. Broil until bubbly. Serve hot with homemade vanilla ice cream.

Yield: 8 servings

Broiled Coconut Icing

1/2 cup plus 1 tablespoon
   packed brown sugar
5 tablespoons melted butter

1/4 cup cream
1/2 cup shredded coconut

❧ Combine the brown sugar, butter, cream and coconut in a small bowl, stirring to mix well. Broil as directed in cake recipe above.

My mother made *Lazy Daisy Cake* every time we watched "Wizard of Oz" on T.V. It became an annual tradition to divert our attention from the scary wicked witch.

Sarah Hardin

Double Lemon Cake

1½ cups cake flour
1 teaspoon baking powder
1/16 teaspoon salt
Peel of 2 lemons
3/4 cup sugar
3/4 cup unsalted butter or
   margarine, softened

3 eggs
1 teaspoon lemon extract
Lemon Glaze (below)
Lemon Frosting (at left)

❧ Preheat the oven to 325 degrees; grease an 8½-inch springform pan. Sift the cake flour, baking powder and salt into a medium bowl. Cut lemon peel into small pieces. Combine the peel and sugar in a food processor or blender container; process at medium speed until the peel is almost as fine as the sugar.

❧ Cream the sugar mixture and butter in the large mixer bowl of an electric mixer at medium speed until light and fluffy. Beat in eggs 1 at a time. Stir in the lemon extract. Mix in the flour mixture. Spoon into the prepared springform pan, smoothing lightly with a spatula.

❧ Bake for 35 minutes or until a cake tester inserted into the center comes out clean. Remove to a wire rack; brush on the Lemon Glaze, distributing it evenly and allowing it to run down the side and absorb into the cake. Remove the side of the springform pan. Let the cake cool for 10 minutes or until cool enough to handle; remove to a platter. Let cool completely. Spread the Lemon Frosting over the top and side of the cake. Serve with lemon sherbet.

Yield: 12 servings

Lemon Glaze

2/3 cup confectioners' sugar,
   sifted

1/3 cup lemon juice

❧ Combine the confectioners' sugar and lemon juice in a small bowl; stir until smooth and well combined.

For *Lemon Frosting*, combine 1½ cups confectioners' sugar, 1½ tablespoons unsalted butter or margarine, softened, 1/16 teaspoon salt, grated peel of 1 lemon and 2 tablespoons lemon juice in a small mixer bowl. Beat at medium speed until fluffy and smooth, adding water as needed for a spreadable consistency.

Texas Peach Bellini Cake

2¹/₂ cups flour
2¹/₄ teaspoons baking powder
¹/₂ teaspoon salt
2 cups sugar
4 eggs
1 cup vegetable oil

¹/₂ cup champagne
¹/₂ cup peach schnapps
1 teaspoon almond extract
Peaches and Cream Frosting
(below)

❧ Preheat the oven to 350 degrees; butter and flour two 9-inch round cake pans. Sift the flour, baking powder and salt into a medium bowl. Beat the sugar and eggs in the large mixer bowl of an electric mixer at medium speed until well combined. Stir in the oil, champagne, peach schnapps, almond extract and flour mixture. Beat at low speed for 1 minute. Pour the batter into the prepared cake pans.

❧ Bake for 35 to 40 minutes or until a cake tester inserted into the center comes out clean. Cool in the pans on wire racks for 10 minutes. Remove from the pans and let cool completely on the racks.

❧ Place 1 cake layer on a serving plate; spread the top with half the Peaches and Cream Frosting. Top with the remaining layer; spread the remaining Peaches and Cream Frosting on the top, leaving the side unfrosted.

Yield: 12 servings

This is a beautiful cake that's frosted with fresh peaches and cream.

Peaches and Cream Frosting

2¹/₄ cups sour cream
2 tablespoons whipping cream
1 teaspoon almond extract

6 cups sliced fresh peaches
1 cup confectioners' sugar

❧ Combine the sour cream, whipping cream, almond extract and peaches in a bowl; mix well. Add the confectioners' sugar and stir until well combined.

Butterscotch Pound Cake

1 (2-layer) package butter-
    pecan cake mix
2 (4-ounce) packages
    butterscotch instant
    pudding mix
1 cup water

¾ cup vegetable oil
4 eggs
1 teaspoon vanilla extract
1 teaspoon butter flavoring
Caramel Icing (below)

❧ Preheat the oven to 350 degrees; grease and flour a tube pan. Combine the butter pecan cake mix, butterscotch pudding mix, water, oil, eggs, vanilla and butter flavoring in a large bowl; beat until smooth and well mixed. Pour into the prepared tube pan.

❧ Bake for 45 to 60 minutes or until a cake tester inserted in the center comes out clean. Cool in the pan on a wire rack for 10 to 15 minutes or until cool enough to handle. Remove from the pan and let cool completely on the rack. Pour the Caramel Icing over the cake.

Yield: 12 servings

Caramel Icing

1½ cups packed brown sugar
½ cup sugar
1 cup half-and-half

3 tablespoons butter
1 teaspoon vanilla extract

❧ Combine the brown sugar, sugar, half-and-half, butter and vanilla in a medium saucepan. Attach a candy thermometer to the side of the pan. Bring the sugar mixture to a boil over medium-high heat, stirring constantly. Boil until the thermometer registers 232 degrees (soft-ball stage). Remove from the heat and let cool until lukewarm. Beat until thick and of a spreadable consistency.

Brown Sugar Pound Cake

3 cups sifted flour
1 teaspoon baking powder
1 cup butter or margarine,
    softened
1/2 cup shortening
1 pound light brown sugar

1 cup sugar
5 eggs
1 cup milk
1 teaspoon vanilla extract
1 cup chopped pecans
1 tablespoon flour

Sift 3 cups flour and baking powder into a medium bowl. Cream the butter and shortening in a large bowl. Add the brown sugar and sugar; beat until light and fluffy. Beat in the eggs 1 at a time. Add the flour mixture alternately with the milk, beating well after each addition. Stir in the vanilla and a mixture of the pecans and 1 tablespoon flour. Pour into a greased and floured tube pan. Place in a cold oven. Bake at 325 degrees for 1¼ hours or until a cake tester inserted into the center comes out clean. Cool in the pan on a wire rack for 10 to 15 minutes. Remove from the pan to cool completely.

Yield: 12 servings

No-Frost Pumpkin Cake

1 (29-ounce) can pumpkin
1 cup sugar
1 (13-ounce) can evaporated
    milk
3 eggs
2 teaspoons cinnamon

1/2 teaspoon salt
1 (2-layer) package yellow
    cake mix
1 cup pecans, toasted, lightly
    salted
3/4 cup butter, melted

Preheat the oven to 350 degrees. Combine the first 6 ingredients in a large bowl, mixing until well blended and smooth. Pour into a 9x13-inch cake pan. Sprinkle the cake mix over the mixture in the pan. Top with the pecans and drizzle with the butter. Bake for 50 to 60 minutes or until a cake tester inserted into the center comes out clean. Cool in the pan. Serve with whipped cream.

Yield: 12 servings

Root Beer Cake

1 (1-layer) package white
   cake mix
1 (12-ounce) can root beer

1 tablespoon root beer extract
1 (12-ounce) can vanilla
   frosting

❧ Prepare the cake mix according to package directions, substituting the root beer for the liquid. Bake according to the package directions. Let cool on a wire rack. Add the root beer extract to the vanilla frosting and blend. Spread over the cake.

Yield: 8 servings

Earthquake Cake

1 (3-ounce) can flaked
   coconut
1 cup chopped pecans
1 (2-layer) package German
   chocolate cake mix

8 ounces cream cheese
1/2 cup margarine or butter,
   softened
3 1/2 cups confectioners' sugar

❧ Preheat the oven to 350 degrees. Grease and flour a 9x13-inch cake pan. Sprinkle the coconut and pecans over the bottom of the pan. Prepare the cake mix according to package directions and pour over the pecans.

❧ Cream the cream cheese and margarine in a medium bowl until light and fluffy. Beat in the confectioners' sugar until fluffy and well blended. Spoon over the cake batter, smoothing gently with the back of a spoon.

❧ Bake for 1 hour or until a cake tester inserted into the center comes out clean. Cool in the pan on a wire rack. Cut into squares to serve.

Yield: 16 servings

Zinfandel Delight Cake

2¼ cups flour
2¼ teaspoons baking powder
½ teaspoon cinnamon
½ teaspoon ground cloves
½ teaspoon salt
¼ cup butter, softened
¼ cup shortening
1 cup sugar
3 tablespoons grated orange
    peel

⅔ cup zinfandel
⅓ cup buttermilk
1 tablespoon Grand Marnier
½ cup ground walnuts
4 egg whites
¼ cup sugar
Orange Cream Frosting
    (at right)

❧ Preheat the oven to 375 degrees; grease and flour two 9-inch round cake pans. Combine the flour, baking powder, cinnamon, cloves and salt in a medium bowl; stir to mix well.

❧ Cream the butter and shortening in a large bowl until light and fluffy. Add 1 cup sugar and orange peel; beat until well blended and fluffy. Beat in the flour mixture. Add a mixture of the zinfandel, buttermilk and Grand Marnier and beat well. Stir in the walnuts.

❧ Beat the egg whites in a large bowl until foamy. Add ¼ cup sugar gradually, beating until stiff peaks form. Fold into the cake batter. Pour into the prepared cake pans.

❧ Bake for 25 to 30 minutes or until a cake tester inserted into the center comes out clean. Cool in the pans on wire racks for 10 to 15 minutes or until cool enough to handle. Remove from the pans and let cool completely on the racks. Spread the Orange Cream Frosting between the layers and over the top and side of the cake. Garnish with walnut pieces and shredded orange peel.

Yield: 12 servings

A Thyme to Remember

For Orange Cream Frosting, Beat 6 tablespoons butter, softened, and 2 tablespoons sour cream in a small bowl until smooth and well blended. Beat in 1 tablespoon orange juice concentrate, 1 tablespoon Grand Marnier and 1 pound confectioners' sugar until light and fluffy.

Buttermilk Glaze

½ cup sugar   ¼ cup butter
¼ cup buttermilk

❧ Combine the sugar, buttermilk and butter in a small saucepan. Cook for 7 minutes, stirring constantly. Pour or spread over a cooled cake.

Yield: Enough frosting for one 12-serving single layer cake

Buffalo Chip Cookies

4 cups flour   2 cups packed brown sugar
1 teaspoon baking soda   2 teaspoons vanilla extract
1 teaspoon baking powder   4 eggs
2 cups rolled oats   2 cups chopped pecans
2 cups butter, softened   2 cups crushed cornflakes
2 cups sugar   2 cups chocolate chips

❧ Preheat the oven to 350 degrees. Combine the flour, baking soda, baking powder and rolled oats in a medium bowl; stir until well mixed.

❧ Cream the butter, sugar and brown sugar in a large bowl until smooth, fluffy and well blended. Beat in the vanilla extract and eggs until well blended and smooth. Beat in the flour mixture. Stir in the pecans, cornflakes and chocolate chips.

❧ Drop by tablespoonfuls onto cookie sheets, allowing about 8 cookies per sheet. Bake for 8 to 10 minutes or until golden brown. Remove from the cookie sheets and cool on wire racks.

Yield: 60 servings

When I got married I only knew how to make chocolate chip cookies.

Pam Edmunds

Clipper Chipper Cookies

2½ cups flour
1 teaspoon baking soda
½ teaspoon salt
1 cup butter, softened
¾ cup sugar
¾ cup packed light brown
    sugar
1 tablespoon vanilla extract

1 tablespoon Tia Maria
1 tablespoon Frangelica
2 eggs
4 cups milk chocolate chips
1 cup walnut halves, or
    ½ cup chopped walnuts
½ cup chopped pecans
½ cup macadamia nuts

❧ Combine the flour, baking soda and salt in a medium bowl; stir to mix well. Cream the butter, sugar, brown sugar, vanilla extract, Tia Maria and Frangelica in a bowl until smooth, fluffy and well blended. Beat in the eggs. Add the flour mixture gradually, beating well after each addition. Stir in the chocolate chips, walnuts, pecans and macadamia nuts. Chill, covered, in the refrigerator for 12 hours.

❧ Preheat the oven to 325 degrees. Drop by teaspoonfuls onto ungreased cookie sheets. Bake for 10 to 13 minutes or until golden brown. Cool on the cookie sheets; remove to wire racks.

Yield: 48 servings

Aunt Nib's Cornflake Cookies

1 cup shortening
1 cup butter, softened
3 cups sifted confectioners'
  sugar

1 tablespoon vanilla extract
3 cups sifted flour
3 cups cornflakes
2 cups pecans

❧ Preheat the oven to 350 degrees. Cream the shortening, butter, confectioners' sugar and vanilla in a large bowl until fluffy, smooth and well blended. Add the flour a little at a time, mixing well after each addition. Stir in the cornflakes and pecans. Drop by tablespoonfuls onto ungreased cookie sheets. Bake for 15 minutes. Remove to wire racks to cool.

Yield: 84 servings

Cream Cheese Cookies

½ cup butter or margarine,
  softened
3 ounces cream cheese,
  softened
1 cup sugar

1 cup flour
½ cup chopped toasted
  pecans
1 teaspoon vanilla extract

❧ Preheat the oven to 350 degrees. Cream the butter and cream cheese in a large bowl until fluffy, smooth and well blended. Mix in the sugar and flour. Add the pecans and vanilla; mix well. Drop by teaspoonfuls onto ungreased cookie sheets. Bake for 10 to 12 minutes or until the edges of the cookies are barely brown. Remove to wire racks to cool.

Yield: 24 servings

Candied Cherry Florentines

2/3 cup sugar
1/2 cup butter
2 tablespoons honey
2 tablespoons milk
1 cup almonds, sliced
1/2 cup flour

2 tablespoons minced candied
  cherries
2 tablespoons minced candied
  orange peel
1/2 teaspoon vanilla extract
Easy Chocolate Glaze (at right)

❧ Grease twelve 5-inch disposable aluminum tart pans about 2½ hours before serving.

❧ Combine the sugar, butter, honey and milk in a 2-quart saucepan. Bring to a boil over medium heat, stirring frequently. Cook until a candy thermometer registers 232 degrees (soft ball stage) or until a small amount spins a 2-inch thread as it falls from the spoon, stirring constantly. Stir in the almonds, flour, candied cherries, candied orange peel and vanilla. Spoon 1 tablespoonful into each tart pan, keeping the mixture warm over very low heat.

❧ Preheat the oven to 350 degrees. Place the tart pans on 2 baking sheets. Bake for 10 minutes or until the centers of the cookies are golden brown and the edges are browned. Cool in pans on wire racks for 5 minutes or until firm. Loosen the cookies from the pans with a blunt knife; cool on the racks. Repeat until all the batter has been used.

❧ Spread a thin layer of the Easy Chocolate Glaze on the bottom of the cookies. Place glazed side up on wire racks to cool. Store, covered in a cool place for up to 3 days.

Yield: 18 servings

A Thyme to Remember

For *Easy Chocolate Glaze*, combine ¾ cup sugar, ¼ cup water, 2 tablespoons light corn syrup and 1 tablespoon butter in a saucepan; stir well. Bring to a boil over medium heat, stirring constantly. Boil for 2 minutes, stirring constantly. Remove from the heat; stir in ½ cup chocolate chips. Continue stirring until the chips are melted and the glaze is smooth. Keep warm over low heat.

Forgotten Cookies

2 egg whites
1/16 teaspoon salt
3/4 cup sugar
1 cup chocolate chips

1/2 teaspoon vanilla or almond
  extract
1 cup pecans (optional)

❧ Preheat the oven to 350 degrees. Beat the egg whites in a large bowl until foamy. Add the salt and beat until stiff peaks form. Add the sugar, chocolate chips, vanilla and pecans if desired. Drop by teaspoonfuls onto ungreased cookie sheets. Place in the oven. Turn off the heat and let stand in the oven for 12 hours.

Yield: 36 servings

Butter, butter, and

more butter. That's what

makes those cookies

good. (Cooking advice

from a 4-year-old.)

Mary Pat Smith

Fresh Ginger Cookies

2 1/4 cups flour
1 teaspoon baking soda
1/2 teaspoon salt
2 tablespoons grated
  gingerroot

3/4 cup butter, softened
1 cup sugar
1/4 cup molasses
1 egg
Sugar for rolling

❧ Combine the flour, baking soda and salt in a medium bowl; stir well. Cream the gingerroot, butter and 1 cup sugar until smooth, fluffy and well blended. Beat in the molasses and egg. Add the flour mixture; beat just until combined. Chill, covered, in the refrigerator for 1 hour.

❧ Preheat the oven to 350 degrees. Pinch off pieces of dough and shape into 1 1/2-inch balls; roll in sugar. Arrange 2 inches apart on ungreased cookie sheets. Bake for 15 minutes or until the edges start to brown. The centers will be slightly soft. Let stand on the cookie sheets for 1 minute; remove to wire racks to cool completely. Store in an airtight container.

Yield: 30 servings

Gumdrop Bar Cookies

2 cups flour
1/2 teaspoon salt
1 teaspoon cinnamon
2 tablespoons water
4 eggs
2 cups packed brown sugar

1 cup gumdrops, cut into
  small pieces
3/4 cup chopped walnuts
Orange Butter Frosting
  (below)

❧ Preheat the oven to 350 degrees; grease a 9x13-inch baking pan. Sift the flour, salt and cinnamon into a medium bowl; stir. Combine the water and eggs in a large bowl; beat until light and foamy. Add the brown sugar and beat until well blended. Add the flour mixture; mix well. Stir in the gumdrops and walnuts. Pour into the prepared baking pan.

❧ Bake for 25 minutes or until a cake tester inserted into the center comes out clean. Spread the Orange Butter Frosting over the cake. Let cool on a wire rack; cut into squares.

Yield: 24 servings

Orange Butter Frosting

1/4 cup butter, softened
2 cups confectioners' sugar
2 egg yolks

2 tablespoons orange juice
Grated peel of 1 orange

❧ Combine the butter, confectioners' sugar, egg yolks, orange juice and orange peel in a medium bowl; beat until smooth and fluffy.

I learned to cook from

books. My mother was

some help. I married during

World War II and we

had meager resources.

Rationing was in effect.

Jean Bremner

Holiday Mincemeat Cookies with Mocha Frosting

3 cups flour
1 teaspoon baking soda
1/2 teaspoon salt
1 cup shortening
1 1/2 cups sugar

3 eggs
1 1/3 cups mincemeat
Mocha Frosting (below)
72 pecan halves, toasted

❧ Preheat the oven to 375 degrees. Sift the flour, baking soda and salt into a medium bowl; stir.

❧ Cream the shortening and sugar in a large bowl until smooth, fluffy and well blended. Add the eggs and beat until smooth. Add the flour mixture; mix until combined. Stir in the mincemeat. Drop onto ungreased cookie sheets.

❧ Bake for 8 to 10 minutes. Let cool. Spread the Mocha Frosting over each cookie. Top each with 1 pecan half.

Yield: 72 servings

Mocha Frosting

1 pound confectioners' sugar
2 to 3 (or more) tablespoons
    cold coffee

1/2 cup melted butter

❧ Combine the confectioners' sugar, coffee and butter in a small bowl. Beat until smooth and fluffy, adding sugar or coffee as necessary for a spreadable consistency.

Our daughter was asked to be in a commercial where she had to eat s'mores around an open campfire. After several takes she had reached her limit and was turning green but still trying her best to look hungry and happy.

Barbara Hickey

Key Lime Squares

1 cup flour
¼ cup confectioners' sugar
½ cup margarine, softened
1 cup sugar
2 eggs, beaten

2 tablespoons flour
3 tablespoons Key lime juice
¼ teaspoon salt
Confectioners' sugar for
   dusting

❧ Preheat the oven to 350 degrees; grease and flour an 8-inch square baking pan. Combine 1 cup flour and ¼ cup confectioners' sugar in a medium bowl; cut in the margarine using a pastry blender until the mixture resembles coarse cornmeal. Spoon into the prepared baking pan and press over the bottom. Bake for 15 minutes.

❧ Combine the sugar and eggs in a medium bowl; stir to mix well. Stir in 2 tablespoons flour, Key lime juice and salt until well blended. Pour over the hot crust. Bake for 20 minutes. Remove to a wire rack and let cool. Dust with confectioners' sugar. Cut into 2-inch squares.

Yield: 16 servings

Texas Gold Bars

1 (2-layer) package yellow
   cake mix
1 egg, slightly beaten
½ cup margarine, melted
1 pound confectioners' sugar

8 ounces cream cheese,
   softened
2 eggs, slightly beaten
1 tablespoon vanilla extract

❧ Preheat the oven to 300 degrees. Combine the cake mix, 1 egg and the margarine in a large bowl; beat until well mixed. Press into an ungreased 9x13-inch baking pan.

❧ Combine the confectioners' sugar, cream cheese, 2 eggs and vanilla in a medium bowl; beat until thoroughly blended. Pour into the prepared pan. Bake for 55 to 60 minutes. Let cool in the pan on a wire rack for 12 hours before cutting into bars.

Yield: 36 servings

Apricot Sour Cream Pie

1 cup dried apricots, chopped
1 cup sour cream
1 cup sugar
1 tablespoon cornstarch
1 tablespoon melted butter

4 egg yolks, well beaten
1 teaspoon vanilla extract
1 (9-inch) unbaked pie shell
4 egg whites
1/4 cup sugar

❧ Preheat the oven to 400 degrees. Soak the apricots in warm water to cover in a medium bowl for 1 hour; drain.

❧ Combine the sour cream, 1 cup sugar, cornstarch, butter and egg yolks in a bowl; blend thoroughly. Stir in the apricots and vanilla. Pour into the pie shell. Bake for 10 minutes and reduce oven temperature to 325 degrees. Bake for 15 to 20 minutes longer or until the filling is set. Let cool on a wire rack.

❧ Increase oven temperature to 375 degrees. Beat the egg whites in a large bowl until foamy. Add 1/4 cup sugar gradually, beating until stiff peaks form. Spread over the cooled pie, sealing to the edge. Bake for 8 minutes.

Yield: 6 servings

The "Make-in-the-Pan" Pie Crust goes well with any one-crust pie, including the Prize-Winning Lemon Chess Pie, Rhubarb Pie, or Chocolate Bourbon Pie.

"Make-in-the-Pan" Pie Crust

1 1/2 cups flour
1 1/2 teaspoons sugar
1 teaspoon salt

1/2 cup vegetable oil
2 tablespoons milk

❧ Preheat the oven to 400 degrees. Combine the flour, sugar and salt in a 9-inch pie plate; stir with a fork to mix well. Blend the oil and milk in a measuring cup. Pour into the flour mixture and stir to mix well. Press over the bottom and up the side of the plate. Bake for 12 minutes or until set.

Yield: 6 servings

Three-Berry Pie

Egg Pie Pastry (below)
3/4 to 1 cup sugar
2 tablespoons cornstarch
1/2 teaspoon cinnamon
1/16 teaspoon salt
2 cups blueberries

1 cup raspberries
1 cup blackberries
1 tablespoon lemon juice
2 tablespoons butter, cut into
  small pieces

❧ Preheat the oven to 400 degrees. Line a 9-inch pie plate with half the Egg Pie Pastry. Chill, covered, in the refrigerator until ready to use. Combine 3/4 to 1 cup sugar, cornstarch, cinnamon and salt in a medium bowl. Place the blueberries, raspberries and blackberries in a large bowl. Add the lemon juice and toss gently. Add the sugar mixture; toss gently. Spoon into the prepared pie plate; dot with the butter.

❧ Arrange the remaining Egg Pie Pastry over the berries. Trim the excess dough, leaving a 1-inch overhang. Moisten the edges of the top and bottom pastry with water; turn the top pastry under the bottom. Crimp the edges with a fork. Cut several slits in the top with a sharp knife to allow steam to escape. Brush water lightly over the top. Sprinkle with additional sugar. Bake for 40 to 45 minutes. A lattice top pastry may be used instead of a full top pastry.

Yield: 6 servings

Egg Pie Pastry

1 egg, slightly beaten
1/4 cup plus 1 tablespoon
  cold water
1 teaspoon white vinegar

3 cups flour
1 teaspoon (or less) salt
1 1/4 cups shortening

❧ Beat the egg, water and vinegar in a medium bowl until well mixed. Combine the flour and salt in a large bowl; stir. Cut in the shortening using a pastry blender until the pieces are the size of peas. Add the egg mixture; stir with a fork until the mixture forms a ball. Divide the dough into halves. Roll out each portion on a floured work surface.

Bourbon Pie

½ (10-ounce) package
  marshmallows
1 (5-ounce) can evaporated
  milk

1 cup whipping cream
3 tablespoons bourbon
1 (8-inch) chocolate crumb
  pie shell

❧ Combine the marshmallows and evaporated milk in a saucepan. Cook over medium heat until the marshmallows are melted, stirring constantly. Let cool.

❧ Beat the whipping cream in a large bowl until soft peaks form. Add to the marshmallow mixture; fold in. Fold in the bourbon. Pour into the chocolate crumb pie shell. Chill, loosely covered, in the refrigerator for 3 to 4 hours before serving Store in the refrigerator.

Yield: 8 servings

Grandma's Buttermilk Pie

½ cup butter
1½ cups sugar
3 tablespoons flour
3 eggs, beaten

1 cup buttermilk
1 teaspoon vanilla extract
¹/16 teaspoon nutmeg
1 (9-inch) unbaked pie shell

❧ Preheat the oven to 350 degrees. Cream the butter and sugar in a large bowl until smooth, fluffy and well blended. Beat in the flour and eggs. Stir in the buttermilk, vanilla and nutmeg until blended. Pour into the pie shell. Bake for 45 to 50 minutes or until set.

Yield: 6 servings

Chocolate Bourbon Pie

1 1/4 cups sugar
1/4 cup plus 2 tablespoons
    baking cocoa
1/2 cup flour
1/2 teaspoon salt
4 egg yolks
1 1/2 cups milk

1/2 cup butter
1/2 cup bourbon
1 teaspoon vanilla extract
1 baked (9-inch) pie shell
4 egg whites
1/2 teaspoon cream of tartar
1/4 cup plus 2 tablespoons sugar

Mix 1 1/4 cups sugar, cocoa, flour, salt, egg yolks and milk in the top of a double boiler over simmering water. Cook for 20 minutes or until smooth and slightly thickened, stirring constantly. Stir in the butter, bourbon and vanilla. Cook until the mixture thickens to a pudding consistency. Pour into the pie shell.

Preheat the oven to 325 degrees. Beat the egg whites in a large bowl until foamy. Add the cream of tartar; beat until soft peaks form. Add the remaining 1/4 cup plus 2 tablespoons sugar gradually, beating until stiff peaks form. Spread over the hot pudding mixture, sealing to the edge. Swirl the top of the meringue attractively. Bake until golden brown. Chill in the refrigerator for an hour. May chill and top with cinnamon whipped cream instead of the meringue. For special occasions, serve with little chocolate cups of Bailey's Irish Cream.

Yield: 8 servings

I learned to make any kind

of pie by memory. One

summer, when I was 8 or 9

years old, I made a different

pie each day for my father.

Barenda Hino

Coffee Butterscotch Pie

1 teaspoon instant coffee
1/2 cup water
1 envelope unflavored gelatin
2 tablespoons cold water
2 eggs, separated
1 cup milk
1/4 teaspoon salt

2 cups packed dark brown
   sugar
2 tablespoons butter
3 tablespoons sugar
1 teaspoon vanilla extract
1 baked (9-inch) deep-dish
   pie shell

❧ Dissolve the instant coffee in 1/2 cup water in a cup or small bowl. Sprinkle the gelatin over the cold water to soften.

❧ Beat the egg yolks slightly in the top of a double boiler over hot water. Stir in the coffee, milk, salt and brown sugar. Cook until slightly thickened, stirring constantly; remove from the heat. Add the butter and softened gelatin; stir until the butter melts and the gelatin dissolves. Chill, covered, in the refrigerator until the mixture begins to thicken.

❧ Beat the egg whites in a large bowl until soft peaks form. Add the sugar gradually, beating until stiff peaks form. Fold into the gelatin mixture; fold in the vanilla. Spoon into the pie shell. Chill in the refrigerator for 3 hours or until firm. Serve with whipped cream.

Yield: 8 servings

Prize-Winning Lemon Chess Pie

1½ cups sugar
1 tablespoon cornmeal
1 tablespoon flour
4 eggs
¼ cup cream or milk

¼ cup melted butter
Grated peel and juice of
1 lemon
1 unbaked (9-inch) pie shell

❧ Preheat the oven to 350 degrees. Combine the sugar, cornmeal and flour in the large mixer bowl of an electric mixer; mix lightly at low speed. Add the eggs, cream, butter, lemon peel and lemon juice; beat briefly at low speed. Beat briefly at medium speed. Pour into the pie shell.

❧ Bake for 40 to 50 minutes or until a cake tester inserted into the center comes out clean. Garnish with Crystallized Violets (below). Crystallized violets may also be purchased in a specialty food store.

Yield: 8 servings

Crystallized Violets

Violets
1 egg white, at room
    temperature

Few drops of water
1 cup superfine sugar

❧ Rinse the petals and pat dry. Beat the egg white and water in a bowl until frothy. Using a small paint brush, coat each petal with the egg white mixture. Sprinkle the sugar evenly on both sides; mold the petals back to the original shape with a wooden pick. Place the petals on waxed paper. Let stand for 12 to 36 hours or until dry.

❧❧❧

My mother was a good cook but my father taught me to make my favorite dish— popcorn. Shake it in a pan with one tablespoon of oil over a medium high flame. Then add melted butter and salt.

Barbara Bradfield

❧❧❧

Best Pecan Pie

½ cup butter or margarine
1¼ cups sugar
½ cup light corn syrup
3 eggs, slightly beaten

1 teaspoon vanilla extract
1½ cups chopped pecans
1 baked (9-inch) pie shell

❧ Preheat the oven to 375 degrees. Combine the butter, sugar and corn syrup in a saucepan; stir to mix. Cook over low heat until the butter is melted, stirring often. Do not boil. Let cool slightly.

❧ Add the eggs, beating until well blended. Stir in the vanilla and pecans. Pour into the pie shell. Bake for 40 to 45 minutes or until the pie is set and the center is soft.

Yield: 8 servings

Rhubarb Pie

1 pound rhubarb, cut into
    small pieces
1 cup sugar
¼ cup flour
1 unbaked (9-inch) pie shell

¼ cup butter
1¼ cups sugar
¼ cup plus 1 tablespoon flour
2 egg yolks

❧ Preheat the oven to 425 degrees. Combine the rhubarb, 1 cup sugar and ¼ cup flour in a large bowl; mix well. Pour into the pie shell.

❧ Combine the butter, 1¼ cups sugar, remaining flour and egg yolks in a medium bowl; mix until crumbly. Spoon over the rhubarb and pat in place. Bake for 15 minutes. Reduce the oven temperature to 375 degrees. Bake for 30 to 40 minutes longer or until the filling is bubbly and the top is golden brown.

Yield: 8 servings

Better-than-Romance Chocolate Pie

Chocolate Pecan Crust (below)
1 square unsweetened
    chocolate
1/2 cup unsalted butter
3/4 cup packed brown sugar

1 1/2 to 2 teaspoons instant
    coffee
2 eggs
Coffee Whipped Cream (at right)

❧ Preheat the oven to 375 degrees. Press the Chocolate Pecan Crust into a 9-inch pie plate. Bake for 15 minutes.

❧ Melt the unsweetened chocolate in a double boiler over hot water. Cream the butter in a bowl until fluffy. Add the brown sugar and beat until smooth, fluffy and well blended. Beat in the melted chocolate, coffee and eggs until well blended. Pour into the Chocolate Pecan Crust. Chill, covered, in the refrigerator for 5 hours or longer. Spread the Coffee Whipped Cream over the filling shortly before serving. Garnish with grated unsweetened chocolate.

Yield: 8 servings

Chocolate Pecan Crust

1/2 (11-ounce) package pie
    crust mix
1 ounce unsweetened
    chocolate, grated

1/4 cup packed brown sugar
3/4 cup finely chopped pecans
1 teaspoon vanilla extract
1 tablespoon water

❧ Combine the pie crust mix, chocolate, brown sugar and pecans in a bowl; stir to mix. Drizzle in the vanilla and water, stirring constantly with a fork to a make a crumbly mixture.

For *Coffee Whipped Cream,* combine 2 cups whipping cream, 2 tablespoons instant coffee and 1/2 cup confectioners' sugar in a large bowl; beat just until soft peaks form.

Audrey's Rum Cream Pie

1 (9-ounce) package chocolate
   wafers
3/4 cup butter, melted
1 envelope unflavored gelatin
1/4 cup cold milk
3 eggs, separated

1/2 cup sugar
1 cup milk
1/8 teaspoon salt
1/4 cup dark rum
1 cup whipping cream

❧ Place the chocolate wafers in a food processor container;
process at medium speed until finely ground, pulsing as necessary.
Combine the chocolate crumbs and butter in a small bowl; mix
well. Pat into an 8x13-inch glass dish. Chill, covered, in the
refrigerator for 1 hour.

❧ Soften the gelatin in 1/4 cup cold milk in a small bowl. Place
the egg yolks in the top of a double boiler over hot water; beat
slightly. Beat in the sugar and 1 cup milk until blended. Cook for
10 minutes or until the mixture coats a spoon, stirring constantly.

❧ Remove from the heat. Add the gelatin mixture and the salt;
stir until the gelatin is dissolved. Add the rum gradually, stirring
constantly. Chill, covered, in the refrigerator until thickened.

❧ Beat the egg whites in a large bowl until stiff peaks form. Beat
the whipping cream in another large bowl until soft peaks form.
Add the egg whites to the gelatin mixture; fold in gently. Add
the whipped cream; fold in gently. Spoon into the chocolate crust.
Garnish with grated sweet chocolate or crushed chocolate cookies.
Chill in the refrigerator until just before serving.

Yield: 8 servings

A Handful of Heaven

DECADENT DESSERTS

"There was never
anything else for me but
medicine. My mother
had pictures of
stethoscopes I drew
when I was six years old
and in the first grade."
—*Robert Rehmet, M.D.,*
Anesthesiologist

Butterscotch Apples

6 large tart apples, peeled,
  sliced
1/2 cup packed brown sugar
1 1/2 teaspoons cinnamon
1/4 teaspoon nutmeg

2 tablespoons flour
1/4 cup orange juice
1/2 cup packed brown sugar
1/3 cup flour
1/4 cup margarine

❧ Preheat the oven to 375 degrees. Grease an 8- or 9-inch round baking dish. Arrange the apples in the dish.

❧ Combine 1/2 cup brown sugar, cinnamon, nutmeg and 2 tablespoons flour in a small bowl; stir. Sprinkle evenly over the apples. Pour the orange juice over the apples.

❧ Combine the remaining 1/2 cup brown sugar and 1/3 cup flour in a small bowl; stir. Cut in the margarine with a pastry blender until the mixture resembles coarse meal. Spread over the apples.

❧ Bake, covered, for 20 minutes; uncover. Bake until lightly browned and tender.

Yield: 4 servings

Almond Cheesecake

16 ounces cream cheese,
  softened
3 eggs
1/2 teaspoon almond extract

2/3 cup sugar
1 cup sour cream
1 teaspoon vanilla extract
3 tablespoons sugar

❧ Preheat the oven to 350 degrees. Grease a 9-inch pie plate. Combine the cream cheese, eggs, almond extract and 2/3 cup sugar in a food processor or blender container; process at medium speed until smooth and creamy. Pour into the prepared pie plate. Bake for 25 minutes. Let cool for 20 minutes.

❧ Beat the sour cream, vanilla and 3 tablespoons sugar in a medium bowl until blended and smooth. Pour over the cooled cream cheese mixture. Bake for 10 minutes.

Yield: 12 servings

Orange Bavarian

3 envelopes unflavored gelatin
1 cup cold water
1/2 cup boiling water
Juice of 1 lemon

3 1/2 cups orange juice
1 1/4 cups sugar
2 cups whipped cream

❧ Soften the gelatin in the cold water in a large bowl; stir in the boiling water. Stir in the lemon juice, orange juice and sugar, mixing well. Chill until the gelatin begins to set.

❧ Fold the whipped cream into the gelatin mixture. Chill, covered, in the refrigerator until set and ready to serve.

Yield: 10 servings

Coconut Cheesecake with Mango Sauce

1½ cups graham cracker
    crumbs
1½ cups sweetened shredded
    coconut
¼ cup sugar
1 cup melted unsalted butter
32 ounces cream cheese,
    softened

¾ cup sugar
3 eggs
1 egg yolk
1 (15-ounce) can Coco Lopez
1 cup whipping cream
1 cup shredded coconut
2 large mangoes, sliced

❧ Wrap foil 2¾ inches up the outside of a springform pan. Combine the graham cracker crumbs, 1½ cups coconut, ¼ cup sugar and butter in a medium bowl; mix thoroughly. Press over the bottom and up the side of the pan. Chill in the refrigerator while preparing the filling.

❧ Preheat the oven to 325 degrees. Beat the cream cheese and ¾ cup sugar in a large bowl until smooth and fluffy. Add the eggs and egg yolk, one at a time, beating well after each addition. Beat in the Coco Lopez, whipping cream and 1 cup coconut just until blended. Pour into the prepared pan. Bake for 1½ hours or until puffed and golden brown. Cool on a wire rack. Chill, covered, in the refrigerator.

❧ Place half the mango slices in a food processor or blender container; process at medium speed until puréed. Stir in the remaining mango slices. Spoon over each serving of cheesecake.

Yield: 12 servings

Rose Blossom Cheesecake

½ cup cold butter
1½ cups flour
1 egg
1 tablespoon cold water
24 ounces cream cheese,
    softened
½ cup butter, softened

¾ cup sugar
3 eggs
1 teaspoon nutmeg
1 teaspoon rose extract, or
    2 tablespoons rose water
½ cup currants

Rose water may be found

in specialty groceries.

❧ Preheat the oven to 400 degrees. Cut ½ cup butter into the flour in a bowl with a pastry blender until the mixture resembles coarse meal. Stir in the egg and cold water with a fork until the mixture forms a dough. Roll to fit a 10-inch quiche dish; place in the dish. Line the pastry with waxed paper and fill with rice or beans. Bake for 15 minutes. Let cool on a wire rack. Remove the rice and waxed paper.

❧ Reduce the oven temperature to 350 degrees. Beat the cream cheese and ½ cup butter in the large mixer bowl of an electric mixer at medium speed until smooth and fluffy. Add the sugar and eggs gradually, beating well after each addition. Stir in the nutmeg, rose extract and currants. Spoon into the pastry shell. Bake for 30 minutes. Turn off the oven; let the cheesecake stand in the oven for 15 minutes. Remove to a wire rack; let cool to room temperature. Chill, covered, in the refrigerator.

Yield: 14 servings

Dessert Cheese Ring

3 envelopes unflavored gelatin
1 cup cold water
1 cup orange juice
1 cup creamed cottage cheese
8 ounces Neufchâtel cheese,
    softened
3 ounces Roquefort cheese,
    softened
1 cup whipping cream,
    whipped
Orange or grapefruit sections
    or slices of other fruits

❧ Soften the gelatin in the water in the top of a double boiler. Cook over simmering water until the gelatin is dissolved, stirring constantly. Stir in the orange juice. Let cool.

❧ Beat the cottage cheese, Neufchâtel cheese and Roquefort cheese in the large mixer bowl of an electric mixer at medium speed until smooth. Add the gelatin mixture gradually, beating at low speed until the mixture is smooth and well blended.

❧ Set the bowl in ice water. Chill until the mixture is slightly thickened, stirring constantly. Fold in the whipped cream. Spoon into a lightly oiled 1½-quart ring mold. Chill for 3 hours or until firm.

❧ Dip the bottom of the mold briefly into hot water; invert onto a serving plate. Fill the center with orange or grapefruit sections or other assorted fruits.

Yield: 8 servings

For *Fast Chocolate Glaze*,

combine 2 ounces

unsweetened chocolate and

2 tablespoons butter in a

saucepan. Cook over low

heat until both are melted

and well blended, stirring

constantly. Add 1 cup

confectioners' sugar and

4 tablespoons whipping

cream, whisking briskly

until smooth.

Cream Puffs with Chocolate Glaze

1 cup water
½ cup butter
1 cup sifted flour
4 eggs

Vanilla Custard Filling
(below)
Fast Chocolate Glaze (at left)

❧ Preheat the oven to 350 degrees. Combine the water and butter in a saucepan over medium-high heat. Cook until the butter is melted and the liquid boiling, stirring constantly. Add the flour immediately; stir briskly to form a ball. Remove from the heat.

❧ Add the eggs one at a time, beating constantly with an electric mixer at medium speed. Drop the dough by spoonfuls onto an ungreased baking sheet. The mixture will make 10 puffs. Bake for 1 hour or until brown and crisp.

❧ Let cool on wire racks. Cut off the tops and scoop out the excess soft dough just before serving. Fill with the Vanilla Custard Filling and reposition the tops. Top with the Fast Chocolate Glaze.

Yield: 10 servings

Vanilla Custard Filling

1½ cups sugar
¾ cup flour
½ teaspoon salt

8 egg yolks, beaten slightly
4 cups milk
4 teaspoons vanilla extract

❧ Combine the sugar, flour salt, egg yolks and milk in the top of a double boiler; mix well. Cook over hot water until the mixture coats a spoon, stirring constantly. Let cool. Stir in the vanilla.

Heavenly Orange Cream Custard

2 cups milk
2 cups whipping cream
6 egg yolks
3 eggs

½ cup sugar
Grated peel of 1 orange
1½ teaspoons vanilla extract

❧ Preheat the oven to 325 degrees.

❧ Combine the milk and whipping cream in a saucepan, mixing well. Bring just to a boil over medium heat, stirring occasionally. Let cool.

❧ Beat the egg yolks, eggs and sugar in a large bowl until smooth and light in color. Stir the milk mixture into the eggs a little at a time. Stir in the orange peel and vanilla. Pour into 6 custard cups.

❧ Arrange the cups in a large baking pan. Pour boiling water into the pan to come ⅔ of the way up the sides of the cups. Cover the baking pan with foil.

❧ Bake for 40 to 50 minutes or until a knife inserted near the center comes out clean. Remove from the water bath and let cool.

Yield: 6 servings

Raspberry Clouds

16 ounces cream cheese,
  softened
1 cup confectioners' sugar
1/4 teaspoon vanilla extract

2 cups whipping cream
2 (16-ounce) cans raspberry
  pie filling

❧ Beat the cream cheese, confectioners' sugar and vanilla in the large bowl of an electric mixer at medium speed until light and fluffy. Add the whipping cream gradually, beating until well blended.

❧ Line a baking sheet with waxed paper. Spoon the mixture into 12 mounds, shaping them into 3-inch shells with the back of a spoon.

❧ Freeze for 2 to 12 hours. Fill each shell with the raspberry pie filling just before serving. Top with whipped cream if desired.

Yield: 12 servings

Chocolate Rum Pots de Crème

4 ounces semisweet chocolate   2 tablespoons dark rum
4 egg yolks   4 egg whites

❧ Melt the chocolate in the top of a double boiler over hot water. Stir in the egg yolks and rum. Remove from the heat.

❧ Beat the egg whites in a large bowl until stiff peaks form. Fold into the chocolate mixture.

❧ Pour into individual serving dishes. Chill, covered, in the refrigerator.

Yield: 4 servings

If all else fails,

serve chocolate.

Donna Beavers

Crème Brûlée

3 cups whipping cream
6 tablespoons sugar
6 egg yolks

2 teaspoons vanilla extract
½ cup packed light brown
   sugar

❧ Preheat the oven to 325 degrees. Pour the whipping cream into the top of a double boiler. Heat over boiling water. Add the sugar, stirring until dissolved.

❧ Beat the egg yolks in a medium bowl until light in color. Stir a small amount of the hot mixture into the egg yolks; stir the egg yolks into the hot mixture. Add the vanilla. Strain the mixture into a shallow baking dish.

❧ Place in a large pan and add hot (not boiling) water to come halfway up the sides of the baking dish.

❧ Bake for 1 hour or until a knife inserted near the center comes out clean. Remove from the water and let cool. Invert onto a serving plate.

❧ Place the brown sugar in a heavy saucepan. Cook over medium heat until the brown sugar melts and caramelizes (turns dark brown), stirring constantly. Pour over the custard. The custard may be made the day before serving. Chill it for 12 hours, loosely covered with waxed paper. Add the caramelized topping no more than 2 hours ahead.

Yield: 6 servings

Eclair Cake

2 (4-ounce) packages vanilla
   instant pudding mix
3 cups milk
3 cups frozen whipped
   topping

1 (16-ounce) package graham
   crackers
Chocolate Eclair Icing (below)

❧ Combine the pudding mix and milk in a large bowl; beat until well blended. Fold in the whipped topping. Layer the pudding mixture and whole graham crackers in a 9x13-inch dish, starting and ending with the crackers. (There should be 4 layers of crackers, 3 layers of pudding.) Spread the Chocolate Eclair Icing over the top. Chill, covered, in the refrigerator for 24 hours before serving. Cut into squares and serve.

Yield: 12 servings

Chocolate Eclair Icing

3 tablespoons margarine or
   butter
2 teaspoons light corn syrup
2 ounces unsweetened
   chocolate

3 tablespoons water
1 1/2 cups confectioners'
   sugar
1 teaspoon vanilla extract

❧ Combine the margarine, corn syrup, chocolate and water in a saucepan; mix to blend. Cook over medium-low heat until the margarine and chocolate have melted, stirring constantly. Remove from the heat and beat until smooth. Stir in the confectioners' sugar and vanilla.

The icing will be thin like a glaze but will set when refrigerated.

Coffee Flan

1 cup sugar
2 cups milk
½ vanilla bean
4 eggs
1 egg yolk
¼ cup coffee extract

1 cup whipping cream
1 cup sugar
1 teaspoon coffee beans or
    chocolate-covered coffee
    beans

❧ Preheat the oven to 350 degrees. Place 1 cup sugar in a heavy saucepan. Cook over medium heat until melted and golden brown (just beginning to caramelize), stirring constantly. Pour into 6 custard cups or individual molds.

❧ Combine the milk and vanilla bean in a saucepan. Bring to a boil, stirring frequently. Discard the vanilla bean. Combine the eggs, egg yolk, coffee extract, whipping cream and 1 cup sugar in a medium bowl, stirring to blend. Stir a small amount of the hot mixture into the egg mixture; stir the egg mixture into the hot mixture.

❧ Strain the mixture into the caramel-lined custard cups. Place in a large baking pan. Add lukewarm water to come ⅔ of the way up the sides of the cups. Bake for 35 minutes, adding more water as necessary to keep it from boiling. Remove from the water bath and let cool before serving.

❧ Unmold the custards by running a knife around the edges of the cups and inverting onto serving plates. Top with coffee beans. Garnish with fresh mint leaves.

Yield: 6 servings

Traditional Flan

3/4 cup sugar
4 egg whites
6 egg yolks
1 teaspoon vanilla extract
1 (12-ounce) can evaporated
  milk

3/4 cup milk
1 (14-ounce) can sweetened
  condensed milk

❧ Preheat the oven to 350 degrees. Place the sugar in a heavy saucepan. Cook over medium heat until the sugar caramelizes (turns dark brown), stirring constantly. Pour into a 9-inch round baking dish and swirl to cover the bottom. Let cool.

❧ Beat the egg whites with a fork in a large bowl until foamy. Add the egg yolks; stir well. Add the evaporated milk and milk; mix well. Stir in the vanilla and condensed milk. Strain through a sieve into the dish and cover with foil.

❧ Place the dish in a large pan and pour in water to a depth of 1/2 inch. Bake for 1 to 1 1/4 hours or until a knife inserted near the center comes out clean. Remove from the water bath. Chill in the refrigerator for 24 hours. Invert the flan onto a serving plate 1 to 2 hours before serving.

Yield: 8 servings

There is nothing

more beautiful than a

woman cooking a meal

for those she loves.

Barbara Bradfield

Luscious Low-Fat Flan

¼ cup sugar
1 (12-ounce) can evaporated
   skim milk
¼ cup skim milk
¾ cup egg substitute
¼ cup sugar

⅛ teaspoon salt
¼ cup frozen orange juice
   concentrate
½ teaspoon almond extract
½ teaspoon vanilla extract

For a coffee flan, replace

the orange juice concentrate

with ¼ cup coffee–flavored

liqueur. Decorate

with chocolate shavings

or coffee beans.

❧ Preheat the oven to 325 degrees. Place ¼ cup sugar in a heavy saucepan. Cook over medium heat until the sugar begins to caramelize (melt and turn golden brown), stirring constantly. Pour into six 6-ounce custard cups; let cool.

❧ Combine the evaporated skim milk and skim milk in a medium saucepan; mix well. Heat until bubbles form around the edge of the pan.

❧ Combine the egg substitute, ¼ cup sugar, salt, orange juice concentrate, almond extract and vanilla in a large bowl; stir well. Stir a small amount of the hot milk mixture gradually into the egg mixture; stir the egg mixture into the hot mixture. Pour into the custard cups.

❧ Place the cups in a large shallow pan and pour in water to a depth of 1 inch. Bake for 30 to 45 minutes or until a knife inserted near the center comes out clean. Remove the cups from the water bath.

❧ Chill, covered, in the refrigerator for 4 to 48 hours. Loosen the edge of the custard with a knife or spatula; invert onto plates. Garnish with mint leaves and fresh fruit.

Yield: 6 servings

Brown Sugar Ice Cream

6 egg yolks
1½ cups packed light brown
    sugar
1½ cups whipping cream

4½ cups half-and-half or
    light cream
2¼ teaspoons vanilla extract

❧ Cook the egg yolks and brown sugar in a heavy saucepan over low heat until thick and well blended, whisking constantly. Combine the whipping cream and half-and-half in another saucepan; stir to mix well. Bring just to a boil over medium-high heat.

❧ Stir a small amount of the hot cream mixture into the egg yolk mixture; stir the egg yolk mixture into the hot cream mixture. Cook over low heat for 6 minutes or until the mixture coats the back of a spoon, stirring constantly. Do not boil. Strain the mixture into a bowl. Stir in the vanilla. Let cool for 30 minutes or to room temperature, stirring occasionally.

❧ Chill, covered, in the refrigerator for 5 hours or until very cold. Pour into the bowl of an ice cream freezer and process according to the manufacturer's directions.

Yield: 16 servings

Coffee Ice Cream Dessert

24 chocolate sandwich
  cookies, crushed
1/3 cup margarine, softened
1 quart (or more) coffee ice
  cream, softened
3 ounces bitter chocolate
1 cup sugar

2 tablespoons margarine
2 (5-ounce) cans evaporated
  milk
2 cups whipping cream,
  whipped
1 cup chopped pecans

❧ Combine the crushed cookies and margarine in a medium bowl; stir to mix well.

❧ Press into a 9x13-inch freezer-proof dish. Freeze for 15 minutes. Spread the ice cream over the cookie crust. Freeze, covered, for 20 minutes.

❧ Combine the bitter chocolate, sugar, 2 tablespoons margarine and evaporated milk in a saucepan; stir well. Cook over medium heat until the chocolate is melted and the mixture is thickened, stirring constantly. Let cool. Spread over the ice cream. Freeze until firm.

❧ Spread the whipped cream over the chocolate mixture; sprinkle the pecans over the top. Freeze until ready to serve; remove from the freezer 15 minutes before serving. Cut into squares. May substitute 4 cups whipped topping for whipped cream.

Yield: 16 servings

Bittersweet Chocolate Sorbet

6 ounces bittersweet chocolate
1/2 cup sugar

1 1/2 cups water
Edible flowers

❧ Melt the chocolate in the top of a double boiler over hot water or in a microwave-safe dish in the microwave. Let cool.

❧ Combine the sugar and water in a small saucepan; stir to mix well. Cook over high heat until the mixture is clear, stirring occasionally. Let cool. Pour the chocolate and the sugar mixture into a bowl; mix well. Chill, covered, in the refrigerator for 1 to 2 hours.

❧ Pour into the container of an ice cream freezer and process according to the manufacturer's directions. Remove to a plastic container. Cover and freeze. Let soften slightly before serving. Garnish each serving with an edible flower.

Yield: 4 servings

Luscious Lavender Flower Ice Cream

1 cup sugar
4 cups half-and-half
4 cups whipping cream

2 teaspoons vanilla extract
1/4 teaspoon salt
1/4 cup fresh lavender flowers

❧ Combine the sugar, half-and-half, whipping cream, vanilla, salt and lavender flowers in a bowl; stir to mix well.

❧ Pour into the container of an ice cream freezer and process according to the manufacturer's directions. Remove to a plastic container. Cover and freeze. Let soften slightly before serving.

Yield: 16 servings

A Thyme to Remember

This is an intense, sweet dessert of pure chocolate; however, it is light enough to serve on a hot summer evening.

Lavender leaves and flowers can be used in vinegars, jellies, salads, ice creams and custards. English lavender is the hardiest of the species.

I never learned to cook from anyone. I was very clumsy in the kitchen. But when I was 22 and married, I realized that I would be hungry if I didn't learn to cook.

Linda Eichenwald

Lemon Cream Sherbet

2 cups sugar
1 cup fresh lemon juice

6 cups milk
1 cup whipping cream

❧ Combine the sugar and lemon juice in a bowl; mix well. Add the milk and whipping cream, stirring to blend well.

❧ Pour into the container of an ice cream freezer and process according to the manufacturer's directions. Remove to a plastic container. Cover and freeze. Let soften slightly before serving.

Yield: 16 servings

Cookies and Cream Cake

16 ounces chocolate sandwich
   cookies, crushed
1/3 cup melted margarine
1/2 gallon vanilla ice cream,
   softened

1 (12-ounce) jar fudge sauce
12 ounces frozen whipped
   topping

❧ Combine the crushed chocolate cookies and margarine in a medium bowl; mix well. Reserve 1½ cups of the mixture. Press the remaining mixture into a 9x13-inch freezer-proof dish.

❧ Spread the ice cream over the cookie crust. Top with the fudge sauce, whipped topping and reserved cookie crumb mixture. Freeze for several hours before serving.

Yield: 16 servings

Tortoni

2 cups crushed vanilla wafers
3 tablespoons (or more) melted
  butter
1 tablespoon almond extract
½ gallon vanilla ice cream,
  softened

2 (10-ounce) jars apricot
  preserves
½ cup toasted almond slices

❧ Butter a 9x13-inch freezer-proof dish. Combine the crushed vanilla wafers, butter and almond extract in a medium bowl; mix well. Reserve ½ cup of the mixture. Press the remaining mixture onto the bottom of the baking pan.

❧ Spread half the ice cream over the cookie crust. Spread with the preserves and sprinkle with half the almonds. Top with the remaining ice cream. Sprinkle remaining crumbs and almonds over the top. Freeze until firm.

Yield: 16 servings

Watermelon Granita

4 cups watermelon juice
2 tablespoons lemon juice

½ cup sugar
Mint leaves or edible flowers

❧ Combine the watermelon juice, lemon juice and sugar in a bowl; stir until the sugar dissolves.

❧ Pour into the container of an ice cream freezer and process according to the manufacturer's directions. Remove to a plastic container. Cover and freeze. Let soften slightly before serving. Serve in chilled glasses. Garnish with fresh mint leaves or edible flowers.

Yield: 8 servings

Daisies, hollyhocks and pansies are some of the edible flowers that can be used as garnishes. Float the blossoms in cold drinks or use to decorate summer ices like *Watermelon Granita* or *Lemon Cream Sherbet.* Blossoms are best if picked when they first open.

Vienna Bread Pudding

1 (1-pound) loaf Vienna
   bread, cut into 1¹/₂-inch
   cubes
6 eggs
1¹/₂ cups sugar

4 cups milk
1 cup light cream
2 teaspoons vanilla extract
¹/₃ cup golden raisins
Caramel Sauce (below)

❧   Spread the bread cubes on a baking sheet. Let dry for 12 hours. Preheat the oven to 325 degrees. Butter a 9x13-inch baking pan. Beat the eggs in a large bowl. Blend in the sugar. Add the milk, cream and vanilla gradually, beating until well blended. Combine the bread cubes and raisins in a large bowl; toss to mix. Pour in the milk mixture; stir to mix well. Pour into the baking pan.

❧   Bake for 60 to 70 minutes or until a knife inserted near the center comes out clean. Cover lightly with foil if the bread begins to brown excessively. Serve warm or chilled in Champagne glasses. Top with warm Caramel Sauce.

Yield: 12 servings

Caramel Sauce

¹/₂ cup butter
¹/₂ cup packed brown sugar
¹/₂ cup sugar

¹/₂ cup whipping cream
1 teaspoon vanilla extract

❧   Combine the butter, brown sugar, sugar and whipping cream in a heavy medium saucepan. Bring to a boil over medium heat, stirring frequently. Boil for 1 minute, stirring constantly. Cool slightly. Stir in the vanilla. The sauce can be stored, covered, in the refrigerator for up to 5 days. Warm before serving.

My *Vienna Bread Pudding*

convinced my

husband to marry me.

Susan Bruck

White Chocolate Bread Pudding

6 cups whipping cream
2 cups milk
1 cup sugar
20 ounces white chocolate,
    broken into pieces
4 eggs
15 egg yolks

1 large (24-inch) loaf dry
    French bread, sliced
1 cup whipping cream
16 ounces white chocolate,
    broken into pieces
2 ounces dark bittersweet
    chocolate, grated

❧ Preheat the oven to 350 degrees. Combine 6 cups whipping cream, milk and sugar in a large saucepan; mix well. Cook over medium heat until hot, stirring constantly. Remove from the heat and add 20 ounces white chocolate. Stir until melted.

❧ Combine the eggs and egg yolks in a large bowl. Stir a small amount of the hot cream mixture into the eggs; stir the eggs into the hot mixture. Arrange the bread slices in a 9x13-inch baking pan. Pour in half the egg mixture, pushing the bread down so it absorbs the liquid. Pour in the remaining egg mixture. Bake, covered with foil, for 1 hour; uncover. Bake for 30 minutes or until set and golden brown.

❧ Bring 1 cup whipping cream to a boil in a saucepan. Remove from the heat. Add 16 ounces white chocolate; stir until smooth. Spoon over each serving of bread pudding. Top with the grated bittersweet chocolate.

Yield: 16 servings

This recipe is decadent and

simply delicious—great for

special occasions.

Butterscotch Sauce

1¼ cups packed brown
    sugar
2/3 cup light corn syrup
¼ cup butter

1 (5-ounce) can evaporated
    milk
1 teaspoon vanilla extract

❧ Combine the brown sugar, corn syrup and butter in a saucepan; mix well. Cook over medium heat for 1 minute or until thick, stirring constantly. Let cool. Add the evaporated milk and vanilla; stir until well blended. Stir in chopped pecans if desired.

Yield: 6 servings

Chocolate Fudge Sauce

1 cup semisweet chocolate
    chips
2/3 cup light corn syrup

1 (5-ounce) can evaporated
    milk

This is a very thick,

rich sauce.

❧ Combine the chocolate chips and corn syrup in a saucepan. Cook over low heat until the chocolate melts, stirring constantly. Remove from the heat; let cool. Add the evaporated milk gradually, stirring constantly.

Yield: 32 servings

Cinnamon–Amaretto White Chocolate Sauce

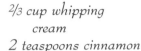

2/3 cup whipping
  cream
2 teaspoons cinnamon

6 ounces white chocolate,
  chopped
2 tablespoons amaretto

❧ Combine the whipping cream and cinnamon in a small saucepan, stirring to mix well. Bring to a boil. Remove from the heat and cover. Let stand for 15 minutes.

❧ Place the white chocolate in a medium bowl. Return the whipping cream to a boil. Pour through a strainer into the chocolate. Let stand for 2 minutes; stir until smooth. Stir in the amaretto. Serve at room temperature or slightly warm.

Yield: 8 servings

This sauce makes a delicious

topping for ice cream or cake.

Or it can be used as a

fondue: Simply warm the

sauce, then dip in the

chunks of fruit or angel food

cake. To store, keep covered

in the refrigerator.

Lemon Dessert Sauce

1/2 cup sugar
1 tablespoon cornstarch
1 cup water
3 tablespoons butter or
   margarine

1/2 teaspoon grated lemon
   peel
1 1/2 tablespoons lemon
   juice

❧ Combine the sugar, cornstarch and water in a saucepan; stir to mix well. Cook over low heat for 5 minutes or until thickened, stirring constantly.

❧ Remove from the heat; stir in the butter, lemon peel and lemon juice. Let cool for 2 minutes before using, stirring once.

❧ Serve over warm gingerbread or use to fill cream puffs.

❧ The sauce can be made ahead and stored, covered, in the refrigerator. Reheat on Low in the microwave or on the stovetop over low heat.

Yield: 4 servings

Serious Chocolate Freezer Soufflés

1/2 cup flour	2 tablespoons butter
3/4 cup baking cocoa	1 teaspoon vanilla extract
3/4 cup sugar	8 egg whites, at room
1/4 teaspoon salt	temperature
2 cups milk	1/4 teaspoon cream of tartar
6 egg yolks, beaten	1/4 cup sugar

❧ Butter individual ramekins or a 2-quart soufflé dish with a 2-inch foil collar attached. Dust with sugar.

❧ Whisk the flour, cocoa, 3/4 cup sugar and salt in a medium saucepan until combined. Add the milk gradually, whisking until well blended. Cook over medium heat just until boiling, stirring constantly. Remove from the heat.

❧ Stir a small amount of the hot cocoa mixture into the egg yolks; stir the egg yolks into the hot mixture. Stir in the butter and vanilla. Let cool.

❧ Beat the egg whites in a large bowl until soft peaks form. Add the cream of tartar and 1/4 cup sugar, beating until stiff peaks form. Fold into the cocoa mixture. Spoon into the ramekins, smoothing gently with the back of spoon. Freeze until firm.

❧ Remove the soufflés from the freezer 30 to 40 minutes before baking. Preheat the oven to 350 degrees. Bake the ramekins for 25 minutes (bake the 2-quart soufflé for 1 1/2 hours). Serve with a hot chocolate sauce.

Yield: 6 servings

Chocolate Torte Royale

2 egg whites
1/4 teaspoon salt
1/2 teaspoon vinegar
1/2 cup sugar
1/4 teaspoon cinnamon
1 cup semisweet chocolate
  chips

2 egg yolks, beaten
1/4 cup water
1 cup whipping cream
1/4 cup sugar
1/4 teaspoon cinnamon
Whipped cream
Pecan halves

❧ Preheat the oven to 275 degrees. Cover a baking sheet with parchment paper; draw an 8-inch circle in the center.

❧ Beat the egg whites, salt and vinegar in a large bowl until soft peaks form. Combine 1/2 cup sugar and 1/4 teaspoon cinnamon in a small bowl. Add gradually to the egg whites, beating until very stiff peaks form and all the sugar is dissolved.

❧ Spread over the circle on the baking sheet, making the center 1/2 inch thick and mounding the edge to 1 3/4 inches high. Form decorative ridges on the outer edge with the back of a teaspoon.

❧ Bake for 1 hour; turn off the oven. Let dry in the oven with the door closed for 2 hours. Peel off the paper.

❧ Melt the chocolate chips in the top of a double boiler over hot water. Cool slightly. Spread 2 tablespoonfuls of the chocolate in the meringue shell.

❧ Add the egg yolks and water to the remaining chocolate; stir to blend well. Chill, covered, in the refrigerator until the mixture is thick.

❧ Combine the whipping cream, 1/4 cup sugar and 1/4 teaspoon cinnamon in a large bowl. Beat until stiff peaks form. Spread half over the chocolate in the meringue shell. Fold the remainder into the egg mixture; spread over the chocolate in the shell. Chill in the refrigerator for 3 to 12 hours. Top with whipped cream and pecans.

Yield: 8 servings

Kahlúa Brownie Torte with Kahlúa Frosting

1 (24-ounce) package
   brownie mix
Kahlúa
½ cup chopped walnuts or
   pecans

Kahlúa Frosting (below)
Chocolate shavings or
   chocolate-covered coffee
   beans

❧ Grease two 8-inch round cake pans. Prepare the brownie mix according to the package directions for cake-type brownies, substituting Kahlúa and water in equal portions for the liquid required. Stir in the walnuts. Pour into the cake pans.

❧ Bake and cool according to the package directions. Spread the Kahlúa Frosting between the layers and over the side and top. Chill in the refrigerator for several hours before serving. Garnish with chocolate shavings or chocolate-covered coffee beans.

Yield: 12 servings

Kahlúa Frosting

2 cups whipping cream
½ cup packed brown
   sugar

2 tablespoons instant coffee
   powder
2 teaspoons Kahlúa

❧ Beat the whipping cream in a large bowl until soft peaks form. Add the brown sugar, coffee powder and Kahlúa, beating until stiff peaks form.

Godiva Chocolate Two-Minute Mousse

2 eggs
2 tablespoons Godiva
    Chocolate Liqueur
2 teaspoons instant espresso

1 cup semisweet chocolate
    chips
¾ cup hot milk
Whipped cream

❧ Combine the eggs, liqueur, espresso powder and chocolate in a blender container. Pour in the hot milk gradually, processing constantly at high speed for 1 to 2 minutes or until smooth. Pour into 4 small bowls or stemmed dessert dishes. Chill, covered, for 1 hour or longer. Serve topped with dollops of whipped cream.

Yield: 4 servings

Turtle Trifle

The recipe may be varied

by adding rum or a liqueur

and by topping with

different candy.

1 (22½-ounce) package
    brownie mix with
    chocolate syrup
1 cup coarsely chopped
    pecans, toasted
3 (4-ounce) packages
    butter pecan instant
    pudding mix

6 cups milk
1½ cups caramel topping
16 ounces frozen whipped
    topping, thawed
2 chocolate candy bars,
    chopped
½ cup coarsely chopped
    pecans, toasted

❧ Prepare and bake the brownies according to the package directions, adding 1 cup pecans. Cool and crumble. Whisk the pudding mix and milk in a large bowl until smooth and creamy. Chill, covered, until thickened. Microwave the caramel topping on Medium until thinned to pouring consistency, stirring every 30 seconds. Layer the brownies, pudding, caramel topping and whipped topping ⅓ at a time in a large serving bowl. Top with the chopped candy bars and ½ cup pecans.

Yield: 24 servings

Fan-Tan Fudge

2 cups sugar
1/2 cup butter
1 cup milk
1 (7-ounce) jar marshmallow
   creme

1 (12-ounce) jar chunky
   peanut butter
1 teaspoon vanilla extract

❧ Butter an 8- or 9-inch square heat-proof dish. Combine the sugar, butter and milk in a saucepan; stir to mix. Cook over low heat until the sugar dissolves, stirring constantly. Bring to a full boil over medium-high heat, stirring constantly. Cook for 15 minutes, stirring constantly. Remove from the heat. Add the marshmallow creme, peanut butter and vanilla, stirring until well mixed. Pour the mixture into the dish. Let cool; cut into squares. Store, covered, in the refrigerator.

Yield: 64 servings

The Brigittine Monk's Fudge

4 1/2 cups sugar
1 (12-ounce) can evaporated
   milk
9 ounces semisweet chocolate
9 ounces bittersweet chocolate

1 (7-ounce) jar marshmallow
   creme
1 cup butter
1 teaspoon vanilla extract
2 cups chopped walnuts

❧ Butter a 9x13-inch heat-proof dish. Combine the sugar and evaporated milk in a saucepan; stir to mix. Bring to a boil over medium heat, stirring constantly. Cook for 6 minutes over medium heat, stirring constantly. Remove from the heat.

❧ Stir in the semisweet chocolate, bittersweet chocolate, marshmallow creme, butter, vanilla and walnuts. Beat until well mixed and thickened. Spoon into the dish, smoothing with the back of the spoon. Let cool to room temperature. Chill, covered, in the refrigerator for 12 hours. Cut into squares.

Yield: 60 servings

❧ ❧ ❧

My dad remembers this

original recipe from his

youth. That version used

cornstarch instead of

confectioners' sugar since it

dates from World War II

and the sugar shortage.

When Daddy served in the

War, Grandma made candy

CARE packages for him and

this was a staple of every

Christmas package.

Sarah Hardin

❧ ❧ ❧

Peanut Butter Roll

2 cups sugar
2/3 cup light corn syrup
1/4 teaspoon salt
1/2 cup boiling water
2 egg whites

1 teaspoon vanilla extract
1 (1-pound) package
   confectioners' sugar
1 cup (or more) peanut butter

❧ Combine the sugar, corn syrup, salt and boiling water in a large heavy saucepan. Cook until the sugar is completely dissolved, stirring constantly. Cook until the candy spins a thread, 230 to 234 degrees on a candy thermometer. Set aside to cool slightly.

❧ Beat the egg whites in a large mixer bowl until stiff peaks form. Add the hot syrup to the stiffly beaten egg whites gradually, beating constantly. Beat in the vanilla and continue beating until the mixture is thickened and stiff. Do not overbeat or the mixture will crystallize.

❧ Sprinkle the confectioners' sugar evenly on a work surface. Pour the candy onto the confectioners' sugar. Roll into a thin even layer. Spread with peanut butter. Roll as for a jelly roll. Cut the roll into slices of the desired thickness.

Yield: 24 servings

Buttermilk Pralines

2½ cups sugar
1 teaspoon baking soda
1 cup buttermilk

¼ teaspoon salt
3 tablespoons margarine
2½ cups pecan halves

❧ Grease foil-lined baking sheets. Combine the sugar, baking soda, buttermilk and salt in a large heavy saucepan; stir to mix. Cook over high heat for 5 minutes, stirring constantly. Stir in the margarine and pecans. Cook for 5 minutes or until a soft ball forms when a small amount of the mixture is dropped in cold water (232 degrees on candy thermometer), stirring constantly.

❧ Remove from the heat and let cool for 2 minutes. Stir until the mixture loses its gloss and is creamy. Drop by tablespoonfuls onto the prepared baking sheets.

Yield: 24 servings

Pretty Party Mints

3 ounces cream cheese, softened
3½ cups (or more) sifted confectioners' sugar

2 or 3 drops of oil of peppermint
Food coloring as desired

❧ Combine the cream cheese and confectioners' sugar in a bowl and beat until the consistency of pastry dough. Add the oil of peppermint and food coloring; knead until well blended. Shape by ¼ teaspoonfuls into small balls. Press into candy molds dusted with additional confectioners' sugar. Unmold onto waxed paper. Let stand until firm and dry. Store in an airtight container. Mints may be frozen for later use.

❧ For chocolate mints, omit the food coloring and oil of peppermint if desired and add 1 tablespoon baking cocoa mixed with ½ teaspoon vanilla extract before shaping.

Yield: 84 servings

Children's Favorite Lollipops

2 cups sugar
2/3 cup light corn syrup
1 cup water

1/2 teaspoon oil of peppermint
Food coloring as desired
Wooden candy sticks

❧ Combine the sugar, corn syrup and water in a large heavy saucepan. Cook until the sugar is completely dissolved, stirring constantly. Cook to 290 degrees on a candy thermometer; do not stir but wipe the side of the pan with a wet cloth to remove any sugar crystals. Reduce the heat so that there will be no discoloration of the syrup. Cook to 310 degrees on the candy thermometer. Remove from the heat.

❧ Add the oil of peppermint and food coloring and stir just enough to blend. Spoon enough hot syrup onto a greased pan to make the size lollipop desired. Insert the stick into the hot syrup. Repeat with the remaining syrup and sticks. Let stand until cooled completely before removing from the pan.

Yield: 32 servings

Orange Pineapple Marmalade

2 oranges, quartered, seeded
1 (15-ounce) can crushed
  pineapple, drained

4 cups sugar
2 tablespoons lemon juice

❧ Place the oranges in a food processor container; process until ground. Combine the crushed pineapple, sugar, lemon juice and oranges in a deep microwave-safe 2½-quart dish; stir to mix well. Microwave on High for 10 minutes or until the mixture boils, stirring after 6 minutes. Microwave for 3 minutes longer.

Yield: 32 servings

The Final Touch

NUTRITIONAL CHARTS AND INDEX

"During my surgery
residency, I noticed that many
surgeons were not very
sensitive to the needs of
women with breast cancer.
I knew that I could do a
better job and decided to
focus on this primarily
female health problem."

—*Alison L. Laidley, M.D.,*

Breast Surgeon

Nutritional Profiles

The editors have attempted to present these family recipes in a format that allows approximate nutritional values to be computed. Persons with dietary or health problems or whose diets require close monitoring should not rely solely on the nutritional information provided. They should consult their physicians or a registered dietitian for specific information.

Nutritional information for these recipes is computed from information derived from many sources, including materials supplied by the United States Department of Agriculture, computer databanks, and journals in which the information is assumed to be in the public domain. However, many specialty items, new products, and processed foods may not be available from these sources or may vary from the average values used in these profiles. More information on new and/or specific products may be obtained by reading the nutrient labels. Unless otherwise specified, the nutritional profile of these recipes is based on all measurements being level.

- Artificial sweeteners vary in use and strength so should be used "to taste," using the recipe ingredients as a guideline. Sweeteners using aspartame (NutraSweet and Equal) should not be used as a sweetener in recipes involving prolonged heating, which reduces the sweet taste. For further information on the use of these sweeteners, refer to the package.
- Alcoholic ingredients have been analyzed for the basic information. Cooking causes the evaporation of alcohol, which decreases alcoholic and caloric content.
- Buttermilk, sour cream, and yogurt are the types available commercially.
- Cake mixes which are prepared using package directions include 3 eggs and ½ cup oil.
- Chicken, cooked for boning and chopping, has been roasted; this method yields the lowest caloric values.
- Cottage cheese is cream-style with 4.2% creaming mixture. Dry curd cottage cheese has no creaming mixture.
- Eggs are all large. To avoid raw eggs that may carry salmonella, as in eggnog or 6-week muffin batter, use an equivalent amount of commercial egg substitute.
- Flour is unsifted all-purpose flour.
- Garnishes, serving suggestions, and other optional information and variations are not included in the profile.
- Margarine and butter are regular, not whipped or presoftened.
- Milk is whole milk, 3.5% butterfat. Low-fat milk is 1% butterfat. Evaporated milk is whole milk with 60% of the water removed.
- Oil is any type of vegetable cooking oil. Shortening is hydrogenated vegetable shortening.
- Salt and other ingredients to taste as noted in the ingredients have not been included in the nutritional profile.
- If a choice of ingredients has been given, the profile reflects the first option. If a choice of amounts has been given, the profile reflects the greater amount.

Abbreviations

Cal — Calories

Prot — Protein

Carbo — Carbohydrates

T Fat — Total Fat

Chol — Cholesterol

Fiber — Dietary Fiber

Sod — Sodium

g — grams

mg — milligrams

Pg #	Recipe Title (Approx Per Serving)	Cal	Prot (g)	Carbo (g)	T Fat (g)	% Cal from Fat	Chol (mg)	Fiber (g)	Sod (mg)
13	Asparagus Sandwiches	46	1	5	2	42	5	1	130
13	Antipasto	363	15	26	24	57	13	4	2075
14	Spinach and Feta Phyllo Triangles	167	4	7	15	75	29	1	243
15	Onion Puffs	276	9	15	20	66	49	1	489
15	Parmesan Chips	40	1	2	3	70	9	<1	83
16	Shrimp Rémoulade	613	17	14	56	80	135	4	837
17	Mexican Swirls	180	5	13	12	61	29	1	244
17	Mexican Egg Rolls	305	19	28	13	38	53	3	592
18	Tomato Basil Santa Fe Pizza	581	31	31	40	59	86	3	966
18	Party Meatballs with Sweet-Sour Sauce	142	10	13	6	37	45	<1	485
19	Corn and Crab Fritters	246	16	21	11	41	107	2	739
20	Crabmeat Cheesecake with Pecan Crust*	435	10	19	37	154	146	1	616
21	Salmon Mousse	142	9	1	12	72	47	<1	278
22	Shrimp Cocktail Mold	59	5	9	<1	4	34	<1	471
22	Syrian Grand Fromage	346	7	5	34	87	20	1	393
23	Smoked Catfish Pâté	118	6	1	10	73	38	<1	268
23	Last of the Red Hot Hams	210	11	8	15	64	40	1	559
24	Roquefort Timbales	463	14	16	38	74	271	1	644
25	Bleu Cheese and Spiced Walnut Terrine	286	11	6	24	75	48	1	704
26	Bleu Cheese Mousse on Endive/Apple and Walnuts	39	2	1	3	77	8	<1	90
26	Pecan Cheddar Cheese Torte	344	10	21	26	65	38	2	236
27	Mushroom Strudels	94	1	5	8	72	18	1	141
28	Cheddar Cream Cheese Chutney	270	9	18	19	61	41	2	259
28	Mexican Cheese Ball	214	9	1	19	81	61	<1	284
29	Hill Country Cheese Pecan Spread	149	4	3	14	83	33	1	276
29	Pecan Spread with Chipped Beef	138	4	2	13	82	30	<1	446
30	Spicy Peanut Dip	116	2	7	9	69	0	1	367
30	Ancho Chile Salsa	340	8	11	27	76	22	2	437
31	Authentic Mexican Green Sauce	32	1	6	1	22	0	2	68
31	Tuscan Tomato Bruschetta	160	5	31	2	10	0	2	311
32	Hot Onion Dip	176	6	2	16	82	41	<1	266
32	Easy and Elegant Shrimp Dip	76	5	1	6	68	51	<1	129
33	Almond Tea	73	<1	18	0	0	0	<1	2
33	Kentucky Mint Tea	66	<1	17	<1	0	0	<1	2
34	Honey Mint Lemonade	78	<1	22	0	0	0	<1	1
34	Fiesta Sangria	105	1	9	<1	2	0	2	8
35	James' Champagne Party Punch	83	<1	5	0	0	0	0	6
35	Hot Cranberry Punch	91	<1	23	<1	1	0	<1	4
36	Vintage Grapefruit Punch	51	<1	13	<1	1	0	<1	5
36	Frozen Cappuccinos	114	1	21	3	27	11	0	15

Pg #	Recipe Title (Approx Per Serving)	Cal	Prot (g)	Carbo (g)	T Fat (g)	% Cal from Fat	Chol (mg)	Fiber (g)	Sod (mg)
39	Asparagus with Sweet and Savory Dressing	151	5	12	11	60	0	3	985
40	Tomato and Grilled Eggplant	471	9	24	40	74	5	10	229
40	Marinated Dill Carrots	108	<1	26	<1	<1	0	3	441
41	Walnut Sauce for Green Beans	200	1	2	21	95	9	<1	167
41	Broccoli with Bacon and Parmesan	460	12	33	32	61	41	2	639
42	Fusilli Salad with Sun-Dried Tomatoes and Peas	433	15	79	7	14	0	7	794
43	Asian Noodle Salad/Ginger Sesame Vinaigrette	472	14	50	26	48	0	9	667
44	Bow Ties with Tomatoes	414	11	53	17	39	0	3	500
44	Vermicelli Chicken Salad	458	21	36	26	51	37	4	402
45	Rosemary Chicken Fettucini Salad	582	43	43	26	41	76	3	470
46	Chicken and Roast Corn Salad	777	44	62	41	47	105	14	278
48	Asian Chicken Salad	665	45	35	39	52	97	8	864
48	Dried Cherry Chicken Salad	740	38	31	54	64	131	4	356
49	Cilantro Chicken Salad	386	46	17	15	35	110	5	1074
49	Chicken and Artichoke Rice Salad	1058	58	26	80	68	200	7	1857
50	Paella Salad	288	20	24	12	39	85	2	756
50	Wild Rice Salad	499	20	46	28	49	42	6	269
51	West Indies Crabmeat Salad	409	22	3	34	76	106	1	614
51	Exotic Curried Shrimp Salad	434	32	4	31	66	322	2	693
52	Bouillabaisse Salad with Caviar Dressing	379	17	6	32	76	187	1	559
52	Crunchy Pea Salad	223	7	11	18	69	5	4	257
53	Ham and Pea Salad with Dill Mustard Dressing	219	13	12	14	55	33	4	409
53	Botswana Bean and Banana Salad	205	8	42	5	18	0	8	555
54	Spanish Salad with Avocado Dressing	454	8	18	42	79	15	8	345
54	White Corn Salad	150	3	24	5	28	3	2	335
55	Spicy Black Bean and Corn Salad	396	7	36	26	57	0	8	1401
56	Corn Bread Salad with Lime Juice and Cilantro	324	6	37	18	48	49	4	794
57	Cranberry Cashew Green Salad	1037	12	34	96	82	21	4	721
58	Asian Water Chestnut and Cashew Salad	542	8	56	35	55	0	8	555
58	Atomic Salad	140	2	2	14	89	1	1	194
59	Molded Spinach Salad	227	5	10	19	74	19	1	287
60	Warm Spinach Toss	134	5	11	9	57	1	3	280
61	Wheat Berry Salad with Spinach	485	15	89	12	21	0	5	788
62	Apple and Walnut Salad with Feta	596	5	23	56	82	24	3	291
63	Raspberry Applesauce Salad	144	2	36	<1	1	0	2	50
63	Mango Salad	425	7	55	22	44	57	1	227
64	Orange Mandarin Salad	213	3	38	6	25	22	<1	180
64	New Wave Waldorf Salad	294	2	24	22	65	22	3	118
65	Apple-Orange-Avocado Salad with Crème Fraîche	375	3	24	32	72	10	8	55
66	Orange Kiwi Salad	467	7	38	34	63	16	4	897

Pg #	Recipe Title (Approx Per Serving)	Cal	Prot (g)	Carbo (g)	T Fat (g)	% Cal from Fat	Chol (mg)	Fiber (g)	Sod (mg)
66	Apple Pineapple Salad	300	2	33	20	56	31	3	119
67	Five Fruit Salad with Peanut Butter Dressing	168	2	16	11	59	0	2	21
67	Refreshing Cranberry Sauce	140	<1	37	<1	0	0	2	17
68	Baked Fruit Salad	160	1	42	<1	1	0	2	10
68	Frozen Fruit Salad	266	2	42	12	37	17	2	47
69	Cranberry Horseradish Mousse	178	2	30	6	30	13	1	47
69	Honey Mustard Salad Dressing	336	<1	25	27	71	0	<1	73
70	Caesar Salad Dressing	826	15	4	84	91	131	<1	868
70	Sesame Dressing	200	<1	2	22	96	0	<1	742
73	Homespun Bran Rolls	220	4	30	9	38	18	1	170
74	Dilly Bread	138	6	23	2	16	23	1	307
74	Easy Cheese Bread	309	13	38	12	34	83	3	577
75	Aunt Effie's Monkey Bread	179	3	20	10	50	22	1	140
76	Parmesan Wine Bread	252	8	33	10	36	52	2	472
76	Italian Flat Bread	161	5	12	11	59	9	<1	441
77	Orange Oatmeal Bread	186	4	36	4	17	26	2	330
77	Pizza Loaf	264	11	33	10	35	48	2	765
78	Featherbeds	140	3	22	4	28	19	1	140
79	Jalapeño Blue Corn Muffins	251	4	22	17	59	59	2	451
80	Ball Park Soft Pretzels	164	5	33	1	5	18	1	200
80	French Bread Spread	368	7	21	28	69	49	2	545
81	Chunky Gazpacho	250	3	17	20	69	0	4	972
81	Carrot Coriander Soup	139	5	18	6	37	20	3	211
82	Creamy Vegetable Soup	206	7	15	14	58	27	2	872
82	Spinach and Cucumber Soup	200	4	8	17	76	60	1	564
83	Mushroom Brie Soup	249	9	11	20	69	60	1	792
84	Roasted Potato and Garlic Soup	299	10	40	12	34	23	4	669
85	Wild Rice Soup	240	11	20	12	46	32	2	829
85	Minestrone	220	14	21	10	38	27	5	1626
86	Cold Curried Crabmeat Soup	201	8	6	16	69	70	<1	206
86	Crawfish and Corn Soup	790	24	39	63	69	304	3	1624
87	Post Thanksgiving Turkey Soup	110	11	11	3	21	18	2	474
87	Mulligatawny Soup	232	22	18	8	30	49	2	440
88	White Chili	275	30	21	7	23	63	6	861
88	Acapulco Chili	254	32	27	2	8	67	9	750
91	Apricot Almond Coffee Cake	516	5	72	25	42	85	2	279
92	Blueberry Coffee Cake	487	4	60	27	49	85	2	271
93	Chocolate-Raspberry Coffee Cake	475	7	54	26	49	103	2	569
94	Gift of the Magi Bread	445	5	65	21	40	35	3	281
95	Mother's Cinnamon Bread	229	5	39	6	23	20	1	210

Pg #	Recipe Title (Approx Per Serving)	Cal	Prot (g)	Carbo (g)	T Fat (g)	% Cal from Fat	Chol (mg)	Fiber (g)	Sod (mg)
96	Waldorf Salad Bread	141	2	18	7	41	21	1	117
97	Apricot Bread	260	3	47	7	24	18	2	210
98	Chocolate Chip Banana Nut Bread	363	4	43	21	50	48	2	206
99	Cream Cheese Carrot Bread	268	3	25	18	59	42	1	192
100	Cranberry Bread	256	5	39	10	33	18	2	220
101	Plum Bread	255	4	34	12	43	57	1	216
102	Pumpkin Coconut Bread	306	3	33	19	53	44	2	246
103	Quick Little Apricot Sweet Rolls	183	2	26	9	40	27	1	120
103	Strawberry Nut Bread	284	3	32	17	51	35	1	161
104	Chocolate Zucchini Bread	242	3	29	13	48	27	2	161
104	Raisin Bran Muffins	343	6	60	10	26	1	3	615
105	Apple Cheddar Corn Bread	252	6	37	9	33	48	2	279
105	Baked French Toast	591	16	41	41	62	431	1	405
106	Hazelnut Meusli	292	8	58	5	15	0	7	9
106	Breakfast Bars	113	2	25	1	6	14	1	120
107	Jalapeño and Swiss Cheese Chicken Crepes	502	34	12	35	63	201	<1	503
108	Chayote Squash Stuffed with Shrimp	158	9	21	4	25	71	4	630
109	Brown Sugar Ham Loaf	456	42	32	17	34	180	<1	1707
109	Sausage Spinach Bread	374	22	32	18	43	59	2	1024
110	Twenty-Four-Hour Wine/Cheese Omelet Casserole	194	11	10	12	29	115	<1	319
111	Breakfast Blintz Soufflé	593	16	43	41	61	288	3	582
112	Stilton Cheese Soufflé with Chives	265	16	11	18	30	123	<1	967
112	Louisiana Crawfish Tarts	425	14	23	31	66	147	1	482
113	Autumn Apple Quiche	463	19	24	33	63	175	2	735
114	Three Cheese Spinach Quiche	430	14	19	34	70	153	2	527
115	Asparagus Brunch con Queso	542	36	10	40	66	409	1	1555
115	Huevos con Esparragos	440	17	12	37	74	302	1	406
116	Goat Cheese, Artichoke and Smoked Ham Strata	825	43	28	61	66	298	4	2191
117	Ham Roll-Ups with Wine Sauce	585	23	15	47	72	170	1	782
118	Marinated Shrimp and Avocado	430	17	11	36	74	135	3	1382
119	Roquefort Mousse	223	6	4	21	81	71	1	448
120	African Butternut Squash Fritters	123	4	24	1	10	29	1	253
120	Vegetable Spoon Bread	339	6	29	23	59	97	4	670
121	Old Nellie's Grits	310	10	9	26	76	98	<1	919
121	Hominy Chile Bake	364	10	42	18	44	42	7	1203
122	Baked Apricots	222	2	42	4	16	10	4	49
122	Cranberry Pear Conserve	240	1	62	<1	2	0	5	2
125	Beef au Poivre	563	42	6	38	62	139	2	117
125	Gingered Beef	549	42	2	37	63	139	<1	550
126	Marinated Flank Steak with Chipotle Glaze	653	49	27	39	54	117	1	500

Pg #	Recipe Title (Approx Per Serving)	Cal	Prot (g)	Carbo (g)	T Fat (g)	% Cal from Fat	Chol (mg)	Fiber (g)	Sod (mg)
127	Chutney Marinade for Steak	197	2	6	18	83	0	<1	1772
127	South African Zulu Bobotie	286	18	17	17	52	127	1	692
128	Famous Cincinnati Three-Way Chili	490	38	44	17	32	81	2	847
129	Mexican Lasagna	452	25	32	25	49	127	3	899
130	Bavarian Meat Loaf	336	26	17	18	49	133	1	806
131	Terrific Taco Pie	594	27	34	39	59	91	3	1131
132	Continental Beef Stew	457	38	27	20	39	87	6	1353
133	Saint Patrick's Day Corned Beef Casserole	671	29	27	50	67	108	3	928
134	Herb Marinated Leg of Lamb	289	37	2	13	41	116	<1	360
135	Pork Chops with Peanut Sauce	305	29	5	19	56	59	1	185
136	Thai Nipa Peanut Dressing	74	2	4	6	70	1	1	27
136	The Quintessential Pork Loaf	333	18	16	22	60	104	2	229
137	Pork Piccata	385	25	39	14	32	62	2	376
138	Baked Country Pork Ribs	287	16	21	16	49	62	1	739
138	Daddy's Best Texas Pork Ribs	635	29	71	28	38	111	<1	1842
139	Chinese Risotto with Shiitake Mushrooms	531	18	78	17	28	17	6	1381
140	Pork Roast with Apples and Bourbon	314	30	12	13	38	80	1	576
141	Marinated Pork Tenderlin Sandwiches	706	43	39	35	46	124	1	2288
142	Sausage Spaghetti Pie	470	24	28	30	56	146	2	811
143	Chicken Niçoise with Latticed Potatoes	327	24	26	14	39	65	2	319
143	Cusseta Barbecue Sauce for Chicken	145	<1	3	16	93	0	<1	499
144	Cherry Chicken	326	36	34	4	12	94	1	658
144	Chutney Barbecued Chicken	584	37	49	28	42	113	4	1803
145	Apricot Chutney Chicken	467	43	51	8	16	113	3	335
146	Shortcut Thai Peanut Chicken	1034	59	123	35	30	39	8	2162
146	Big-D Chicken	214	25	7	9	39	79	1	335
147	Duck Gumbo	1071	100	31	58	50	412	2	524
147	New Year's Casserole	377	18	17	27	64	47	6	1308
148	Indonesian Grilled Turkey	366	38	5	21	52	91	1	589
149	Sesame Crusted Salmon with Ginger Vinaigrette	417	24	22	24	54	68	1	1806
150	Salmon Soy Steak	443	26	5	36	72	68	<1	3998
151	Seafood Mosaic Ballotine	198	17	3	13	57	69	1	176
152	Parmesan Sauce for Fish	119	3	1	12	88	24	<1	278
152	Grilled Tuna with Oriental Marinade	338	30	7	19	54	44	1	2679
153	New Orleans Stuffed Eggplant	419	18	19	31	66	164	5	776
154	Pasta Primavera with Scallops	482	22	54	22	39	30	8	650
154	Greek Pasta with Shrimp	459	30	43	19	37	181	6	838
155	Fettuccini and Spicy Shrimp	293	25	28	9	28	170	2	556
155	Barbecued Shrimp	1035	30	2	102	88	393	<1	1069
156	Authentic Shrimp Curry	316	17	10	24	66	135	2	171

Pg #	Recipe Title (Approx Per Serving)	Cal	Prot (g)	Carbo (g)	T Fat (g)	% Cal from Fat	Chol (mg)	Fiber (g)	Sod (mg)
156	Green Peppercorn Sauce	172	1	2	17	86	56	<1	348
159	Cabbage and Sweet Pepper Medley	133	2	8	10	69	8	2	425
160	Braised Red Cabbage with Apples and Wine	113	2	16	3	22	0	3	24
160	Carrots with Apricot Brandy Sauce	198	2	15	12	51	0	4	764
161	Carrot Soufflé	285	4	28	18	56	148	2	296
161	Cauliflower and Peas with Ginger	171	6	15	10	53	0	6	47
162	Corn and Black Bean Tart with Chili Crust	528	19	52	29	48	69	10	914
163	Corn Pudding	578	12	63	35	51	237	6	1008
164	Spicy Baked Eggplant	121	5	12	7	48	56	4	119
164	Grilled Portobello Mushrooms/Honey Marinade	323	8	19	27	70	0	8	85
165	Vidalia Onion Pie	239	6	12	19	70	111	1	562
165	Baked Sweet Red Onions	46	1	5	3	50	<1	1	169
166	Sake Potatoes	229	4	33	6	23	16	3	668
166	Garlic Mashed Potatoes	266	7	9	23	76	37	1	151
167	Sweet Potato Puff	618	6	89	29	41	53	4	242
167	Golden Squash Patties	144	4	16	7	44	53	3	375
168	Tomato Cheese Pie	481	25	15	36	67	95	1	475
168	Mexican Vegetable Casserole	754	31	81	35	41	91	8	1338
169	Red Chile Enchiladas	1036	38	55	77	65	101	11	1248
170	Rainbow Vegetable Loaf	280	15	12	19	62	255	2	599
171	Vegetable Trio	225	2	20	16	61	41	3	267
171	Old South Corn Bread Dressing	675	27	88	24	32	321	7	2167
172	Cranberry Wild Rice	408	13	79	6	13	0	6	91
172	Fresh Basil Pesto Sauce	289	9	11	24	73	11	3	343
173	Garden Herb Seasoning for Vegetables	3	<1	1	<1	15	0	<1	156
173	Roquefort Sauce	97	3	4	6	59	19	<1	216
174	Jalapeño Hot Mustard	16	<1	4	<1	2	0	<1	104
174	Bell Pepper Mustard	40	1	4	3	59	0	1	352
177	Chocolate Carrot Cake	1413	13	155	86	53	199	6	804
178	Chopped Apple Cake with Caramel Frosting	497	5	80	19	33	70	2	338
179	Commander's Carrot Cake	1176	11	118	77	57	133	5	712
180	One-Egg Devil's Food Cake	440	5	69	18	36	40	3	413
181	No-Fat Mocha Cake	317	7	72	2	6	4	6	289
182	Aztec Chocolate Cake	881	13	97	55	53	141	5	479
183	Cranberry Upside-Down Cake	811	7	82	52	56	199	3	559
184	Kahlúa Cake	652	5	78	33	45	79	1	380
185	Mother's Lazy Daisy Cake	363	4	56	14	35	86	1	260
186	Double Lemon Cake	331	3	49	14	38	88	<1	83
187	Texas Peach Bellini Cake**	593	7	75	30	45	93	2	235
188	Butterscotch Pound Cake	573	4	85	24	38	86	0	609

Pg #	Recipe Title (Approx Per Serving)	Cal	Prot (g)	Carbo (g)	T Fat (g)	% Cal from Fat	Chol (mg)	Fiber (g)	Sod (mg)
189	Brown Sugar Pound Cake	644	8	81	34	46	133	2	249
189	No-Frost Pumpkin Cake	498	8	61	26	46	90	4	550
190	Root Beer Cake	485	4	86	14	26	0	1	496
190	Earthquake Cake	474	4	57	27	50	57	1	425
191	Zinfandel Delight Cake	488	5	79	17	30	27	1	315
192	Buttermilk Glaze	68	<1	9	4	50	11	0	45
192	Buffalo Chip Cookies	217	3	29	11	44	31	1	132
193	Clipper Chipper Cookies	186	2	21	11	52	22	1	105
194	Aunt Nib's Cornflake Cookies	91	1	8	6	62	6	<1	33
194	Cream Cheese Cookies	114	1	13	7	52	14	<1	50
195	Candied Cherry Florentines	218	2	29	11	45	16	1	64
196	Forgotten Cookies	39	<1	7	1	30	0	<1	12
196	Fresh Ginger Cookies	111	1	16	5	39	20	<1	131
197	Gumdrop Bar Cookies	234	3	44	6	21	58	1	90
198	Holiday Mincemeat Cookies/Mocha Frosting	117	1	16	6	43	12	<1	53
199	Key Lime Squares	148	2	21	6	39	27	<1	114
199	Texas Gold Bars	164	2	24	7	37	25	<1	149
200	Apricot Sour Cream Pie	476	7	69	20	38	164	2	220
200	"Make-in-the-Pan" Pie Crust	282	3	25	19	60	1	1	391
201	Three-Berry Pie	843	8	97	48	51	46	6	467
202	Bourbon Pie	317	3	33	17	49	44	<1	137
202	Grandma's Buttermilk Pie	505	6	66	25	44	149	<1	367
203	Chocolate Bourbon Pie	484	7	59	21	39	144	2	419
204	Coffee Butterscotch Pie	391	5	68	12	27	65	<1	251
205	Prize-Winning Lemon Chess Pie	349	4	48	16	41	132	<1	196
206	Best Pecan Pie	538	5	59	34	54	111	2	268
206	Rhubarb Pie	408	3	73	12	27	69	1	165
207	Better-than-Romance Chocolate Pie	675	6	51	52	67	166	2	199
208	Audrey's Rum Cream Pie	512	7	38	36	62	173	1	453
211	Butterscotch Apples	504	2	102	12	21	0	5	155
212	Almond Cheesecake	247	5	16	18	66	103	0	138
212	Orange Bavarian	186	3	35	5	22	16	<1	10
213	Coconut Cheesecake with Mango Sauce	814	11	48	67	72	223	2	397
214	Rose Blossom Cheesecake	367	6	16	32	76	150	<1	296
215	Dessert Cheese Ring	266	12	6	22	74	76	<1	429
216	Cream Puffs with Chocolate Glaze	533	11	65	26	44	308	1	316
217	Heavenly Orange Cream Custard	487	10	24	40	72	439	<1	109
218	Raspberry Clouds	393	4	32	28	64	96	1	148
219	Chocolate Rum Pots de Crème	227	9	14	16	58	213	1	63
220	Crème Brûlée	587	5	34	49	74	376	0	59

Pg #	Recipe Title (Approx Per Serving)	Cal	Prot (g)	Carbo (g)	T Fat (g)	% Cal from Fat	Chol (mg)	Fiber (g)	Sod (mg)
221	Eclair Cake	420	5	68	14	31	8	2	532
222	Coffee Flan	538	8	76	22	35	243	0	99
223	Traditional Flan	355	11	51	12	30	187	0	150
224	Luscious Low-Fat Flan	157	9	28	1	7	3	<1	175
225	Brown Sugar Ice Cream	265	4	24	18	60	135	0	47
226	Coffee Ice Cream Dessert	456	5	40	31	60	104	1	208
227	Bittersweet Chocolate Sorbet	331	3	50	14	37	2	3	3
227	Luscious Lavender Flower Ice Cream	332	3	17	29	77	104	0	83
228	Lemon Cream Sherbet	208	3	31	9	36	33	<1	51
228	Cookies and Cream Cake	440	5	53	24	48	32	1	296
229	Tortoni	305	4	47	13	36	36	1	124
229	Watermelon Granita	61	<1	16	<1	2	0	<1	3
230	Vienna Bread Pudding	527	10	70	24	40	173	1	395
231	White Chocolate Bread Pudding	982	15	76	68	63	411	1	350
232	Butterscotch Sauce	374	2	75	9	21	25	0	164
232	Chocolate Fudge Sauce	50	1	9	2	31	1	<1	13
233	Cinnamon-Amaretto White Chocolate Sauce	202	2	15	14	63	31	0	27
234	Lemon Dessert Sauce	182	<1	27	9	41	23	<1	88
235	Serious Chocolate Freezer Soufflés	363	13	52	13	31	234	4	257
236	Chocolate Torte Royale	295	3	33	19	54	94	1	102
237	Kahlúa Brownie Torte with Kahlúa Frosting	560	6	57	35	56	107	<1	348
238	Godiva Chocolate Two-Minute Mousse***	269	7	29	17	51	112	2	59
238	Turtle Trifle	423	5	62	17	36	14	2	463
239	Fan-Tan Fudge	81	1	10	4	45	4	<1	45
239	The Brigittine Monk's Fudge	173	2	24	9	43	9	1	41
240	Peanut Butter Roll	228	3	45	5	1	0	1	90
241	Buttermilk Pralines	172	1	23	9	45	<1	1	104
241	Pretty Party Mints	23	<1	5	<1	14	1	0	3
242	Children's Favorite Lollipops	68	0	18	0	0	0	0	8
242	Orange Pineapple Marmalade	108	<1	28	<1	0	0	<1	<1

*Nutritional profile does not include crab claw fingers
**Nutritional profile does not include Peach Schnaaps
***Nutritional profile does not include Godiva Chocolate Liqueur

Index

258

Recipe Contributors

Lindalyn Adams (Reuben)
Bettye Adin (Louis)
Elaine Agatston (Stephen)
Evelyn Alexander (Sam)
Chris Anderson (Paul)
Kay Anderson (Allan)
Nancy Armstrong (W. Mark)
Mary Bankhead (Jack)
Joan Beck (Jay)
Jaree Bierig (Paul)
Roland Black, M.D.
Gabriella Bondy (Robert)
Glenna Bowls
Barbara Bradfield (John)
Jean Bremner (Normand)
Sue Brooks (Quentin)
Letrice Brown (Don)
Susan Bruck (William)
Sita Burman (Sudeep)
Carol Bywaters (T. W.)
Shannon Callewart (Craig)
Susan Candy (Errol)
Barbara Chapman (Brooks)
Martha Chisolm (Jack)
Linda Coon (John)
Ellen Crim (Randy)
Marty Curtis (R. Stephen)
Anne Darrouzet (Michael)
Suzette Derrick (Howard)
Corrine Donica (Stephen)
Maxine Driggs* (Guy)
Pamela Edman (Clare)
Linda Eichenwald (Heinz)
Mary Geisler (Gerald)
Mildred Geist (Frederick)
Nancy Goode (James)
Rosemary Goodman (James)
Chris Grafton (Edwin)
Landis Griffeth, M.D.

Terri Griffeth (Landis)
Deborah Guerriero (Charles)
Elizabeth Gunby (Robert)
Stephanie Haley (Robert)
Lynn Hamilton (J. Kent)
Wendy Hansen (Phillip)
Sarah Hardin (Mark)
Betty Hayes (H. Thomas)
Rulan Hebeler (Robert)
Barenda Hino (Peter)
Estelle Howell (James)
Cynthia Hudgins (Robert)
Susan Hughes (John)
Kay Hyland (John)
Rebecca Lacour (Thomas)
Norma Laycock (Royce)
June Leib (Luis)
Marion Leucke (Percy)
Nancy Liebes (George)
Gail Loeb (Peter)
Kellie Martin (Cory)
Marianne McConnell (Thomas)
Tom McConnell, M.D.
Christine McDanald (Conway)
Kate Meler (J. D.)
Sheryl Miller (Mark)
Lynn Mock (Presley)
Barbara Munford (Robert)
Carol Nace (Edgar)
Elizabeth Naftalis, M.D. (Richard)
Karen Nielson (Thomas)
Joanna North (Robert)
Hazel Pearson (B. Daniel)
Sarah Rathjen (Kurt)
Karen Reardon (William)
Sandra Rian (Roger)
Victoria Salem (Samuel)
Susan Scott (Troy)
Linda Secrest (Leslie)

Valerie Senter (Donald)
Nancy Shelton (James)
Marcia Simon (Theodore)
Randi Smerud (Michael)
Mary Pat Smith (Bruce)
Virginia Sone (Law)
Willie Sparkman (Robert)
Sandra Steinbach (Hebert)
Robin Stephens (Stacy)
Carole Strother (W. Kemp)
Judi Sudderth (Jerry)
Grace Talkington (Perry)
Roena Tandy (Charles)
Barbara Tenery (Robert)
Janet Tenery (Rob)
Karen Uhr (Barry)
Karen Vandermeer (Robert)
Tammy Vines (Victor)
Jenny Waddell (Gary)
Sally Wagner (K. James)
Karen Wang (Stanley)
Tina Westmoreland (Matthew)
Lori Whitlow (Warren)
Lee Williams (Oscar)
O. B. Williams, M.D.
Libby Wilnite-Luterman (David)
Zazelle Wingo (Richard)
Jean Wootan (Richard)
Liny Yollick (Bernard)
Joyce Zopolsky (Paul)
*deceased

A Thyme to
Remember

Order Information

Name _____ (Please Print)

Street Address _____

City _____ State ___ Zip ___

Phone _____

The Aldredge House

5500 Swiss Avenue

Dallas, Texas 75214

214.823.2972

Your Order	Qty	Total
A Thyme to Remember $22.00 per book		$
Texas residents add 8.25% sales tax $1.82 per book		$
Shipping and handling $3.00 per book		$
Total		$

Method of Payment: [   ] VISA   [   ] MasterCard

[   ] Check payable to D.C.M.S.A. Cookbook

Account Number _____ Expiration Date _____

Cardholder Name _____

Signature _____

Photocopies accepted.